Seeking the Historical Cook

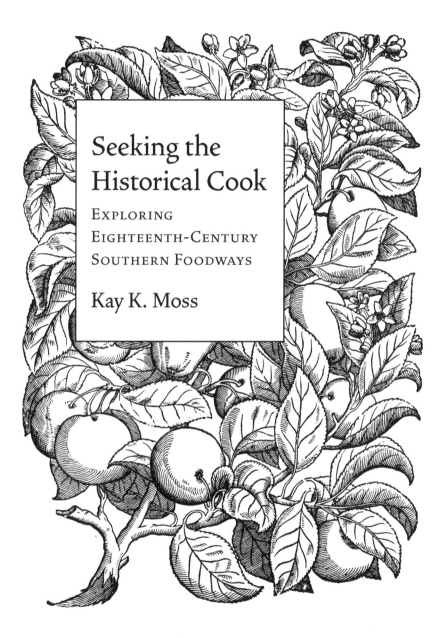

Seeking the Historical Cook

Exploring
Eighteenth-Century
Southern Foodways

Kay K. Moss

The University of South Carolina Press

© 2013 University of South Carolina

Published by the University of South Carolina Press
Columbia, South Carolina 29208

www.sc.edu/uscpress

Manufactured in the United States of America

22 21 20 19 18 17 16 15 14 13
10 9 8 7 6 5 4 3 2 1

Library of Congress Cataloging-in-Publication Data
Moss, Kay.
  Seeking the historical cook : exploring eighteenth-century southern foodways /
Kay K. Moss.
    pages cm
  Includes bibliographical references and index.
  ISBN 978-1-61117-259-1 (hardcover : alk. paper) — ISBN 978-1-61117-260-7
(pbk. : alk. paper) 1. Cooking—Southern States—History—18th century.
2. Cooking, American—Southern Style—History—18th century. 3. Food
habits—Southern States—History—18th century. I. Title.
  TX715.2.S68M678 2013
  641.597509'033—dc23
                        201204554

This book was printed on a recycled paper with 30 percent
postconsumer waste content.

CONTENTS

ILLUSTRATIONS

PREFACE

MARCH 11: *How dreary to be still at my penmanship while I hear my younger sister and brothers shouting with glee at Blind Man's Bluff in the orchard. The peach trees are just beginning to show pink.*

I am thrilled with my birthday gift from Mother and Father, a beautiful blank book covered in yellow, blue, and gray marbled paper. I shall title it "A Friend to the Memorie" and fill it with directions for cookery.

MAY 24: *However beautiful my copybook and clever my title, filling it with advice on cookery is decidedly tiresome. I am trying ever so hard to transcribe all the details of my grandmother's best receipts. I'll never match her elegant hand. I just hope to learn to set out as appetizing a table as she. Anyone who knows me might guess what I entered first in my new copybook. Yes, Grandmother's Quaking Pudding. In springtime she turns this pudding into a tansy with spinach and sorrel. In summer we pick raspberries for her to add. Delicious! I do admire all her delicate custards, especially when flavored with rose water. When grandmother adds fresh lemon peel or candied orange sweetmeats, I declare the pudding perfect.*

JULY 1: *Today, weary from chopping weeds in the garden, I gladly sat down and took up my pen. Mother reminded me I mustn't neglect to include everyday dishes in my collection. A vision of her special Onion Pie came to my mind, and she was flattered to dictate directions. Of course it is as much potato and apple and egg pie as it is onion. She revealed her secret ingredient—generous mace. Mother told me she copied that receipt from a neighbor's cookery book when she was my age, and has been making her own versions of it ever since. I have noticed she adds other vegetables in season or even leftover meats. It suits me best of all when I discover bits of ham amongst the potatoes and apples. I will make a note to remember ham for my special touch to Onion Pie. That makes it more of a Sea Pie and good enough to take along to a corn husking or barn raising.*

SEPTEMBER 3: *My sister Kathryn and her husband are visiting from York, here to help with the harvest. She seems pleased that I am making good progress with my "Friend to the Memorie." Her compliments improved my mood, for I have been finding it a prodigious task.*

Kathryn reminded me of our aunt's exceptional Beef a la Mode. She has heard of this receipt being shared all the way from Virginia to South Carolina, maybe beyond. I begged her to write those directions. There seem to be so many receipts for boiling or stewing beef and mutton, with so many odd names. Whether simple "Stewed Beef in Soup" or "Hodgepodge," or the elegant-sounding "a la Mode," "a la Daub," or "Olla Podrida," all those dishes seem similar. Each family fancies different seasonings. Usually we ladle meat, vegetables, and broth up together. To set out a table for guests the broth serves as soup, while the meat is set in the center with vegetables arranged around. Kate told me she once saw a clever cook tossing a pudding into the same pot with the simmering meat and vegetables. What a wonderful idea! A one pot meal, good enough for company, seems splendidly practical to me. When I become a housewife, like Kathryn, I'm sure I will want to spend as little time as possible wrestling dirty pots. (Perhaps one day I may have a servant or a daughter to tend to heavy chores.)

NOVEMBER 30: *We just received word: Father's friend from Charlottetown is coming next week. He is bringing his whole family— including Fredrick! Grandmother, Mother and I are bustling with preparations. I want to cook something all by myself that will absolutely amaze everyone (especially Fredrick). The most luscious thing I can think of is Cousin Suzanne's Sweet Egg Pye. This evening I will walk over to her house with pen and "Friend" to collect the receipt. I am becoming rather proud of my growing book of cookery.*

DECEMBER 8: *I love winter when there is more time for visitors and visiting. Our house is running over with guests. And the company is lively. How wonderful it would have been if Suzanne had seen the dinner table this afternoon. Every dish was beautiful and delicious. Fredrick ate two servings of my Egg Pye! After dinner we strolled down by the creek.*

The journal entries above are fictional thoughts of an imaginary girl living on the Carolina frontier in the last quarter of the eighteenth century; however, dozens of cookery manuscripts from real girls and women and one young man survive. Reading between the lines of these personal cookery books, one glimpses the scribe, the historical cook—perhaps a girl simply performing the task of penmanship practice, a young woman looking toward marriage, a housewife collecting *receipts* (recipes) from friends and relatives, an experienced cook preparing a cookery book as a gift to a younger friend, a girl adding to a commonplace book inherited from her grandmother, even a young gentleman creating a book of recipes to offer for sale at a fair.

One manuscript, with Virginia provenance, was penned in a beautiful hand into a book covered in marbleized paper. Both the script and the receipts suggest this book may have been brought from England to Tidewater

Pre-1744 Virginia Cookery Book Collection of the Museum of
Early Southern Decorative Arts, Old Salem Museums & Gardens

Virginia. Quite English in flavor, this manuscript contained seventeenth- and
eighteenth-century standbys along with unusual and perhaps unique receipts.
Toward the end of the volume the handwriting changed several times, reflecting continuation of the collection, perhaps by subsequent generations. One of
the later entries was dated 1744 by a Jane Randolph, who may or may not have
been the Jane of another cookery manuscript. Thus I refer to the body of this
source as the "pre-1744 Virginia manuscript."

A book attributed to Dorothea Christina Schmidt was apparently brought
to Liberty County, Georgia, from Stuttgart, Germany, in 1790. The initial
seventy-nine pages were filled with cookery receipts in German, some translated for this collection. An additional twenty pages contained directions for
cookery, medicine, dyes, and other household matters. These were predomi-
nantly written in English and by several hands. The date 1772 on page eighty-
two suggests an earlier date for the German portion.

A copybook titled "Anne Cameron Writing Book" was inscribed, on the
first page, "A Friend to the Memory, Recipes, Mrs. R. Cameron. Fairntosh,
Orange Co. No. Carolina," and in another hand, "October the 15th, 1816."
Two additional segments, one dated 1834 and another undated, were inserted
in the 1816 memorandum. Cookery, household hints, and medicines were
intermingled—Minced Pies, Ink, and a remedy for Chin Cough & Croup all
share a page. Many receipts reflected the preceding century; others were quite

Minced Pies.

2 ll Raisins, 1½ ll Suet, 1 ll Brown Sugar, 1 tongue, 1 Pint wine and brandy 3 Apels, 2 Oranges grated, and Juse of one pice.

Naple Biscuit Pudding

Take a Pint of Milk, boil it and pour it over as much Naple Biscuit as will make it thick, then beat up the yolks of 4 Eggs and half the whites, 1 spoonfull of Flour, 2 Oz of powder Sugar, a little Orange flower water, some grated Nutmeg, add them all together, and boil it an hour in a China Bason, well butter the inside of it first. Beat up some butter, sugar, and sack, for sauce.

Plumb Pudding

Shred a pound and half suet very fine, add a pound & half of good Raisins Stoned 6 spoonfulls of flour, as many of Sugar, the

Schmidt Household Book, Alexander & Hillhouse papers, Southern Historical Collection, Wilson Library, the University of North Carolina at Chapel Hill

up to date for 1816. Through subsequent family documents one can trace favorite receipts forward through the nineteenth century. The Camerons were indeed a family of recipe collectors.

Fifteen-year-old student Lancelot Minor Blackford entered in his diary on April 10, 1852: "Employed myself this evening in copying into the Recipe Book I am Preparing for the ladies' fair down in Haover [sic]. There will be some very good drawings in it and some very witty things from Punch & wh: [which] will make it more desirable." He filled spaces between recipes and household hints with clever poems, jokes, and conundrums (riddles) and enlivened it further with the wry humor of his drawings. Surely someone purchased this charming

"A Friend to the Memory," Cameron Family Papers, Southern Historical Collection, Wilson Library, the University of North Carolina at Chapel Hill

cookbook at that Election Day fair in Hanover, Virginia, in spite of its homely cover. Did Blackford make more than one copy?

Blackford obviously copied from a number of sources for his "Recipes in the Culinary Art, Together with Hints on Housewifery &c. [etc.]" Perhaps some were from a family collection. One suspects his personal preferences guided his choices. He mingled traditional favorites with stylish new dishes. This source gives us yet another view of culinary lineage, another link between the eighteenth century and the present.

More tidy cookery volumes survive. You will meet a couple dozen in the pages that follow. Beyond personal cookery books, receipts have been discovered in

This man bought a cookery BOOK!

This one did'nt

Mutton, "Harico"

Take a neck of mutton, cut it into chops and fry them brown. Then put them into a stew pan with a parcel of sweet herbs, 2 or 3 cloves, a little mace, and pepper and salt to your taste. Cover them with boiling water and let them stew slowly for about an hour. Then cut some carrots and turnips into dice, slice some onions and cut up a head of celery; put them into a stew pan and keep it closely covered except when you are skimming off the fat. Let the whole stew gently for an hour longer and then send it to table in a deep dish, with gravy about it. You may make a similar harico of veal steaks or of beef cut very thin.

"Recipes in the Culinary Art . . . ," Blackford Family
Papers, Southern Historical Collection, Wilson Library,
the University of North Carolina at Chapel Hill

letters, journals, and odd blank spaces of account books. Some even survived two centuries on scraps of paper. Some were dated, signed, or of an identifiable locale, but many are of undetermined origin. All are interesting, especially where they are seen to fit into our culinary heritage.

That Virginia schoolboy formalized his cookery book with a preface, in which he declared "it is intended to be an intellectual pantry." I cannot think of a better way to describe the objective of the present collection.

This then is our intellectual pantry.

ACKNOWLEDGMENTS

This book grew from the fruits of countless pleasant days exploring methods, ingredients, and recipes while cooking and dining with fellow culinary history enthusiasts. I am indebted to many who so generously contributed to this project. The list is long and includes foodways interpreters, culinary historians, and experienced Southern cooks as well as armchair foodies and novices who sometimes offered the freshest insights of all.

Adventurous cooks and diners have tested these recipes. Their discoveries, suggestions, and questions seasoned this study. Together, we have explored early foodways for nearly four decades at the Schiele Museum Backcountry Farm and other historical interpretive sites in the Carolinas and Virginia, in twelve years of open hearth cookery classes at John C. Campbell Folk School, with the Pig of Knowledge Society, and at home assisted by daring friends and family members. These are the *we*, the *curious cooks*, of this book. While I find it impossible to list all these important people, I hope each will be proud to note how her or his experiences enriched this work. I am grateful for their energy and wisdom and all the delightful events we have shared. We sat down together at three dozen thoroughly memorable Harvest Day feasts. A salamagundy dinner party shed light on varying interpretations of this elegant dish. Most recently several teams have explored the challenge of organizing amazing one pot dinners. One interesting spread emerging from a single pot included beef a la mode, hodge-podge of pork and veal with autumn vegetables, a peas pudding, and a quail hidden inside a rice "snowball."

Patient readers each offered key suggestions that molded form and style as well as content. Much gratitude goes to Kathryn Hoffman, independent researcher and muse; Suzanne Simmons, eighteenth-century backcountry lifeways specialist, Schiele Museum; Steve Watts, primitive skills specialist, Schiele Museum; Claire Pittman, retired history professor and poet; James Daniel, independent researcher; and Kate Carter, historical interpreter. I am also grateful for pertinent observations from all those who reviewed earlier drafts and selected passages. Several readers lobbied for additional receipt interpretations; I agreed and added many.

Each member of my family played a role—in the kitchen, by the fire, and at the dining table, as well as reading drafts—Susan, Ken, Mary Glenn, and

Talley Krause; Meg Moss, Nathan and Adam Sears; but most of all Fred Moss who always appreciates and encourages the cook. On one particularly memorable rainy winter weekend a granddaughter, daughter, husband and I took turns reading aloud from William Byrd's rather risqué *Secret Diary* while we tested some of his favorite dishes, prepared according to contemporary Virginians' cookery manuscripts.

Research was the fundamental ingredient of this project: part puzzle and treasure hunt, part math problem and science experiment. Special appreciation for generous sharing of resources and advice goes to John White and Matthew Turi, Southern Historical Collection, University of North Carolina; Michelle Doyle and many others, Museum of Early Southern Decorative Arts; Old Salem, Inc.; Ann Tippit, Robert Crisp, Carrie Duran, Alan May, in fact the entire Schiele Museum staff; Ann Gometz and reference staff, Gaston County Public Library; Special Collections Library, Duke University; South Carolina Historical Society; Caroliniana Collection, University of South Carolina; Charleston Museum; Tryon Palace; Carolyn Dilda and Catawba Valley Cooking Guild; and all the individuals who graciously shared family traditions and recipes. I appreciate Teresa Myers Armour's careful drawings of tools, artifacts, and foods from Schiele Museum's Backcountry Farm site.

And, finally, the University of South Carolina Press encouraged this effort from start to finish. Acquisitions editor Alexander Moore welcomed my manuscript and along with assistant director Linda Fogle shepherded it into production. All at the University of South Carolina Press have been unfailingly helpful and supportive, offering clear guidance in their affable manner.

INTRODUCTION

Experiential culinary history lights a pathway for time travel. Whether you simply enjoy experimenting with new combinations of flavors, ingredients, and interesting presentations in your modern kitchen or earnestly wish to reproduce historical hearthside methods, you will discover intriguing foods within these pages. You, clever reader, are invited to join the ranks of those of us seeking the historical cook. The *we* encountered throughout this book includes many adventurous cooks with whom I have explored early foodways. Together, we are the recreated *Curious Cooks*. This book is a tour guide for exploring early Southern foodways.

This study was conceived out of frustration with the more enthusiastic than scholarly prebicentennial furor of the early 1970s. An ever deepening and more sophisticated approach to early American foodways has matured during the intervening four decades. New personal cookery manuscripts have been discovered, and quite a few period cookery books have been republished. Many researchers and cooks have shared insight and experimental results.

Many new sources have come to light in twenty-seven years since the publication of *The Backcountry Housewife: A Study of Eighteenth-Century Foods*. That modest volume has served many as a basic guide to recipes and methods from eighteenth-century America and the homelands of its new settlers, particularly the British Isles, Germany, and France.

In this new work you will find a miscellany of favorite receipts (recipes), musings on historical methods, curiosities from our ancestors, and a few purely whimsical topics. With few exceptions, receipts are new to this volume. Some titles have been repeated from *The Backcountry Housewife*, although the receipts collected here are different. New findings and alternate receipts illustrate each food.

The focus has been the evolution of southern cookery through the eighteenth century, along with related food histories throughout the mid-Atlantic region. Recipes were simplified as they were brought to the New World. European tastes and traditions intermarried Native American and African foodways. New World plants and animals were prepared by Old World methods; while introduced livestock provided meat for that American feast, the barbeque. Turtle feasts, as enjoyed in the Caribbean, became fashionable in South Carolina and elsewhere up and down the Atlantic coast. Journals and receipts document the increasing popularity of the New World pepper, cayenne, often paired with imported mace and nutmeg. African cooks altered the seasonings in traditional dishes and added distinctive touches remembered from home.

Necessity dictated new ingredients to replace old familiar foodstuffs, the most common being corn (maize), also rice in southeastern coastal regions, substituted for European settlers' familiar *corn* (wheat, oats, barley). Wild fruits and vegetables became new staple foods, augmenting produce from gardens and orchards. Deer, bear, turkey, pigeons, squirrels, raccoons, and an abundance of other game appeared on the tables of gentry and common folk alike. Newcomers remarked on the abundance.

Of course, early American foodways reflected what came before and influenced what followed. Many traditions continued into the nineteenth century and even right up to the present. These pages examine histories of selected foods.

Watch for particular flavors and combinations of ingredients that put the eighteenth-century seal on a dish. The majority of these traditional dishes were selected because they are as truly delicious in the twenty-first century as they were over two centuries ago. A few were included to flesh out the historical context or simply for curiosity. With obvious exceptions (we cooked no sea turtles or woodcocks), receipts have been tested. Receipts are given here in their original form. Interpreted versions cut original receipts to manageable quantities, or combine options from closely related receipts. You are challenged to develop your own interpretations of popular dishes.

✍ Sources

Works consulted for this study reveal a range of seventeenth-, eighteenth-, and nineteenth-century sources—personal manuscripts and popular publications, American as well as English and other western European sources. Letters and journals mention foods, although a meal worth writing about was likely to have been uncommon, unusually delightful, or particularly unappetizing. Together these sources yield intriguing stories of ancestors and descendants of popular eighteenth-century dishes. The curious cook can uncover recipe genealogies by tracing a food's evolution through the sources.

Personal manuscripts are as heavy with receipts for special occasions as are cookery books. Many illuminate ideal, often pretentious dishes. Just think of your own recipe collection. Chances are you have collected ideas for dishes that you only tried once, or perhaps never actually get around to preparing. Other recipes in your collection are those old favorites to which you regularly turn. Some may have been passed down from your grandmother. The same was true for eighteenth-century collectors.

A challenge lies in ferreting out common foods and methods. This has been our central aim. In these pages are families of receipts judged to have been widely known and enjoyed—with a nod to special occasion dishes and a few fancies that we just could not resist.

✍ Language

Receipts (recipes) are quoted with all the quirks and inconsistencies of spelling, punctuation, and capitalization of the originals. Context helps us riddle through puzzling spelling when we read "Loyn of Mutton," "yelk of egg," and "Rosten Ears or Coarn." Most of us will easily understand the meaning of *turneps, currans, spinage,* and *orainge* (turnips, currants, spinach, and orange). We may hesitate longer over *flower, sewett, time, sallery, harty Choake,* or *challots* (flour, suet, thyme, celery, artichoke, or shallots) as called for in *bisket, pye,* or *soop* (biscuit, pie, or soup). Such words were spelled phonetically rather than following any standard. Reading receipts out loud will often reveal the meaning, as when we are directed to cook in a *sawspan* (saucepan).

You will also encounter unfamiliar abbreviations: *Ditto* abbreviated *do.* and *etcetera* written *&c.* rather than the familiar *etc.* Some earlier authors used *yr* for *your; wh* for *which; wn* for *when;* as well as *pd* rather than *lb* for *pound.* Meanings generally become clear in context.

The period charm and flavor of the wording slips us further into the mindset of the historical cook. More importantly, beginning with original receipts allows one to draw fresh interpretations. You will find notes and comparisons accompanying many receipts, suggesting choices of method, ingredients, and seasonings where multiple options were documented.

✍ Methods

Basic eighteenth-century cooking methods are examined in some detail as they differ in important aspects from modern practices. Boiling may seem too mundane to mention; however, a pot of boiling water is an unexpectedly versatile tool. Baking techniques at the hearth require practice and can produce a remarkable array of foods. Roasting and broiling are familiar methods, although today's fashionable barbecue and grilling gear ranges far afield from campfire or open hearth. Within these pages you may discover useful old style skills to reintroduce to your backyard "cook-outs."

✍ Genealogies

Receipts collected here were, with few exceptions, well known two centuries ago. We have endeavored to trace each dish's ancestry and direct descendants.

A few mutations showed up along the way. You may be able to determine where your own family's traditional receipts and tastes fit into this broader culinary genealogy.

✍ Historical Mindset—the Invisible Ingredient

When cooking at historic sites, on hearth or camp fire, I try slipping into the mindset of the place and the time. Who am I? Where did I get these foodstuffs? Why am I cooking this particular dish? Sometimes it is 1760 and I have just arrived here in the Carolina backcountry. Other times, the Revolutionary War has reached our part of the country in 1780. Most often the war is over and I am cooking in a prospering household on the west side of the Catawba River. In this mindset I have the whole eighteenth-century experience of settlement, colonies, war, and new country behind me with the freedom to draw from foods and methods that reflect the changes.

These pages offer the reader a primer in historical interpretation. Receipts are grouped in families. Often more than one method is included to allow the reader to choose among historically appropriate options. Just as we may consult several cookbooks or websites when planning a twenty-first-century dish, we can better understand historical cookery through comparisons. Each receipt is given with context. Numerous examples have been drawn from unpublished manuscripts or rare cookery books. These are compared to more accessible published sources. All dishes, concepts, and methods are from the pens of early cooks and diners or from the volumes they consulted. There are generous resources here to guide the adventurous cook in developing eighteenth-century skills, attitudes, and mindset.

Part 1 presents tools and philosophy for slipping into the mindset of the historical cook. Exercises in interpreting and re-creating early receipts provide food for the mind as well as for the body. The reader is guided and challenged to join the ranks of curious cooks exploring early foodways.

Part 2 aids the cook in developing useful and popular techniques from the past. Some dishes can be prepared equally well in an historical setting or in today's kitchen. A pot of boiling water is the same, no matter the heat source. Dutch oven, bake oven, and modern oven require vastly different skills, although baked goods turn out similarly from each. On the other hand, an open fire is essential for eighteenth-century style roasting or broiling.

Part 3 is a collection of receipts, from many sources, but all related to foods of our ancestors and ancestors of our foods. Ours is as personal a collection as any historical source. Personal whim and preference influenced selections, although foods were carefully chosen to illustrate period tastes, interesting techniques, and continuing appeal.

Furniture for the Table. "The furniture for the table, for several years after the settlement of this country, consisted of a few pewter dishes, plates and spoons; but mostly of wooden bowls, trenchers and noggins. If these last were scarce, gourds and hard shelled squashes made up the deficiency. The iron pots, knives and forks, were brought from the east side of the mountains along with the salt and iron on pack horses. . . . In our whole display of furniture, the delft, china and silver were unknown. It did not then as now require contributions from the four quarters of the globe to furnish the breakfast table . . ." Joseph Doddridge, western Virginia and Pennsylvania, 1763–83. Robert Crisp Photograph, courtesy of the Schiele Museum.

You may use this volume as a guidebook for time travel. We hope you enjoy a delicious journey through these pages and in your kitchen, whether you preside over a shiny new stove or beside a thrifty open fire with a mature bed of coals. Receipts will turn out best with a generous measure of the invisible ingredient—historical mindset.

PART I

Discovering and Re-creating

A Curious Cook,
That Has a Good Fancy

A Curious Cook, That Has a Good Fancy shall find out many Novelties, hitherto unknown, and Add much to Cookery; so that future Ages will be ever finding out of new Rarities . . . of this most noble Art and Mystery.

Charles Carter, *Complete Practical Cook* (1730), 1.

CHAPTER 1

Interpreting Historical Receipts

Discovering Methods, Attitudes,
and Feel of the Historical Kitchen

An understanding of any sphere of cookery develops through careful reading and comparison of receipts as well as mindful experience with the actual preparation. In the case of eighteenth-century receipts, interpretation is a skill in itself. The sooner one can block out twenty-first-century attitudes and habits, the nearer one can approach historical accuracy. Trying to follow each receipt exactly, even when it may seem unworkable, frequently rewards the curious cook with surprising, even delightful results.

The ingredients may be unfamiliar and in unusual combinations. Quantities are often vague, as when a receipt directs the cook to add "a little" rose water, sweeten "to taste," or bake "till enough." Methods may be mysterious. How does one *lard* or *force* or *jug*? An old method may seem difficult, unnecessary, or even impossible yet turn out amazingly well to become a new favorite cookery trick.

These opening chapters examine ways to look at old receipts. None are written in a form with which we are familiar. Quantities were sometimes outlandishly large, so that we must cut proportions by one half or more. Early receipts raise multiple questions and present odd challenges. This chapter offers experience in interpreting several useful receipts. In chapter 2 we examine that invisible ingredient, historical mindset, that can help us avoid the pitfalls of adaptation versus interpretation.

✑ The Grand Pudding Surprise

As some variation of Quaking Pudding was discovered in nearly every early source, we reluctantly realized that we must give it a try. And, besides, who could resist such an intriguing name? But how in the world could pouring a raw egg and cream custard into a cloth, tying it into a bundle, and dropping it into boiling water produce anything but a royal mess? Well, as it turned out, a buttered or floured cloth held the contents long enough to transfer the pudding to the pot. Then, boiling water instantly sealed the surface of the egg rich pudding. Wow! We were never again timid with runny puddings and in fact became quite partial to such custards.

To make a quaking Pudding

Take a pint and somewhat more of thick Cream, ten Eggs, put the whites of three, beat them very well with two spoonfuls of Rose-water: mingle with your Cream three spoonfuls of fine flour: mingle it so well, that there be no lumps in it, put it altogether, and season it according to your Tast: butter a Cloth very well, and let it be thick that it may not run out, and let it boyl for half an hour as fast as you can, then take it up and make Sauce with Butter, Rose-water and Sugar, and serve it up. You may stick some blanched Almonds upon it if you please.

W. M., Compleat Cook, 25–26.

This lovely lump of custard is delicious on its own or served alongside fruit pie or rich cake. You may find boiling in a cloth to be your new favorite technique. However, the quaking pudding receipt raises a number of questions:

How many eggs are required? Is it ten eggs plus three more whites? That is what this receipt seems to say. However, examination of numerous other receipts from this period reveals the use of more yolks than whites in custards.

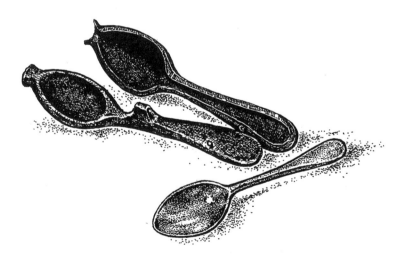

How much is a spoonful? Examination of eighteenth-century spoon molds and pewter spoons reveals that an average spoon, not surprisingly, held about one tablespoonful. By Teresa Myers Armour, courtesy of the Schiele Museum.

We judge this author almost certainly meant ten egg yolks with only three of their whites.

Season it according to taste? With what? How much? About one fourth to one third cup sugar and a dash of salt along with the rose water are appropriate for this receipt. Your taste buds may guide you to use more or less. Eighteenth-century taste buds would have been pleased with less sugar. Other quaking pudding receipts suggested other combinations of seasonings.[1]

How does one boil this mixture in a buttered cloth? Chapter 3 offers a thorough discussion of pudding cloths with tips on preparation.

Is the sauce necessary? The buttery sauce seems redundant as the pudding itself is rich. Similar receipts from early sources document serving quaking pudding without a sauce. Thus we may feel free to consider the sauce optional while operating within the historical compass.

Beyond Quaking Pudding, there are incredible possibilities in this family of custard based receipts—with apple, raspberry, spinach, almond, and ever so much more. Heavier puddings, thick with bread, flour, rice, or suet, are even easier. You will find a wide variety of interesting puddings in Chapter 3.

✍ A Scary Little Fish

To reproduce period fare seriously, one should become familiar with eighteenth-century tastes. Our modern spice cabinets and preferred condiments must be ignored and taste buds reeducated. Then one can discover just how delicious an unfamiliar combination may be. Traditional blends of flavors may seem truly strange and unlikely: mace in savory dishes, mint in peas, caraway in cakes, rose water in puddings, and anchovy lurking in sauces. However, early seasoning combinations are likely to become new favorites in a thoroughly modern kitchen as well as at the open hearth.

We, the band of culinary time travelers, were quite reluctant to experiment with anchovy. Our favorite beef a la mode from a pre-1744 Virginia manuscript is a delicious pot roast that we have cooked many times (initially omitting the anchovy). How chancy it seemed, to risk ruining a mouth watering pot of beef with an anchovy. We chided and challenged and shamed each other into finally adding the smelly little fish and first tried it on an occasion with hungry, unsuspecting guests standing by for dinner. And, voila! The already tasty gravy took on a new delectable depth of flavor, with no hint of fishy taste or smell. We became instant believers in that secret ingredient. You will find an anchovy or two lurking in all sorts of unlikely receipts. Go ahead—try it—we dare you.[2]

The Carolina Housewife's Beef a la Mode is nearly identical to the Virginia receipt from over a century before. However, the language is clearer in this later version.

Beef a la Mode

Take a piece of fleshy beef (the round or thick flank); take off the fat, skin, and coarse parts; beat it well, and flatten it with a rolling-pin or cleaver; lard it with fat bacon; season highly with pepper, salt, cloves, mace, and powdered nutmeg; then put it into a pot where nothing but beef has been boiled, in good gravy. Put in a handful of sweet herbs, a bay leaf, and a few shallots, and let it boil till the meat is tender; then add a pint of claret wine and a few anchovies, and stew until the liquor thickens. If there is more liquor than enough, take out the surplus before you add the wine, etc. When sufficiently cooked, take out the bay leaves and shallots, and serve either hot or cold.

Rutledge, *Carolina Housewife*, 61.

✍ Eighteenth-Century Tastes

When conducting historical cookery classes we have long employed "Beef a la Mode" as an introduction to eighteenth-century tastes as well as techniques in stewing meats. Here we find the four basic categories of seasonings: herbs, spices, tartness, and a magic ingredient to add depth of flavor, today called *umami*.

Sweet herbs included not only parsley, sage, rosemary, and thyme, but also savory, marjoram, bay, chives, mint, sorrel, spinach, and even lettuce. Among *spices*, pepper, mace and nutmeg were greatly favored, along with cloves, cinnamon, ginger, and allspice (Jamaica pepper). Mustard, horseradish, radish, or nasturtium added zip. Wine, vinegar, or lemon provided *tartness*. For that special *depth of flavor*, the common ingredient was a bit of anchovy, shellfish, mushroom, or pickled walnut. Onion, leek, or shallot may fall into this category as well.

A la mode indicated this beef receipt followed the mode or fashion of the day. While today's preferences might tempt you to toss in garlic or oregano, do resist that urge. Those flavors were rarely encountered in eighteenth-century dishes. And don't let a little anchovy scare you as it once scared us.

Beef a la Mode introduces several techniques:

Beating meat was often recommended. Considering the fact that two centuries ago you could have been dealing with a cut from the old milk cow or ox, beating may have been more necessary then than now. Modern meats will generally become tender in the simmering. Since not every *a la mode* receipt called for beating you may choose to omit this step while remaining true to period cookery.

Larding added desired flavor and fat to the dish. To lard, stuff thin strips of fat bacon into slits in the meat. This can be accomplished with a sharp knife or a specialized larding needle. Remember that our ancestors did not have the excessive fat in their diets that we avoid today. Many of today's meats are lean, as they were historically. You will find larding makes a tasty difference when replicating an early dish.

Gravy, as in this receipt, refers to broth. In simmering this Beef a la Mode, a delicious broth naturally develops. It is difficult to imagine why extra gravy is needed. Should you happen to have leftover broth with period appropriate seasonings, by all means add that. Otherwise, simply use water. Commercial broth will change the character of this exceptional dish.

☙ Reading between the Lines

Old dishes waiting to be rediscovered in historical sources may become new favorites. Onion Pie is just such a tasty and attractive dish. This interesting pie is showing up in kitchens and on family dinner tables of cooks who discovered it in open hearth experiments.

An Onion Pie

Wash, and pare some Potatoes, and cut them in Slices, peel some Onions, cut them in Slices, pare some Apples and slice them, make a good Crust, cover your Dish, lay a quarter of a Pound of Butter all over, take a quarter of an Ounce of Mace beat fine, a Nutmeg grated, a Tea Spoonful of beaten Pepper, three Tea Spoonfuls of Salt, mix all together, strew some over the Butter, lay a Layer of Potatoes, a Layer of Onions, a Layer of Apples, and a Layer of Eggs, and so on, till you have filled your Pie, strewing a little of the Seasoning between each Layer, and a quarter of a Pound of Butter in Bits, and six Spoonfuls of Water. Close your Pie, and bake it an Hour and a half: A Pound of Potatoes, a Pound of Onion, a Pound of Apples, and twelve Eggs will do.

Glasse, *Art of Cookery* (1747), 114.

This receipt is an excellent example of the need to read all the way to the end of the receipt before beginning. However, one can hardly go wrong with these familiar ingredients, combined in an interesting form, with an unfamiliar twist in the seasoning. The mysterious flavor of mace is the secret to the popularity of this otherwise homely pie.

Both ingredients and method present challenges for interpretation:

Challenge of ingredients: About three medium onions, three small apples, and two medium potatoes supply a pound of each. With twelve eggs and a quarter pound of butter, this makes a very large pie indeed. This receipt may easily be cut to fit your pie dish, as the proportions need not be exact. A smaller pie bakes in an hour.

Challenge of quantities: With the quarter pound of butter listed twice, one might interpret that a half pound of butter is needed. Your interpretation may depend on personal taste, the quantity of butter available, or how wealthy you wish to appear.

Challenge of variable size: "A grated nutmeg" raises another question. Nutmeg sizes vary quite a bit. Experimentation revealed a whole nutmeg may yield from one teaspoonful to more than two.

Challenge of method: Are the eggs boiled? Or are they raw? When presented with this experiment cookery students have answered the question variously, and the pie turns out very nicely whether prepared with boiled or raw eggs. Furthermore, if boiled, are the eggs chopped or sliced as are the vegetables? Reading additional eighteenth-century sources revealed numerous pies, both savory and sweet, containing chopped boiled eggs, not proof, but credible evidence for using hard boiled eggs in onion pie. One can argue either way.

Sticking to an original receipt can be a challenge. As we do with today's recipes, reading variations of the same dish facilitates interpretation. One receipt may better explain the method, another may clarify quantities, and a third may offer a more tempting seasoning combination. Only after becoming versed in possibilities can one appropriately vary method or ingredients. Throughout these pages you will find interpretations documented through comparison of related receipts. Charting ingredients often aids the comparison.

✍ A Fat Quandary

Comparing two or three recipes is simple; we cooks do it all the time. To compare multiple sources one must be more systematic. I have used several methods ranging from mosaics of sticky notes to orderly charts. For example, the table below compares variations on the odd, once common, sweet egg pie. The chart will clarify our reasoning in the discussion below and our selections of receipts to include in this collection, our "Friend to the Memory."

The table reveals that sweet egg pies began with chopped hard boiled eggs and a quantity of suet, butter, or marrow. Variations held currants or raisins, fresh apples, or sweetmeats (citron, lemon or orange peel, or dates). Each was flavored with wine or brandy, rose water or orange flower water, sugar, and spices. Less typical receipts called for bread crumbs or rice, cream or custard.[3] We are astonished by quantities of fat. High fat dishes were considered special; however, few households had available the quantities called for in early receipts. Compare egg pie receipts for examples of profligate use of fats. It is hard to understand why one would add marrow on top of a suet filled pie as E. Smith suggested or stir in extra butter after baking as in Glasse's directions "To Season a Sweet Egg Pie."

Egg pie was ubiquitous in eighteenth-century cookbooks and personal manuscripts. A survivor from centuries before, this dish was seldom mentioned

The Ubiquitous Sweet Egg Pie

Title	Eggs (boiled)	Fat	Liquid	Sweetmeats	Sugar & Spice	Source
"Egg Pies"	20	Suet (double wt. of eggs)	¼ pt. verjuice, ¼ pt. rose water	½ lb. dates, 1 lb. raisins, 1 lb. currants	¼ lb. sugar, Cinnamon, cloves, mace	England May (1685)
"Egge Pie"	12	Suet (1 lb.)	Sack, rose water (Egg, sack, sugar sauce after baking)	1 lb. currants, Candied orange & lemon peel	Sugar, Nutmeg	England Martha Washington's Booke (17th-century ms.)
"Egg Pies"	24 yolks, 12 whites	Suet (double wt. of eggs)	½ pt. sack, Lemon juice	approx. 1 lb. (currants, candied orange & citron)	½ lb. sugar, spice	South Carolina Horry (c.1770), Pinckney (c.1756)
"Egg-Pye"	20 yolks	Butter (1½ lb.)	½ pt. cream, ¼ cup canary wine, orange flower water (Egg, wine, sugar sauce after baking)	Layers of sweetmeats	Sugar, Nutmeg, cloves, mace	Virginia, Unidentified c.1700 ms.
"Eggs Minc'd Pyes"	6	Suet (double wt. of eggs)	⅓ cup sack, lemon juice & peel	1 lb. currants (opt. candied orange peel & citron)	Sugar, Mace, nutmeg	Virginia, Unidentified c.1700 ms.

The *Ubiquitous Sweet Egg Pie* (continued)

Title	Eggs (boiled)	Fat	Liquid	Sweetmeats	Sugar & Spice	Source
"Egg Pyes"	20 yolks	Suet & marrow (equal to wt. of eggs)		Candied citron & lemon peel	Spice	Virginia, Unidentified c.1700 ms.
"Another Way"	20 yolks		1 qt. custard	Candied citron & lemon peel	Spice	Virginia, Unidentified c.1700 ms.
"Egg Pye"	16 yolks & 1 penny loaf	Butter (1¼ lb.)	½ pt. cream, ¼ c. sack, ¼ c. orange flower water	1½ lb. currants	Sugar, Cloves, mace, nutmeg	Virginia Pre-1744 ms.
"Egg Minc'd-Pyes"	6	Suet (double wt. of eggs)	⅓ c. sack, Lemon juice & peel	1 lb. currants (opt. candied citron & orange peel)	Sugar, Mace, nutmeg	England, Kettilby (1734)
"Egg Pyes"	6	Suet (1½ lb.)	1 or 2 T. brandy	6 apples, 1 lb. currants (opt. sweetmeats)	Sugar, Mace, nutmeg	England, Moxon (1742)
"A Sweet Egg Pye"	12	Butter (¼ lb)	1 pt. white wine, 4 raw eggs	½ lb. currants	Sugar, Nutmeg	England, Glasse (1747)

Title	Eggs (boiled)	Fat	Liquid	Sweetmeats	Sugar & Spice	Source
"To Season an Egg Pye"	12	Suet or marrow (1 lb) (¼ lb. butter after baking)	2–3 T. cream "a little" sack & rose water	1 lb. currants	Cinnamon & nutmeg	England, Glasse (1747 & 1805 American ed.)
"Lent Mince Pie"	6	—	1 gill brandy, 1 gill sack 1 glass red wine, juice of 1 orange	12 pippins 1 lb. currants 1 lb. raisins Candied citron, orange	1 T. sugar Mace, cloves, nutmeg	England, Glasse (1747)
"Mince-pyes without flesh"	12 & 1 lb. rice	Suet	—	Currants, raisins Candied Orange	Nutmeg Sugar	England, Ellis (1750)
"Egg Pyes"	24	Suet (double wt. of eggs) (marrow on top —optional)	½ pt. sack Juice of one lemon	½ lb. pippins 1 lb. currants 3 oz. each candied orange & citron	½ lb. sugar Spice	England E. Smith (1758)
"Egg Mince Pies"	6	Suet (double wt. of eggs)	⅓ c. sweet wine, Lemon juice & peel	1 lb. currants Candied citron, lemon, & orange peel	Sugar Mace, nutmeg	England Rundell (1810)

after 1800. One early cook in Virginia included four different sweet egg pies in her c.1700 personal cookery book.[4] It is interesting that in 1734 Kettilby called these "Egg Minc'd Pyes" as did Rundell in 1810. And indeed it is of the mince pie family. Glasse's "Lent Mince-Pie" and Ellis' "mince-pyes without flesh" are actually sweet egg pies. These pies were little changed from Robert May's 1685 egg pie.[5]

In the South Carolina lowcountry, Harriott Horry copied her Egg Pye from her mother, Eliza Lucas Pinckney, who in turn appears to have copied from Eliza Smith's *The Compleat Housewife*, or a source common to both. The proportion of fat is quite large, twice that of many and eight times that of Glasse's Sweet Egg Pie. The resulting richness is hard to imagine. Eating such a dish is a bit hard to imagine also.[6]

Egg Pyes

Take the Yolks of twenty-four Eggs boil'd hard and half the whites, chop'd with double the quantity of Beef Suet and half a pound of Pippins pared, cored and sliced. Then add to it one pound of Currants wash'd and dry'd, half a pound of sugar, a little salt, some spices beaten fine, the Juice of a Lemon and half a pint of Sack, Candied Orange and Citron cut in Peices of each three Ozs.; Fill the Pastry pans full, the Oven must not be two [sic] hott, three quarters of an hour will bake them.

Horry, *Colonial Plantation Cookbook*, 73.

Horry's high proportion of fat is much more than most of us would find appetizing. Suet was the favored fat for egg pie, although butter is more readily available today and perhaps more agreeable to modern tastes. Of four egg pie receipts in the unidentified c. 1700 Virginia manuscript two were heavy with suet, one called for a generous quantity of butter, the fourth had no fat. The version with no suet or butter was more akin to a custard than to other sweet egg pies. This uncharacteristic version also appeared in the popular 1720 cookery book, *E. Kidder's Receipts*. We found the taste of the buttery version nice enough; but the puddle of melted butter on top was neither attractive nor enticing. However, remember the historical context; fat was a luxury, a sign of prosperity, a status symbol. The richer the dish, the richer the household.[7]

Among egg pie receipts calling for butter, Hannah Glasse left us one that is much leaner than most. Her Sweet Egg Pye is interesting and tasty as is; however, you may vary your egg pie with other sweetmeats or flavorings. This unusual, but delicious pie might have served for breakfast, dinner, or supper. It is lovely for gracing either an eighteenth-century or twenty-first-century table.

A Sweet Egg Pie

Make a good Crust, cover your Dish with it, then have ready twelve Eggs boiled hard, cut them in Slices and lay them in your Pye; throw half a Pound of Currans, clean washed and picked, all over the Eggs, then beat up four Eggs well, and mix with half a Pint of White Wine, grate in a small Nutmeg, and make it pretty sweet with Sugar. You are to mind to lay a quarter of a Pound of Butter between the Eggs, then pour in your Wine and Eggs, and cover your Pye. Bake it half an Hour, or till the Crust is done.

Glasse, Art of Cookery (1747), 113.

Glasse's Sweet Egg Pie (Interpretation, one half receipt)

> Line baking dish with pastry.
> Slice (or dice) 6 hard boiled eggs into dish.
> Sprinkle ¼ pound (¾ cup) currants over eggs.
> Dot with 2 ounces (4 Tablespoonfuls) butter.
> Mix two raw eggs, ½ cup white wine, 1 heaping Tablespoon sugar, ½ teaspoon nutmeg.
> Pour raw egg and wine mixture over boiled eggs and currants.
> Cover with pastry and bake approximately ½ hour.

(Optional enhancements from related receipts: candied lemon or orange peel, shredded apple, rose or orange flower water.)

Yesterday's cook intentionally tucked in extra fat, while today we try to produce lower fat meals. Bear in mind that a moderate amount of fat is part of a healthful diet. A person will perish if eating no fat. And fatty foods were not available at every street corner then, as they are today.

If one wishes to accurately reproduce an upper class meal for guests, copious butter, suet, and bacon will enter the dishes. An everyday meal for the gentry or a meal for the "middling sort" would be less rich; and when interpreting a hardscrabble meal there may be only a little lard or salt pork.

How do we solve the fat quandary when replicating dishes from two centuries ago? Sometimes a less rich version emerges from period sources as with the nice sweet egg pie above. Perhaps some of our ancestors were no more charmed with oozing butter than we are. Use your intuition and an eighteenth-century mindset to determine which receipts can be made lighter without destroying the character.

☙ Sugar "to Taste"

Sugar was also a luxury. You will find receipts simply directing "add sugar to taste." As it became cheaper and more widely available, sugar entered receipts with a heavier hand. The following chronological table illustrates increasing quantities of sugar through more than two centuries. These receipts trace the genealogy of one family of favorite southern pies.

How exciting to discover my long treasured chess pie and a dear friend's inherited transparent pie are directly descended from early eighteenth-century transparent puddings, lemon and orange puddings, and atypical cheesecakes. You can be sure these outstanding pies continue to be featured on holiday tables, mandated by our families. This tradition is likely to continue well into the future as the receipts have been passed along to the next generation of family cooks.

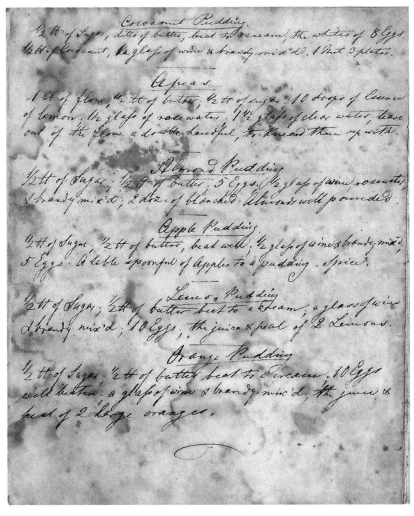

Anna Paulina Schober Commonplace Book, 1805–1821. Collection of the Museum of Early Southern Decorative Arts, Old Salem Museums & Gardens.

Evolution of Transparent Pudding and Chess Pie

Title	Eggs	Butter	Sugar	Flavoring	Additional Ingredients	Source
"Orange-Pudding" *	4 yolks 2 whites	¼ pound	"to taste"	1½ orange skins, boiled and pounded, with juice, or grated raw peels	Orange flower water	English, 1734 Kettilby
"Lemon Cheesecakes" *	6 yolks 4 whites	¼ pound	½ cup	1 lemon, peel and juice	2 tablespoons cream	England, 1747 Glasse
"To make Orange Cheese-cakes" * "lemon cheese cakes are made the same way"	4 yolks 1 white	¼ pound	½ cup	3 orange skins, boiled and pounded (or lemons)	"a little" brandy	Scotland, 1759 Cleland
"A Transparent Pudding" *	4	¼ pound	½ cup	½ teaspoon nutmeg		England, Raffald 1769 and Glasse, 1796
"Lemon Pudding" * (also Orange Pudding)	5	¼ pound	½ cup	1 lemon, peel and juice (or orange)	2 tablespoons wine and brandy	America, 1805 (North Carolina) Schober ms.
"Lemon Pudding" (also Orange Pudding)	3	¼ pound	½ cup	1 lemon (or orange & lime) 1 teaspoon rose water	2 tablespoons white wine and brandy	America, 1828 Leslie (Boston)

Evolution of Transparent Pudding and Chess Pie (continued)

Title	Eggs	Butter	Sugar	Flavoring	Additional Ingredients	Source
"Transparent Pudding" *	4 yolks	¼ pound	½ cup		Dried sweetmeats (dried or candied fruits; perhaps nuts)	America, 1847 (South Carolina) Rutledge
"Transparent Custard" *	4 yolks	¼ pound	½ cup	"flavor to taste"	2 tablespoons thick cream (optional: citron or other sweetmeats)	America, 1872 Mrs. Hill's Southern Practical Cookery
"Orange Custard, No. 2" * (also Lemon Custard)	3	¼ pound	½ cup	Two oranges, juice and grated rind (or lemon)	2 tablespoons mixed wine and brandy	America, 1872 Mrs. Hill's Southern Practical Cookery
"Transparent Tarts"	5	¼ pound	2 cups (brown)		1 pound citron	America, 1950 (South Carolina) Charleston Receipts
"Mrs. Moore's Chess Pie"	2	¼ pound	1 c. (brown) ½ c. (white)	1 teaspoon vanilla	1 teaspoon flour ½ egg shell milk	American, 1951 Brown, The Southern Cookbook
"Transparent Pie"	4 yolks	¼ pound	1 cup	3 tablespoon lemon juice 1½ teaspoon lemon rind	(optional meringue topping)	America, 1953 Rombauer, The Joy of Cooking

Title	Eggs	Butter	Sugar	Flavoring	Additional Ingredients	Source
"Chess Pie"	2	$\frac{1}{4}$ pound	1 cup (brown)	1 teaspoon vanilla	$\frac{1}{2}$ cup nuts	American, 1964 Truax, ed. *Ladies Home Journal Dessert Cookbook*
"Easy Chess Pie or Tarts"	3	$\frac{1}{4}$ pound	2 cups (brown)	Nutmeg "to taste"		America, 1969 North Carolina *The Charlotte (Junior League) Cookbook*
"Transparent Pie"	3	$\frac{1}{4}$ pound	1 $\frac{1}{2}$ cups	1 $\frac{1}{2}$ tablespoon lemon juice	$\frac{1}{8}$ teaspoon salt	South Carolina, 2012 (A Curious Cook bakes this treasured recipe from her North Carolina mother-in-law)
"Chess Tarts"	2	$\frac{1}{4}$ pound	1 c. (brown) $\frac{1}{2}$ c. (white)	1 $\frac{1}{2}$ teaspoon vanilla	1 tablespoon flour 2 tablespoons milk $\frac{1}{2}$ cup pecans	North Carolina, 2012 (The author's long time family favorite)

(*Recipes cut in half to aid comparison.)

Whether labeled *pudding, custard,* or *pie* each of the above receipts was meant to be baked in a crust. Today we would dub them all *pies*.[8]

Note that lemon, orange, and nutmeg were common flavorings in the earlier receipts. While today's chess and pecan pies often call for vanilla, lemon chess pies have remained popular throughout. Nuts, other than almonds, were uncommon in eighteenth-century or nineteenth-century receipts; however, *sweetmeats* (such as candied orange or lemon peel or citron) were appropriate to puddings and pies from that early period.

The differing numbers of eggs may be attributed to varying egg size or to cooks' preferences. Three eggs work well with one quarter pound butter and one half cup sugar. If all ingredients are at room temperature (warm), simply cream together. If cold, melt butter before combining ingredients.

From the table above we can readily see the developing preference for an increasingly sweet pie. You may be surprised to find that the smaller amount of sugar is really sufficient, even in the lemon flavored version.

Transparent Pudding (Interpretation, based on pre-1850 sources)

Mix together:
> ¼ pound butter (melted)
> ½ cup sugar (white or raw)

Beat in:
> 3 large eggs (4 or 5 small)

Add:
> Juice and grated rind of 1 or 2 lemons or oranges
> or ½ teaspoonful nutmeg

Optional:
> 1 teaspoon rose water or orange flower water
> 2 Tablespoons mixed wine and brandy
> and/or candied orange or lemon peels

Pour into pastry lined dish. Bake until browned and set.

Comparing this interpreted receipt with the charted receipts above ties each ingredient to the eighteenth or early nineteenth century. When cooking this ancestral chess pie in an historical mindset use the smaller quantity of sugar; otherwise you may enjoy the double or triple quantity to satisfy a twenty-first-century sweet tooth. The eighteenth- or nineteenth-century version should be referred to as transparent, lemon, or orange pudding. Today's curious cooks' versions may be either transparent pie or chess pie.

The chess pie family tree has other interesting branches—some with greater proportion of milk, cream, or buttermilk; others thick with cornmeal or flour; and flavored with almost anything one can imagine. You may find your own traditional receipt among the variations.

The name *chess* pie may derive from *cheesecake*. However, the early cheesecake receipts in the table above were atypical. More typical eighteenth-century cheese cakes were based on milk curdled with rennet, wine, or eggs. Many also contained ground almonds and Naples biscuits or macaroons. You may wish to trace that genealogy to seek ancestry of your favorite cheesecake.[9]

Throughout this collection you will discover groups of related receipts. In some cases I have done the homework and the math to aid in replicating the dish. In other cases there are options for you to explore, a challenge for thoughtful experimentation.

The next chapter will offer practice in developing your own interpretations. Try preparing a table from the three similar spinach receipts. Compare and interpret. Appropriate choices of ingredients and method will become clear so that you may invent your personal spinach pudding (or dumpling or tansy) in an eighteenth-century mindset.

CHAPTER 2

Developing an Eighteenth-Century Mindset

Interpreting or Adapting?

✎ "Their Way" versus "My Way"

While there are many ways to interpret and combine recipes without straying from the period, there are also many ways to lose historical accuracy when receipts are adapted. Interpretations are documented, based on details from period sources. Adaptations are not documented to the period, but incorporate outside knowledge, modern opinion, or whim.

We recreated historical cooks urge interpretation and combination rather than adaptation; of course there is grey area between. There is so much to learn and so many delightful surprises in store through attempting to work in our ancestors' mindset. Culinary exploration brings new joy to our palates as we seek pure flavors from an ancestral dinner plate. Let's try it *their* way rather than *our* way.

Consider the following three receipts for possible interpretations. From them you may create your own signature springtime specialty, in the mindset of an eighteenth-century cook.

✎ Spring Tonic: Tansy, Pudding, or Dumpling

Foods featuring eggs and greens were traditional in springtime, celebrating those healthful ingredients following the scarcity of winter. Eighteenth-century sources included numerous *tansies*—egg and greens dishes which took a range of forms, as baked or boiled puddings or omelets. Among this family of quiche like puddings many were baked, others were boiled as a savory side dish. Three closely related mid-century variations, with dissimilar titles, follow.

Moxon's "Tansey another Way" and "Herb Dumplin" are very similar to Glasse's "Spinage Pudding." Numerous other tansies, puddings and dumplings were closely related. Note the proportion of bread, eggs, and milk or cream is similar in each of the three receipts. The quantity of herbs varies, as do sweet ingredients and seasonings.

A Spinage Pudding

Take a quarter of a Peck of Spinage, picked and washed clean, put it into a Sauce-pan, with a little Salt, cover it close, and when it is boiled just tender, throw it into a Sieve to drain; then chop it with a Knife, beat up six Eggs, mix well with it half a Pint of Cream, and a stale Roll grated fine, a little Nutmeg, and a quarter of a Pound of melted Butter; stir all well together, put it into the Sauce-pan you boiled the Spinage in, and keep stirring it all the time till it begins to thicken; then wet and flour your Cloth very well, tie it up, and boil it an Hour. When it is enough, turn it into your Dish, pour melted Butter over it, and the Juice of a Seville Orange, if you like it; as to Sugar, you must add or let it alone, just to your Taste. You may bake it; but then you should put in a Quarter of a Pound of Sugar. You may add Bisket in the room of Bread, if you like it better.

Glasse, Art of Cookery (1747), 111.

To make Tansey another Way

Take an old penny Loaf[1] and cut off the Crust, slice it thin, put to it as much hot Cream as will wet it, then put to it six Eggs well beaten, a little shred Lemon-peel, a little Nutmeg and Salt, and sweeten it to your Taste; green it as you did your baked Tansey [with Spinach juice]; so tye it up in a Cloth and boil it; (it will take an Hour and a quarter boiling) when you dish it up stick it with a little candid Orange, and lye a Seville Orange cut in Quarters round your Dish; serve it up with a little plain Butter.

Moxon, English Housewifry, 96.

To make Herb Dumplins

Take a penny Loaf, cut off the out Crust, and the rest in Slices, put to it as much hot Milk as will just wet it, take the Yolks and Whites of six Eggs, beat them with two Spoonfuls of powder Sugar, half a Nutmeg, and a little Salt, so put it to your Bread; take half a Pound of Currants well cleaned, put them to your Eggs, then take a Handful of the mildest Herbs you can get, gather them so equal that the Taste of one be not above the other, wash and chop them very small, put as many of them in as will make a deep Green, (don't put any Parsley amongst them, nor any other strong Herb) so mix them all together, and boil them in a Cloth; make them about the bigness of middling Apples; about half an Hour will boil them; put them into your Dish, and have a little candid Orange, white Wine, Butter and Sugar for Sauce, so serve them up.

Moxon, English Housewifry, 58.

The three receipts offered here can be taken together to develop a clearer, simpler, and perhaps more pleasing dish. While the interpreted receipt may not come straight from the pen of any one individual eighteenth-century cook, each detail of the resulting composite dish should be thoroughly documented, traceable to eighteenth-century sources.

✍ Developing Your Way from Their Way

Compare the receipts for "Spinage Pudding," "Tansey another Way," and "Herb Dumplins" to develop a springtime specialty that suits your individual taste preferences and makes best use of available ingredients. (Sketching a table of ingredients and methods may help in the comparison.) Consider each element and base your choices on options drawn from these period sources. Your composite receipt will then be documented completely within eighteenth-century tastes and methods. Evaluation and combination of these three herb receipts into one will require the recreated historical cook to make at least a dozen decisions. And what will you name *your* variation? Will you call it a pudding, a tansy, or a dumpling? Either title fits.

Compare your interpretation to the curious cook's below. You may notice that every detail of "One Curious Cook's Herb Pudding" has been drawn straight from one or another of the three eighteenth-century recipes above. This cook's personal preferences, her favorite greens, and her minimalist (lazy?) approach are in evidence, but all within the compass of the historical sources. Your interpretation and choices may be rather different, perhaps less green, perhaps more sweet, yet be every bit as accurate.

One Curious Cook's Herb Pudding (Interpretation and combination)

> ¼ pound white bread (1 or two hard rolls or half a small artisan loaf), sliced or crumbled
>
> ½ cup cream
>
> 3 medium eggs, beaten
>
> 1 quart chopped raw mild greens (as spinach, sorrel, wild violet leaves)
>
> Add a pinch of salt, a dash of nutmeg, one fourth teaspoonful fresh lemon peel.

Stir all together.

Have ready a pot of boiling water.

Wet a cloth; rub flour into cloth; shake out excess. Pour uncooked pudding into cloth, tie it up tightly. Immediately drop pudding into boiling water.

This down sized receipt requires only 45 minutes boiling.

Turn out onto serving plate. Put a bit of butter on top of warm pudding. Garnish with fresh orange slices. Serve warm or cold.

During a recent hearth cooking course a student created a quite different and equally good greens pudding based on the same three historical receipts. His version was sweetened and included Madeira and candied orange peel. Delicious. Which path will you take? Savory or sweet?

❧ Three Dishes—One Pot

Some of us judge the difficulty of meal preparation by the number of dirty utensils, more than by the time required in the kitchen, especially when dealing with heavy iron pots. If you are of that opinion you will delight in such receipts as Mary Randolph's "Leg of Pork with Pease Pudding" (Chapter 3), Olla and Hodge-podge (Chapter 6), Bradley's "Plum-Pottage, or Christmas-Pottage" (Chapter 8), and "Stew'd Beef in Soup." Toss a sweet pudding into the pot and you have three courses: soup, entrée, and dessert or side dish. In an historical setting, all three dishes may occupy the table together rather than as separate courses.

Stew'd Beef in Soup

Take four Pounds of Beef, indifferently lean, and cut it in eight or ten Pieces. Put these into a Pan that may be close cover'd, and then about three Quarts of Water, and a Pint of White Wine, some Pepper and Salt, some Powder of dry'd sweet Marjoram, a few Cloves powder'd, half a dozen small Turnips cut in Dice, a Carrot or two cut in the same manner, the white Part of a large Leek shred small, some Leaves of white Beet, two Heads of Sallery [celery] shred, and a Piece of Bread-Crust burnt [toasted?]; cover close, and stew this for six Hours, and serve it hot. You may garnish with Lemon sliced.

Bradley, *Country Housewife*, II: 61–62.

This receipt is fairly straightforward to interpret and calls for a familiar combination of ingredients. A period typical way of presenting this dish could be to pile the large chunks of stewed beef in the center of a shallow soup tureen.

Alternately, the beef might be appropriately served separate from the soup. Suppose a pudding boils in the pot along with beef and soup; then we gain three individual dishes, only one dirty pot. These are interpretive decisions, based on ideas straight from various period receipts. Each cook was and is likely to have a personal creative way with this sort of stew soup. We may each develop our own take on this handy method.

An intriguing "Good Soop" from early Virginia is confusing in its wording and may include an undercooked egg. Following this receipt is problematic. Changing it may take us over the line from interpretation into adaptation.

Good Soop

Take a leg of Beef with a knuckel of Veal and the fat end of a Neck of Mutton let them be Chopt all to peices and make broth of them with a Crust of Bread then clean the broth from y^c Meat and put it into an Earthen Pott and put in a point [pint] of white Wine with a bunch of good herbes with good Store of Spinage then take a Hen and larde it with bacon and boyl it in y^c broth and when it is Enough pore the broth into your Dish with the Juice of an Orainge and beat as many Yolks of Eggs as you think will thicken it beat them very well before you put them in and keep them Sturing about for fear they should Curdle then put your Fowl in the Middle of your Dish—with the broth and Sippets

Pre-1744 Virginia cookbook, 59–60.

Lots of questions arise beyond translating the creative spelling and lack of punctuation. Most important is the question of when to add the egg yolks. We would question the safety of adding raw egg to the soup after it is poured into its serving dish. Is that what this anonymous writer intended? That is the idea one gets from the wording. Maybe it was understood the egg should be added near the end of cooking, but the soup not allowed to return to a full boil which might curdle the egg. Perhaps the egg will cook sufficiently if added to a large tureen of very hot soup. Despite these uncertainties, "Good Soop" inspires creative ideas.

"Good Soop" (Variations)

Begin with nicer cuts of meats, either beef alone as in Bradley's stewed beef or the mixture of beef, veal, and mutton suggested in the Virginia receipt.

When done, the meat may be removed from the broth, hashed, made into pie or ragout, or served cold.

The chicken larded with bacon (salt cured pork, bacon or ham) then may be stewed until done in the same broth.

The wine and a good mix of herbs and greens would add nice flavor to the resulting rich broth. Salt and pepper were not mentioned, but perhaps understood. A cautious cook might add bread crumbs rather than raw egg for thickening, or serve the soup as a simple thin herb broth.

Thus we may develop three savory dishes from one pot of soup—soup, boiled beef (or other meats), and stewed chicken. Toss in a pudding and you have four dishes. So, is this variation on "Good Soop" an interpretation, a combination receipt, or an adaptation? Perhaps it may fit into the realm of combination and interpretation, for every detail can be documented to an historical receipt found in this volume. Some might argue, and it would be easy to cross the line into adaptation. That is where historical mindset enters the picture. When a change to a receipt is based on information from the past, we are interpreting; when we alter a dish according to our twenty-first century habits, we are adapting. Of course, adaptation is not a sin unless one is representing changes as historically accurate. Then the "history police" among food historians will challenge.

Among the many "historical" or "colonial" recipe books available, one can often quickly separate the serious collection from the adapted by turning to the baked goods section. A recipe for "Edenton Tea Party Cakes," said to date back to 1774, sets off alarms as it is leavened with soda and flavored with vanilla. (Baking powder should also alert the reader that a receipt is nineteenth-century or later.) Neither of these ingredients was in use in the eighteenth century. I suspect this nice cookie recipe did indeed evolve from an eastern North Carolina favorite. With the soda omitted and rose or orange flower water in place of vanilla, the resulting little cake would have seemed familiar to those Edenton ladies pledging abstinence from tea drinking.[2]

There are myriad truly fabulous dishes from two centuries ago waiting to be recreated. The purists among us are dismayed to find inappropriate foods at historic hearths when there are so many interesting possibilities. Two especially dreadful examples stand out in my mind.

Once, at the height of peach season in South Carolina, the author and a friend, who happens to be the queen of pastries, offered to help with last minute dinner preparation in a Revolutionary War military camp setting. We were directed to make a peach pie. Perfect, we thought, before we were handed a large can of peach pie filling. Not the luscious local peaches we had in mind, but we figured to play down the filling and concentrate on making a nice paste as a demonstration for visitors. Then we were handed a packaged pie crust mix. Yes, there was flour in camp, but neither butter nor lard, only a tub of soft butter substitute. This was a truly embarrassing and sad example of adaptation. What an opportunity for interpreting local seasonal foodways—missed.

Another stumbling block that can trip up the most seasoned open hearth cook is the temptation to prepare modern foods in a historical context. Extreme examples are pizza in a Dutch Oven and reenactors in fine period dress roasting marshmallows over a campfire. One exceptionally skilled lady who loves demonstrating her cooking skills in house museums has adopted a puzzling signature dish. She showcases her hearth baking expertise with a cake made from a strawberry angel food mix, although she has wide experience with period receipts.

All of the above shortcuts and adaptations are fine and fun for the family camping trip or a backyard cookout. Sometimes a campfire pizza may be the goal. After all, you can prepare anything at a campfire or hearth that you can cook in today's kitchen. However, when time traveling, we aim to experience the pure flavors of ancestral foods and methods. It is all in the mindset.

When cooking in an historic setting, be wary of crossing that line between interpretation and adaptation. When any detail of your receipt, method, or presentation cannot be documented by words from the past, you have crossed the line into modern adaptation.

If you are exploring eighteenth-century foodways for new adventures in today's kitchen, you may choose simply to have fun both interpreting and adapting to your tastes and needs. In any case, immersing oneself in the historical mindset invites deeper understanding of the foods of our ancestors and the ancestors of our foods.

PART II

Cookery Methods

This Most Noble Art and Mystery

CHAPTER 3

From a Pot of Boiling Water

Although boiling may seem the most boring of methods, a simple pot of boiling water is a wonderful tool. Early recipes suggested cooking everything from a delicate custard or hearty suet pudding to a tender, moist, savory meat contained in a cloth, animal membrane, jug, or mold submerged in boiling water. The large kettle might hold several items—even a complete meal.

✐ The Pudding

This dish has now been developed to such an extent that it may be regarded as one of the best foods for toothless gourmets.

Karl Von Rumohr, *Essence of Cookery* (1822), 133.

Pudding can take many forms. In consistency it may be a sturdy moist cake, a dumpling, a sausage, or fragile quaking custard. Puddings may be sweet or savory. The base ingredients may be bread, grain, meat (particularly suet), fruit, vegetable, milk, egg. The Christmas pudding and Scots haggis are remnants of this tradition; our hot dog is a descendant. Bread puddings and custards retain popularity as well. Eighteenth-century puddings were boiled or baked. Boiling was the earlier and simpler method, requiring less attention.

Pudding Cloth or Pudding Bag

Depending on its preparation, the pudding cloth or bag may prevent flavors from escaping into the water and protect the contents from dilution. Other foods require passage of water or broth into the cloth, as when cooking rice or dried peas.

A cloth is more convenient to use and easier to clean than a bag. Into the nineteenth century the pudding cloth was most likely of linen. Several authors noted the cloth should be thick or closely woven. "An article less thick, will admit the water, and injure the pudding." Today a square of cotton muslin or sheeting may be substituted, unless the cook is aiming for eighteenth-century accuracy of linen. The size will depend upon the size of your pudding or dumpling. Eighteen inches square is a good average.[1]

Buttered, Floured, or Plain?

Preparation of the cloth depends on the type of pudding. When the food is meant to absorb water, the cloth need not be treated. When the object is to provide a barrier between the pudding and the boiling water, the cloth should either be buttered or wet and floured.

A custard based pudding cooks nicely in a buttered cloth. Egg rich custard forms a protective skin on the surface of the pudding immediately on contact with hot water.

A wet and floured cloth was typically suggested for a suet based, pastry wrapped, or cake like pudding or dumpling and others. This technique provides the best barrier, although it may leave wet flour on the surface for an unappetizing presentation.

One wonders why Hannah Glasse directs to both butter and flour the cloth for her Quaking Pudding, and *Martha Washington's Book of Cookery* directs to wet and butter. Neither of these methods seems as satisfactory as simply buttering or wetting and flouring the pudding cloth.[2]

Since early authors disagreed on the best method; the recreated historical cook may feel free to decide how to prepare the cloth for each different pudding. For most puddings you will not go wrong following the common suggestion: "tie it close up in a cloth well buttered." You will develop your own preferences as you experiment with various puddings and dumplings.

🐟 "Observe Always in Boiling Puddings"

Decide on the appropriate method for treating the cloth for the pudding at hand: wet or dry, buttered, floured, or plain. Use your fingers to thoroughly saturate the cloth with softened butter. Take care to cover the entire area that may come into contact with the pudding mixture. Alternately, wet and flour the cloth when preferred. Rub flour into a thoroughly wet cloth, and shake off excess flour. Both methods work well.

Have a string ready to tie up the bundle; an extra pair of hands helps, too. Lay the prepared cloth in a bowl; pour the mixture into the cloth; catch up corners and tie with string.

"Observe always in boiling Puddings, that the Water boils before you put them into the Pot." The water should boil gently throughout the cooking. Avoid a hard boil that may break apart the pudding.[3]

Several techniques will prevent scorching: Suspend the pudding by looping its string over the handle of the pot; turn the pudding frequently; or put an old

Pudding in Cloth. Consideration of the likelihood of a pudding expanding as it cooks will dictate whether to allow extra space in the bundle or to tie down tightly. By Teresa Myers Armour, courtesy of the Schiele Museum.

earthenware plate in the bottom of the pot. Alternately, some receipts direct placing the pudding in a buttered wooden bowl or ceramic dish before tying the cloth around.

You may judge when the pudding is done by lifting the bundle from the water and tapping it to determine if it has set. A quaking or custard pudding will quake or jiggle; a heavier pudding will feel solid.

When the pudding is done, lift from the water. Allow to cool a few minutes or dip into clean cold water. Set it in a bowl, untie the string, fold the cloth down over the bowl, lay your serving dish over pudding and bowl, and turn it all upside down. Remove the bowl and cloth with care. Do not fret if the pudding should break apart, it will still be good. At any rate, a complementary sauce or an appropriate garnish of sugar, spices, herbs, or edible flowers will do wonders to mask imperfections.

✒ Simple and Unadorned

The convenience of boiling is appealing, as it requires less attention; and when a food is boiled in a cloth, the pot requires less cleaning. The time traveling cook is likely to be won over by these simple and tidy methods for preparing rice, oats, or split peas.

By 1700 rice was widely cultivated in coastal areas and had become a staple food in the southern lowcountry. Carolina Gold, a long grain rice, was well liked in Europe and America throughout the eighteenth and nineteenth centuries, "it being absolutely the best Rice which grows upon the whole Earth." Rice was commonly available in the backcountry as well as in coastal areas where it was grown. During the American Revolution soldiers' rations often included rice.[4]

Rice Puding

Take ¼ lb Rice & ½ lb of Riasons Stone'd tie them in a bag, so, as to give Room to swell—boil it 2 hours—Serve it with Butter Melted

Van Rensselaer, Score of Hospitality, 34.

This American receipt is a condensed version of rice puddings from mid-eighteenth-century English and Scots cookery books. One author advised untying the pudding halfway through cooking to stir in butter, sugar, and nutmeg before tying up close and returning to the pot. A suggestion of white wine and sugar sauce elevated this simple pudding to the captain's table. The receipt survived unchanged into mid-nineteenth-century America as "A Cheap Rice Pudding."[5]

The technique for boiling rice in a cloth continued in its most basic form with frugal housewives. When raisins and apple are omitted the result is simply an attractive ball of rice.

Rice Puddings

If you want a common rice pudding to retain its flavor, do not soak it, or put it in to boil when the water is cold. Wash it, tie it in a bag, leave plenty of room for it to swell, throw it in when the water boils, and let it boil about an hour and a half.

Child, American Frugal Housewife, 63.

A variation on boiled rice pudding, "Carolina Snowball," was in vogue on both sides of the Atlantic by the 1790s. As Hannah Glasse described, "they will look as white as snow, and make a very pretty dish." An early nineteenth-century backcountry North Carolina receipt simplified published English versions.[6]

Snow Balls

Swell rice in [warm] milk, strain it off, and having pared, & coared apples, put the rice around them, tying each up in a cloth; put a clove or cinnamon in each, & boil them well.

Schober commonplace book.

Hannah Glasse's 1796 sauce for Carolina Snowballs is good for any sort of simple pudding. This spiced butter and wine preparation can rescue an uninteresting dish. You are likely to discover many uses for this simple sauce, as we have.

Earthenware Pipkin. Redware vessels, such as this pipkin, are useful near the fire when gently heating milk for swelling rice or melting butter for sauces. However, such ceramics will not withstand a direct flame or contact with red-hot coals. By Teresa Myers Armour, courtesy of the Schiele Museum.

[*Sauce for Carolina Snowballs*]

The sauce is . . . a quarter of a pound of fresh butter melted thick, a glass of white wine, a little nutmeg, and beaten cinnamon, made very sweet with sugar; boil all up together, and pour it into a bason, and send it to table.

Glasse, *Art of Cookery* (1796), 341.

On the other hand an unadorned rice pudding or a plain Peas Pudding boiled in a cloth might have found a place on any table. These basic puddings are first rate accompaniments to savory stewed or fricasseed dishes, today as in past times.

A Peas Pudding

Boil it till it is quite tender, then take it up, untye it, stir in a good Piece of Butter, a little Salt, and a good deal of beaten Pepper; then tye it up tight again, boil it an Hour longer, and it will eat fine.

Glasse, *Art of Cookery* (1747), 124.

Peas Pudding (Interpretation)

   4 ounces (approximately one half cup) dried peas
Tie a bit loosely in a cloth, allowing space for the pudding to swell.

Drop into pot of boiling water for one hour.

Remove from pot, untie, and stir in seasoning.

> 1 tablespoon butter, ¼ teaspoon salt, and pepper to your taste are about right for this quantity of peas.

Tie up tight and boil another hour.

"It will come out of the pot as firm as a bread-pudding."[7]

This rather homely dish is surprisingly tasty. Stir in a little fresh or dried mint for an interesting period touch. With herbal garnish or a savory sauce peas pudding becomes a pleasing side dish.

Groats (cracked or cut oats) were handily prepared in similar fashion. Oats were raised in the southern colonies; however, the extent to which oats went for animal feed and how much for humans is unclear. Oats were certainly familiar to resettled Europeans.

Optional ingredients with oats might include raisins and currants, suet, or sweet herbs. Within a more complicated English receipt we are instructed to boil "in a cloth one quart of groats with two or three onions in them." Presoaking is not necessary. One cup of steel cut oats with a small chopped onion, tied loosely in a cloth and boiled for an hour produces an unexpectedly tasty dish. With the addition of salt and pepper and one half cup or more of "what herbs you like best" it is even more savory. The trick lies in tying the cloth just loosely enough to allow the groats to swell, but tightly enough for the pudding to form a solid ball.[8]

To make an Oatmeal Pudding boil'd

Take the biggest oatmeal, mince what herbs you like best and mix with it, season it with pepper and salt, tye it strait in a bag, and when it is boild, butter it and serve it up.

May, *Accomplisht Cook*, 154.

Oats Pudding (Interpretation)

With 1 cup groats (steel cut oats) try one fourth cup chopped onion, one half cup shredded raw greens and herbs, salt and pepper. Tie the cloth only slightly loose as the onion and herbs will collapse as the oats swell. One hour is adequate to boil this size pudding.

You may invent your own signature combination of "herbs you like best." I like spinach with sorrel and a little thyme, savory, or marjoram. May listed additional possibilities: spinach, sorrel, endive, violet leaves, leek, onion, savory, thyme, parsley, marjoram, sage. (He also suggested pennyroyal, chicory, or strawberry leaves, which we do not recommend.) Another seventeenth-century author, Hannah Wolley, suggested suet, raisins, and currants as possible refinements to a "dry Oatmeal Pudding." Various oat puddings were boiled in a cloth, in guts, or baked in a dish or pie.[9]

Few puddings are so straightforward as the above methods for rice, peas, or oats. Many early references exist for the custard type rice puddings with which we are familiar. In addition to cinnamon or nutmeg and raisins, as we might expect in rice pudding, rose water was a usual flavoring. Richer puddings were often baked in a dish, perhaps in a crust, although some were meant to be boiled in a cloth.[10]

✍ Custard, Batter, and Bread Puddings

As I originally divided this section into Custard, Batter, and Bread Puddings, it became apparent many puddings defy such categorization. Puddings, both sweet and savory, were thickened with some combination of egg, flour, and bread. From 1672 we inherit "many Puddings taught in one" thickened with egg and bread, a good basic pudding with many variations.

To make a green Pudding to Butter

[Basic Pudding Receipt:] Take a Quart of Cream and boil it, then put in twelve Eggs, yolks and whites well beaten, and one Manchet [small loaf or roll of white bread] grated small, a little salt, beaten Spice and some Sugar: [One half cup sugar is about right]

[Variations:] Then colour it well with some Juice of Spinage, or if you will have it yellow, colour it with Saffron, so boil it in a wet Cloth flowred as before, and serve it in with Wine, Sugar and Butter, and stick it with blanched Almonds split in halves, and pour the sauce over it, and it will look like a Hedgehog. [Further variations suggested: Stick it with candied orange or lemon peel or strew with caraway comfits. If baked, add marrow and dates.] . . . thus you have many Puddings taught in one.

Wolley, *Queen-like Closet*, 92.

If the cream is boiled, allow it to cool before mixing. This initial boiling is not essential. In similar receipts the number of eggs varied from eight to twelve. Puddings with fewer eggs required additional bread or flour for thickening. Compare quaking pudding, raspberry pudding, and almond pudding to the "green" pudding above. All are custards variously thickened.

Thickening agents varied widely among period receipts. Bread, flour, and egg, singly or in combination, were utilized for puddings and pies as well as for soups, stews, and sauces. When cooking in an eighteenth-century context we often may substitute one thickener for another.

Berries or flowers were proposed for interesting flavor and eye appeal. Other fresh or dried fruits are appropriate. From the same seventeenth-century source, Rasberry Puding produces a delicious lump of berry studded custard. Although the quantity of bread is vague, the pudding will turn out fine with a little or a lot.

To make a Rasberry Puding

Take a Quart of Cream and boil it with whole Spice a while, then put in some grated Bread, and cover it off the Fire, that it may scald a little; then put in eight Eggs well beaten, and sweeten it with Sugar; then put in a Pint or more of whole Rasberries, and so boil it in a Cloth, and take heed you do not boil it too much, then serve it in with Wine, Butter and Sugar.

You may sometimes leave out the Rasberries, and put in Cowslip Flowers, or Gooseberries.

Wolley, *Queen-like Closet*, 93.

Differing interpretations of *some* will make it more custard or more bread pudding. A little rose water or rose brandy is a delicious and appropriate addition.

Raspberry Pudding (Interpretation)

    1 quart cream (half and half, or milk)
    (Option: Bring to boil with whole nutmeg or stick cinnamon; allow to cool; remove spice.)
    Add 1 cup (or more) of crumbled fresh bread or grated stale bread.
    8 eggs, well beaten
    ½ cup sugar
    1 pint raspberries (or other berries. We are uncertain about cowslips, but common violet flowers or rose petals may be added.)
    (Optional: 1 or 2 teaspoons rose water or rose brandy)
Tie up in buttered (or wet and floured) cloth and boil approximately 1 hour.

This sort of pudding will generally look naked when first turned onto its serving dish. The suggested wine, butter, sugar sauce is nice, or you may simply sprinkle the pudding with sugar and garnish with additional berries or edible flowers such as rose petals or common violet blossoms (not African violet).

Almond puddings fit into two unrelated families: The early Virginia receipt below provides an especially nice example of an almond pudding. The other common type (suet based), typically known as "white pudding" such as "Almond Puding in Guts," was not selected for this collection.[11]

Although almonds were an imported luxury, Europeans and Americans seem to have been quite fond of them in puddings and cakes. German author von Rumohr considered cooked almonds unwholesome. "Ground almonds are often added to sweet pudding mixtures, but make them heavy and indigestible." Apparently this was a minority opinion in Germany as well as elsewhere. Receipts for almond puddings were found in nearly all period sources. Some were meant to be boiled; others were baked as pies.[12]

Allmond Puding

Take a quart of Cream and two Eggs beat them and Strain them into the Cream and Grait an Nutmeg in and a penny loaf [approximately ½ pound bread] and Six spoonsfull of flower and half a pound of Allmonds beaten fine Mix them alltogether and Sweeten it with good Sugar [½ cup] then fflower [*sic*] the bag and boyl it and when it is Enough Melt butter with a little Orainge or Rosewater beaten thick and pore it over the pudding with a little Sack and Stick it thick with blanch'd Allmonds.

Pre-1744 Virginia cookbook, 51.

If you process the almonds yourself with mortar and pestle, you will add rose water or orange flower water near the end of beating to keep the nut meal from *oiling* or clumping. If you begin with commercial almond flour you may duplicate that flavor by adding one or two teaspoonfuls of rose water. The suggested garnish of slivered almonds and perhaps a dribble of sack (sherry or madeira) are pleasing finishing touches.

The quantity of bread crumbs and flour make the pre-1744 Virginia Allmond Puding a hybrid between custard, batter pudding, and bread pudding. This receipt was among the simplest of almond puddings. The proportion of cream and egg is conservative. Even so, this pudding is quite delicious and sufficiently rich for most folks. You may find the butter sauce unnecessary.

Three other Virginia receipts for almond pudding called for *biskets* (likely Naples biscuits) rather than bread for thickening, added melted butter, and were baked in a paste as a pie rather than boiled. *The Virginia Housewife* departed from earlier practice by thickening almond pudding with crackers or rice flour.[13]

"Before potatoes became widespread in England, people used to eat a pudding made of a flour and water batter with their roast beef. This was wrapped in a cloth and then boiled, and it is still [in 1822] cooked in this way in the country." This German food writer also mentioned the addition of eggs with butter, marrow, or suet to a batter pudding, noting that "it can be made sweet or savory by the addition of further ingredients." A French lady in Virginia wrote scornfully of American fondness for such puddings. "At dinner they de-vour, literally *devour*, boiled pasties called puddings." A Swedish adventurer noted, "Pudding or pie, the Englishman's perpetual dish, one seldom saw among the Dutch" in the mid-Atlantic colonies.[14]

Batter puddings were quite ordinary. This family of puddings included both sweet and savory members and contained everything from fruits, sugar, and spices to meats and herbs. Most authors expected the cook to know how to add flour enough to make the batter "a proper thickness." We are fortunate that Hannah Glasse furnished guidance: six spoonfuls of flour for a quart of milk. Eliza Leslie recommended eight. Both authors proposed six eggs per quart of milk, or even eight "if you have plenty." *The Frugal American Housewife* lived up to her name in a basic receipt for flour batter pudding. She suggested that country folk use five or six eggs with a quart of milk; while city folk, who must buy eggs, could get by with only three.[15]

A Batter Pudding

Take a Quart of Milk, beat up six Eggs, half the Whites, mix [with one half cup of the milk] six Spoonfuls of Flour, a Tea Spoonful of Salt, and one of beaten Ginger; then mix all together, and boil it an Hour and quarter, pour melted But-ter over it. You may put in eight Eggs, if you have Plenty for Change, and half a Pound of Prunes, or Currans.

                              Glasse, *Art of Cookery* (1747), 108.

For best results the eggs should be well beaten, "the pudding should be very light and spongy and this is achieved by beating foaming eggs into the mix-ture, filling it with air bubbles which will expand on heating." Cooks agreed to tie the cloth a bit loosely, allowing room for the pudding to swell.[16]

Basic Batter for Boiled or Baked Puddings (Composite interpretation)

For every 1 cup of milk add 2 eggs (perhaps omit half the whites) and 2 level tablespoonfuls flour.

Stir a little of the milk into the flour before adding the well beaten eggs and the remaining milk.

This proportion of egg and flour should adequately thicken puddings containing juicy ingredients. If you find the batter too heavy, cut back on flour or egg.

[Option: Add about 1 cup berries, chopped apple, leftover meats, or other ingre-dients, and season as appropriate.]

A batter pudding functioned as a side item for a full dinner or a meal in itself. From the 1750 English countryside comes "a very cheap, wholesome, satiating, and pleasant dinner" consisting of a boiled apple pudding. An apple pudding could be in yeast dough, wrapped in pastry, or in batter. "But if this dish is to be made better, milk and eggs may be mixed with the flour instead of water and yeast." Thus we assume a batter pudding was preferred, at least by some, to pastry or yeast dumplings.

To make a Farmer's Family boiled cheap Apple-pudding

Cut apples very small even to mincing, and mix them thoroughly well with the batter; then put it into a pudding bag or cloth tied up, leaving room enough for its swell: This boil an hour or an hour and half, and eat it with milk and sugar or better with sugar and melted butter.

Ellis, *Country Housewife's Family Companion*, 284.

The taste for both batter and pastry dumplings persisted well into the nine-teenth century. *The Kentucky Housewife* included a milk, egg, and flour batter with cranberries. Blackberries, blueberries and their kin have long been seasonal favorites. Both families of berries are widely distributed in the wild and would have been available on both sides of the Atlantic. Overlapping common names create confusion.[17]

Whortleberries, cranberries, huckleberries, and blueberries are members of a common genus. These berries were not only enjoyed fresh, but dried for storage. Blackberries, raspberries, brambleberries, and dewberries share another genus. Where do scald berries fit into this picture? Englishman, William Ellis, identified *scald berries* as blackberries. Were his blackberries the same as ours?

Scald-berry [Blackberry] Puddings

We stir them in batter as we do plumbs, and boil them in a bag or cloth. These ways of improving scald-berries are in such common practice . . . that in some families they are thus prepared during almost the scald-berry season. For sauce to such a pudding, they strew a little sugar over it.

Ellis, *Country Housewife's Family Companion*, 315.

What sort of batter? Ellis could have intended egg, milk, and flour batter; a bread pudding, a yeast batter; or even a suet pudding. Compare Raspberry Pudding above. Each method works well for fruit puddings or dumplings. In early America a corn meal batter offered yet another.

The English batter pudding became Indian pudding in the New World. Corn meal took the place of wheat flour. One Englishman traveling in the southern backcountry was "Kindly treated at a Dutch Blacksmith's, who lives with an Indian Squaw. Got a very hearty supper of a sort of Dumplings made of Indian Meal and dried Huckleberries which serves instead of currents."[18]

Other fruits could be used: "Our meal this day [Christmas 1796] was the most scanty we have had for some time. We had some apples on board our boat, of which, together with some coarse meal, we endeavoured to make an apple pudding; it was a rough kind of one, but such as it was, it constituted our only food for this day."[19]

Although there are recurrent eighteenth-century references to simple dishes of corn meal or hominy, few actual recipes were recorded. Not until 1832 do we find published a receipt that may be similar to Cresswell's "hearty supper" from a half century before and simple enough to have served as Bailey's "rough" Christmas pudding.

Whortleberry Pudding

Whortleberries are good both in flour and Indian pudding. A pint of milk, with a little salt and a little molasses, stirred quite stiff with Indian meal, and a quart of berries stirred in gradually with a spoon, makes a good-sized pudding. Leave room for it to swell; and let it boil three hours.

Child, *American Frugal Housewife*, 64.

Berry Pudding I (Interpretation, one-half receipt)

(Based on boiled Indian pudding from Hannah Glasse's first American edition.[20])

¾ cup cornmeal

2 tablespoons molasses

1 cup of milk (or water, if necessary)

1 to 2 cups berries (or chopped apple)

(Optional: ⅛ teaspoon salt.)

Tie loosely in cloth. Boil for two hours.

This stirs up a heavy but decent rustic pudding, good with fresh blueberries. Other fresh or dried berries or chopped apple might be used. The make do puddings mentioned by eighteenth-century travelers may have been made with water if milk was lacking. Mary Randolph put forth a more sophisticated boiled meal pudding. The added egg takes this pudding to another level.

Berry Pudding II (Interpretation)

(Based on Mary Randolph's Indian meal puddings)

⅓ cup cornmeal

2 tablespoons molasses

1 cup milk

1 or 2 eggs, beaten

1 to 2 cups berries (or chopped apple)
(Optional: ⅛ teaspoon salt.)
Tie loosely in cloth. Boil for two hours.

Randolph noted, "the great art in this pudding is tying the bag properly, as the meal swells very much." With one or two trials you will develop a sense of how loosely the cloth should be tied. It is possible to untie and loosen the cloth halfway through cooking, if necessary. On the other hand if tied too loosely, the pudding may never form a solid ball. Turning the pudding several times during boiling helps distribute the meal and fruit more evenly.[21]

The boiled corn meal pudding is likely to serve more for a history lesson than as your new favorite dish. It is excellent to prepare in an early American context, at an historic site, for a school heritage event, or a scouting activity. There are many more outstanding boiled puddings, such as the quaking, raspberry, or almond puddings to proudly present at your next party. For more appealing corn meal puddings see the Cameron baked "Idian Meal Pudding" and Blackford "Virginia Batter Bread" at the end of this chapter.

You will find bread entering into all sorts of dishes throughout this collection, from boiled herb puddings to baked charlotte to onion soup. Bread was frequently included in puddings as thickening or as the major ingredient. The most basic bread pudding is a boiled loaf, simply a roll soaked in milk, tied in a cloth, and boiled. An unusual clever and richer variation was discovered in the pre-1744 Virginia manuscript.[22]

Boyled Puding

Take a Manchet of the bigness of 3 penny loves then cut out the Top as you do a pye and pick out all the Crumbs and put into it [the crumbs] some milk let it ly tell it is thick then take six Eggs with the Whites and put them to the Milk and bread and Season it with Nutmeg Suger Rose Water and a little Salt according to your Tast then mix them altogether then put it into the Crust of the loaf and lay on the Top Tye it up in a Cloath and boyl it and when it is boyld Eat it with Sack butter and Suger

Pre-1744 Virginia cookbook, 50.

The original receipt was based on a large loaf of bread, weighing one and a half or two pounds. Tests with a smaller, half pound round loaf produced a nice pudding:

Boiled Loaf Pudding (*Interpretation, one-third receipt*)

Cut top from an 8 ounce loaf; pick out the crumbs from inside of loaf.
Soak crumbs in ⅔ cup milk for an hour or more.

Mix with 2 eggs, ¼ cup sugar, one teaspoonful rose water, dash salt, and a
   generous dash of nutmeg.
Fill the bread crust with crumb, milk, and egg mixture; replace lid.
Tie up in a wet floured cloth, drop into boiling water for an hour.
(A large loaf will require triple quantities and longer boiling.)
Serve with wine, butter, sugar sauce if desired.

☙ Paste Puddings, Dumplings

Meats or fruits boiled in pastry were variously named puddings, pies, or
dumplings. Apple or bird dumplings in pastry, simply boiled in a cloth, were
common. Beef steak pie is in fact a large dumpling. The receipt concluded with
a note that pigeons or apples might be prepared similarly as a boiled pie.[23]

How to make a boiled Beef-steak [or Apple or Pigeon] Pie

Cut the meat into steaks of a moderate size, beat them, and season them to your
palate . . . [place steaks into pastry lined dish] lay a close thick cover of dough on
the top, and over that fasten a thick cloth to prevent the water getting in. This
boil in the same manner a pudding is done . . . as it saves the trouble and expence
of heating an oven. . . . Our broken meat is often dressed in this manner, sometimes improved when mixed with some onions and apples.

   To boil a Pye of squab Pigeons, &c.—This is often done with us, and so is
apple-pye, in the same manner as the beef-steak-pye is done.

Ellis, Country Housewife's Family Companion, 311.

Scotswoman Margaret Dods agreed with treating apples and other fruit as in
the beef pie above. Plum, apple, currant, raspberry, strawberry, gooseberry,
and damson either preserved or prepared "as for pies and puddings" were
suggested. Fruit dumplings were to be boiled in a dish as above for two or
three hours. Alternately a pastry fruit dumpling might be rolled and boiled as
below.[24]

To make Raspberry Dumplings

Make a good cold paste, roll it a quarter of an inch thick and spread over it raspberry jam to your own liking, Roll it up and boil it in a cloth one hour at least.
Take it up and cut it in five slices, and lay one in the middle and the other four
round it. Pour a little good melted butter in the dish, and grate fine sugar round
the edge of the dish.

   It is proper for a corner or side for dinner.

Raffald, English Housekeeper, 88 and Glasse,
Art of Cookery (1796), 257.

Few of us today are fond of boiled pastry. These two receipts almost beg to be slipped into the oven. However, if we work in an eighteenth-century mindset, we might agree with *The Country Housewife's Family Companion* that boiling "saves the trouble and expense of heating an oven" and requires less attention from the cook.[25]

✐ Suet Puddings

Suet furnished fat and substance to a large class of puddings and dumplings. Receipts below illustrate suet puddings boiled in a cloth and in gut casing. Other suet puddings were baked as pies; for example see Horry "Egg Pyes" (Chapter 1). Margaret Dods advised, "mutton-suet for puddings is lighter than that of beef; but marrow, when it can be obtained, is better than either."[26]

A South Carolina household book gave a simple and good receipt for a sort of plum pudding. Attribution to "Mrs. Glasse" was puzzling as we have not found this pudding in any edition of Hannah Glasse's *Art of Cookery Made Plain and Easy*. If you wish additional seasoning, nutmeg, cinnamon, ginger, lemon or orange peel, or rose water would be appropriate for this pudding. The quantities are uncharacteristically manageable.

A Pudding Mrs Glasse

Three ounces of Apples chopt & D° [ditto] of currants D° of Sued finely chopt D° of Sugar D° of white bread Crumbs three Eggs but only two of the whites put this into a well flowered Bag & boil it full two hours serve it up with or without Wine Sauce

South Carolina household book.

✐ "Fill your guts"

Both sweet and savory mixtures were boiled in intestine, stomach, skin of a goose neck, or other convenient container procured through butchering. We are most familiar with sausages in gut casings. Robert Burns' "Great Chieftain o' the pudding race," the haggis, is actually a curious sausage cooked in a paunch or maw (stomach bag) or perhaps a calf's bag or caul. Those handy pudding bags are not readily available today as they were in past times.

Several receipts added insight to boiling hogs puddings and others in intestine: "fill your Guts but half full" then "boil them a little, and prick them as they boil, to keep them from breaking the Guts." An ancient poet wrote of a mishap with a pudding in a stomach bag:[27]

> I never thought to give the rascal vent,
> Bounce goes the bag, and covers me all over
> With its rich contents of such varied sorts.

Tying the gut into small puddings was not only for savory sausages. Sweet puddings were also tied into individual servings as in "Very fine Hogs Puddings," a variety of plum pudding.[28]

Very fine Hogs Puddings

Shred four pounds of beef-suet very fine, mix with it two pounds of fine sugar powder'd, two ground nutmegs, some mace beat, a little salt, and three pounds of currants wash'd and pick'd; beat twenty four yolks, twelve whites of eggs, with a little sack; mix all well together, and fill your guts, being clean, and steep'd in orange-flower water; cut your guts quarter and half long, fill them half full; tie at each end, and again thus OOOO ; boil them as others, and cut them in balls when sent to the table.

Smith, *Compleat Housewife*, 134–135.

Mind the instruction to fill them but half full, and remember to prick them. A gentle simmer rather than a rolling boil may also help prevent bursting. We bold hearth cooks have experienced all the pitfalls. Filling the gut casing correctly is tricky indeed. The technique is worth mastering as these little round puddings are interesting additions to a collation of sweets for a party. The above receipt is rather bland.

A multitude of suet puddings, savory and sweet, may be gathered from period cookery books. See the List of Works Cited for sources if your curiosity leads you further down this path.

✍ Jugging

Jugging may be the handiest technique passed down from our ancestors. It requires simple preparation and little attention. Slow simmering in an earthenware pot set in a boiling water bath is not only tidy but produces savory results. Rabbit springs first to mind, as Jugged Hare was mentioned often.

Cloth-covered Ceramic Pot or Jug. Mid-eighteenth-century English authors recommended varying methods to "Stop up your jug close." Raffald directed the common method of tying a cloth over the top. Ellis favored a bladder cover. Glasse simply set a tile on the jug. By Teresa Myers Armour, courtesy of the Schiele Museum.

Other possibilities abound. A Hodge-Podge of Mutton is actually "jugged." Many stewed dishes lend themselves to this method. Hashes or ragouts built around leftover meats are conveniently prepared thusly.[29]

Match your jug (ceramic container) to an appropriate metal pot. The pot should hold a sufficient quantity of water around the jug, so that it will not quickly boil dry. The chosen foodstuffs and seasonings are arranged in the jug. Small birds may be left whole while larger meats or vegetables should be cut into pieces. No extra liquid is required in the jug when beginning with raw meats.

The jugged meal then simmers in its own juices for several hours. If the container is rather full, give it a top to bottom stir halfway through to ensure even cooking. That is a good time to add a splash of wine if desired.

Among "Various Receits" appended to William Ellis' cookery volume was an excellent basic jugged pigeon. Wild passenger pigeons now being extinct and domestic pigeons not readily available, you may substitute other small birds. Perhaps you can make friends with a dove hunter if you promise to share a jugged dove dinner. Quail are a good choice, although rather different, having whiter flesh than wild doves or pigeons.

Jugging Pigeons

Stuff them with parsley chopt very small, some butter, pepper, and salt . . . put one or more so stuft without liquor into a stone or other wide-mouthed earthen pot close tied over with bladder, and so boiled in water till enough.

Ellis, Country Housewife's Family Companion, 449.

Boiling "till enough" taxes the cook's judgment. A contemporary English author suggested one and a half hours, another advised three hours. Of course the time will vary depending on the ingredients and the shape and size of the jug (earthen pot). When giving it a stir after an hour and a half, one may judge how much longer it should cook.[30]

Elizabeth Raffald added mace to her jugged pigeons and poured on a highly seasoned sauce when serving. Her garnish of parsley and red cabbage with optional mushrooms and forcemeat balls sounds wonderful, but turns our dish from simple to labor intensive. Hannah Glasse also proposed a complicated method. Her stuffing combined livers, lemon, nutmeg, suet, egg, and bread crumbs with the parsley, butter, salt, and pepper. *The Frugal Colonial Housewife* put forward a similar stuffing with an added touch of marjoram. A quantity of butter was included in the jug.

After dishing up the birds, a delicious sauce may be developed from the remaining buttery broth by adding a little cream, lemon peel, anchovy, mushrooms, and white wine. Thicken the simmering sauce with a little butter rolled in flour.[31]

✍ A Whole Meal from a Pot of Boiling Water

Such a variety of foods can be boiled, that we may engineer all sorts of meals cooked within one pot. A pudding in a cloth may boil in a pot of soup or stew. This trick is rarely mentioned in cookery books; however, one suspects boiling multiple items in a common pot may have been too mundane to mention.

A rice or peas pudding may be cooked in the pot with stewing meat, with the bonus of broth to flavor the pudding. *The Virginia Housewife* proposed such a dish. William Byrd recorded eating peas pudding with pork on occasion. Perhaps his cook used a similar method.

Leg of Pork with Pease Pudding

Boil a small leg of pork that has been sufficiently salted, score the top and serve it up; the pudding must be in a separate dish; get small delicate peas, wash them well, and tie them in a cloth, allowing a little room for swelling, boil them with the pork, then mash and season them, tie them up again and finish boiling it; take care not to break the pudding in turning it out.

M. Randolph, *Virginia Housewife*, 65.

Scotswoman Dods agreed with boiling a peas pudding in the same pot with pork, also adding cabbage or parsnips to the pot. The French cook Ude advised presenting pork "with green cabbage all round, and a peas pudding." After boiling dried peas soft in a cloth and mashing, he suggested adding egg yolk along with butter and salt before again tying up the cloth for a final boil. I find such a peas pudding turns out solid without added egg, although the egg would guarantee it. My taste buds cry for mint or pepper in this pudding. Both seasonings would have pleased eighteenth-century tastes.[32]

Simple vegetables also cook nicely in a cloth. To accompany a boiled haunch of venison, "serve it with a furniture of Collyflowers, Russia Cabbages, some of the Hertfordshire Turnips cut in dice, and boiled in a Net, and toss'd up with Butter and Cream" or else yellow French turnips or red beet roots. These vegetables were to be arranged around the venison to "afford a pleasant Variety both to the Eye and the Taste." Hard lettuce boiled in a net was an accompaniment to boiled beef. See Chapter 6 for the Cabbage Pudding family of made dishes which may boil handily along with meat or fowl.[33]

A variety of meats might be boiled in a cloth. Von Rumohr wrote: "If you wish to do without the broth, it is a good idea to wrap, or even better, to sew the piece of meat up in a cloth. . . . The meat is then boiled for an appropriate time. . . . The English prepare their boil'd mutton in this way, and it makes a dish which is both succulent and nutritious." This echoes Glasse and Johnson, who wrote that venison or mutton should be boiled in a floured cloth. An 1816 backcountry North Carolina manuscript gave evidence this technique traveled to America and persisted, as Mrs. Cameron gave directions for stuffing a ham with herbs and spices before enclosing in a cloth for boiling.[34]

A turkey or chicken is handily boiled in a cloth as well. The following Scots receipt puts forward an especially nice stuffing. Note that the directions are backwards; the bird must be first stuffed, then rubbed with butter and flour and tied in a cloth, and then boiled until fowl and stuffing are thoroughly done. Cooking time will depend on the size of the fowl. You may prefer to butter and flour the cloth itself rather than the bird.[35]

To boil a Turkey or Fowls with Sellery

Boil your Turkey or Fowls in a Pot of boiling Water, rub Butter and Flour on the Breasts, and tye them up in a Cloth: You may stuff where their Crops were thus: Two Handfuls of Crumbs of Bread, one of Sewet shred small, Lemon-peel, Parsley, Thyme, sweet Marjoram, and a little Onion, all shred small, season it with Pepper, Salt and Nutmeg, wet it with an Egg, and work it together, so stuff them full.

Cleland, New and Easy Method, 89–90.

Bacon would be an appropriate and tasty substitute for suet in this stuffing. Celery sauce or oyster sauce was recommended to accompany this boiled fowl. We have enjoyed sorrel sauce. However, the savory lemon, onion, herb stuffing may adequately flavor the bird to your taste with no sauce needed.

The meat should be seasoned before wrapping and boiling as there is little exchange of liquids through the floured cloth. Venison or mutton was brined in salt water overnight or for as long as a week (not recommended). Alternately "the meat may be wrapped in a cloth dipped in hot water, dusted with flour, and then covered with a layer of salt;" however, Dods added a disclaimer, "We have but little faith in this method."[36]

Johnson and Dods advised against preparing fowl or lamb by this method. "Milk and floured cloths as wrappers are often employed in boiling white meats and poultry, to make them look whiter. The practice is questionable; the milk often curdles, and the flour clots; and both fill up the pores and hang about the meat, which looks as if it had been poulticed."[37]

Boiled, wrapped turkey seems to have persisted. Old southern receipts published in 1881 California by friends of a celebrated African-American cook from South Carolina included a nicely seasoned and stuffed turkey, tied in a

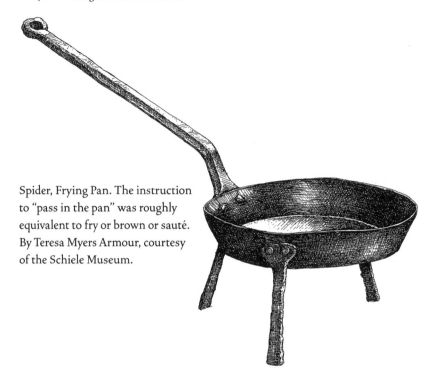

Spider, Frying Pan. The instruction to "pass in the pan" was roughly equivalent to fry or brown or sauté. By Teresa Myers Armour, courtesy of the Schiele Museum.

bag and boiled for two hours. No treatment was recommended for the bag. The suggested "gravy" to serve with this turkey was a mustard seasoned butter, flour, and milk sauce.[38]

✌ Frying?

You may wonder at *frying* in this chapter on boiling. The broad definition of *fry* was to boil in a small amount of liquid. Two 1747 methods for frying beef steaks directed "fry them in Half a Pint of Ale" or alternately "fry them in just as much Butter as will moisten the Pan." Another mid-eighteenth-century author described stewing in a little water as a method for *frying* chicken, lamb, or veal. A receipt to fry pigeons directed first to stew, then to dip in batter and fry; another directed to cut up the pigeons and "pass them in the pan" with lard and butter.[39]

Meats, poultry, fish, and vegetables were fried in a variety of ways—some only seasoned, others battered, breaded, or floured—fried in fat as we would expect or cooked in other liquids—some stewed then browned, others browned then stewed. All sorts of foods were browned in fat and then simmered in a gravy or sauce to create the popular brown fricassees.

❧ Puddings as Ancestors of Batter Breads and Pies

Early sources included numerous boiled puddings, while baking became ever more common by the end of the eighteenth century. In this chapter overlapping methods for apples, berries, meats, and fowls were examined among different boiled puddings. You will find these same ingredients in baked puddings and pies. All manner of puddings may be either boiled in a cloth or baked in a dish, with or without a paste (crust). In many cases puddings were the ancestors of pies.

Baking seems to have been preferred over boiling in affluent households with an oven and servants. Many receipts offered a choice of cooking methods. Several considerations guided the choice—availability of an oven, personal preference, and whether the cook had time for the extra bother of assembling a pie and minding the oven. Many eighteenth-century puddings might be considered pies or casseroles today.

We saw corn meal used in creating hardship puddings. Richer and more fashionable puddings also developed around the new American grain, some boiled, even nicer ones baked. The southerners' beloved spoonbread, egg bread, or batter bread is nothing more than a baked Indian Pudding. A basic version persisted from colonial days to show up in the 1852 Blackford recipe collection. This is simply a cornmeal batter pudding that might be boiled in a bag just as successfully as baked.

Virginia Batter Bread

One pint of meal, one qt. of rich milk, and three eggs, to be beaten well before the other ingredients are put in. Bake in a brisk oven and send in quick.

Blackford, "Recipes in the Culinary Arts," 42.

The Carolina Housewife, contemporary with the Blackford manuscript, added a tablespoonful butter and a little salt to the above batter bread for her "Corn Egg Bread." These no nonsense batter breads would have been recognized a century before, but called puddings. A century later these soft custardy cornbreads came to be known as spoon breads, which traditional southerners continue to enjoy today. Later receipts reveal a step that may have been understood in Blackford's day. If the meal is added to hot milk and set aside to cool before adding to beaten eggs, separation into two layers is prevented. On the other hand layering does not spoil the bread and may have been expected and relished.[40]

Many baked corn meal puddings or breads were made richer with butter and sweetened with molasses or sugar. Compare the following rich cornmeal pudding from central North Carolina with the whortleberry pudding and other boiled Indian meal puddings discussed earlier in this chapter.

Idian [sic] Meal Pudding

10 oz. Butter, 10 oz. Sugar, 10 Eggs, half the whites & 4 oz. meal cream the butter, & Sugar together, then mix them with a Glass of wine, and put it into a baking pan & bake it.

Cameron, "Friend to the Memory," 5.

Indian Meal Pudding (Interpretation from Cameron, two-fifths receipt)

    Cream 4 ounces butter with ½ cup sugar.
    Add 4 eggs (leaving out half the whites)
    1 tablespoonful wine
    ⅓ cup cornmeal.
Bake in a buttered dish.

Be aware, this pudding separates into two layers as do others of this type. Once separation is expected it ceases to be a concern and becomes an interesting feature. You may discourage this separation by stirring once or twice during cooking as the pudding begins to set.

The pudding is tasty and turns out well. Note that this is essentially a transparent pudding with added corn meal. If baked in a crust, this Indian meal pudding becomes a type of chess pie still popular in some parts of the south.

American authors Amelia Simmons, Mary Randolph, and Lettice Bryan each proposed quite different, but equally interesting baked Indian puddings. Their options for additional flavor included cinnamon, nutmeg, brandy, or raisins. Bryan's baked Indian pudding contained suet in place of butter.[41]

The Englishman's flour batter pudding persisted alongside the new American cornmeal puddings. Comparing the ingredients for "Sparrow Dumpling" with "Pigeons in a Hole" and "Chicken Pudding" reveals close relationship despite different cooking methods. Each of these attractive dishes is basically fowl in batter pudding.[42]

Since songbirds are not part of our diet today (and illegal to harvest), we may substitute dove or quail for the sparrow. I have observed several experiments in which cookery students were unwilling to trust eighteenth-century batter pudding proportions. Student cooks added more and more flour until they judged the batter a proper thickness. The result was edible, but heavy and doughy.

Give traditional proportions a try. Although the batter may not seem thick, you may be pleasantly surprised with the resulting light dumpling.

To make a Sparrow Dumpling

Mix half a pint of good milk with three eggs, a little salt, and as much flour [approximately two tablespoonfuls] as will make it a thick batter. Put a lump of butter rolled in pepper and salt in every sparrow [or other small bird], mix them in the batter and tie them in a cloth, boil them one hour and a half. Pour melted butter over them and serve it up.

Raffald, *Experienced English Housekeeper*, 89.

Quail or dove dumplings are delicious, although tedious to eat whilst avoiding tiny bird bones. "Pigeons in a Hole" is another batter pudding, similar to sparrow dumpling but baked rather than boiled. The little birds do indeed appear as if in holes, for the batter puffs around them as this amusing dish bakes.[43]

Pigeons in a hole

Pick, draw, and wash four young pigeons, stick their legs into their belly as you do boiled pigeons. Season them with pepper, salt, and beaten mace, put into the belly of every pigeon a lump of butter the size of a walnut. Lay your pigeons in a pie dish, pour over them a batter made of three eggs, two spoonfuls of flour, and half a pint of good milk. Bake it in a moderate oven and serve them to table in the same dish.

Raffald, *Experienced English Housekeeper*, 65–66.

Although the presentation is different, the following pudding is closely related to "Pigeons in a hole." Using precooked meat makes "Virginia Chicken Pudding" almost foolproof. Although the dish made its appearance under this name in nineteenth-century southern cookery books, you will recognize it as simply another incarnation of batter pudding, made richer with butter and baked rather than boiled.[44]

Chicken Pudding, A Favorite Virginia Dish

Beat ten eggs very light, add to them a quart of rich milk, with a quarter of a pound of butter melted, and some pepper and salt, stir in as much flour [8 Tablespoonfuls] as will make a thin good batter; take four young chickens, and after cleaning them nicely, cut off the legs, wings, &c. put them all in a sauce pan, with some salt and water and a bundle of thyme and parsley, boil them till nearly done, then take the chicken from the water and put it in the batter, pour it in a deep dish, and bake it.

M. Randolph, *Virginia Housewife*, 98–99.

Since one of today's large chickens might yield the meat of two available to Mary Randolph, one might simply halve the above receipt and use one whole chicken. The meat of one chicken with half Randolph's batter yields one large or two medium baked puddings.

William Byrd was dining on chicken pudding a century before Mary Randolph published the receipt. This is another period dish worthy of adopting for twenty-first-century occasions. It is an attractive and tasty chicken casserole for any century.[45]

Glasse suggested baking mutton chops in a batter, seasoned with ginger. Rundell noted "some like loin of mutton." It seems reasonable to assume that the creative cook might substitute any available meat or seasonal ingredients in this standard recipe. This is a fine way to utilize leftovers in any century.

Batter Pudding with Meat

Make a batter with flour, milk, and eggs [to each cup milk add two or three eggs and two tablespoons flour]; pour a little into the bottom of a pudding-dish; then put seasoned meat of any kind into it, and little shred onion; pour the remainder of the batter over, and bake in a slow oven.

Rundell, *New System of Domestic Cookery*, 143.

Jane Randolph and Mary Randolph offered sliced apple puddings to be baked in a batter. This pudding was served with sugar, butter, and nutmeg, or "If your Apples are very sower twill take [much?] more Sugar than any other Pudding."[46]

One can imagine a wide range of sweet or savory, baked or boiled batter puddings featuring meats, fruits, or vegetables. While boiling differs little whether on an electric stove, a gas burner, or a fireplace, baking at the open hearth requires more attention and skill than in your modern oven.

Almost any cake, pie, pudding, or *made dish* can be baked in a bake kettle or Dutch oven, unless the dish is simply too large. If you have access to a wood fired oven, there are no limits. In the next chapter we will explore techniques and receipts that bake well in a Dutch oven.

CHAPTER 4

With a Good
Bed of Coals

Baking Without an Oven

Ovens were not generally available in early settlement days and in simpler homes. Nevertheless there were ways to bake breads, pies, cakes, puddings, and much more. Baking requires even heat on all sides. Two straightforward methods involve burying in hot ashes and coals or baking in a Dutch oven or bake kettle. Through experiments with early receipts and methods, the open hearth cook's intuition develops.

Traditional campers or scouts among us have cooked a potato buried in the campfire. Perhaps you have even prepared an entire meal by this method, packaging meat and vegetables in foil to bake in the coals. So you may be convinced of this possibility, but of course there was no foil available to our ancestors. Leaves and clay answered that need on occasion. On the other hand one can simply bake directly in the ashes and coals.

Potatoes, turnips, onions, winter squash, even eggs or cornbread can be baked on the hearth or in the edge of an outdoor fire. Prepare a nest of warm ashes on a pre-warmed spot of hearth, flat stone, or ground. Set the vegetable or egg into the ashes, insulate with additional ashes, and shovel hot coals on top. With sufficient coals the baking will proceed in the time expected: approximately an hour for a potato.

The egg is the most difficult to judge, but also the most impressive accomplishment. Ten or fifteen minutes is usually about right. The baked (often called *roasted*) egg will be similar to a boiled egg, soft or hard according to heat and cooking time. An over baked egg will explode. That possibility adds excitement to an open hearth cooking experiment.

An ashcake of cornmeal and water, better with a little fat and salt, may be placed directly on warm hearth or stone, before covering with ash and coals. After fishing the corn cake from the ashes, it is dusted off and eaten. Yes, a little ash remains which gives the bread a bit of lye flavor much like a corn

Dutch Oven or Bake Kettle. By Teresa Myers Armour,
courtesy of the Schiele Museum.

tortilla. The corn cake may be wrapped in leaves before burying in the ashes. Cabbage, any garden greens, or edible wild greens such as dock will protect your cornbread.

An English lieutenant observed an ingenious oven in a Cherokee household where "good Indian bread" was baking. "After making a fire on the hearth-stone, about the size of a large dish, they sweep the embers off, laying a loaf smooth on it; this they cover with a sort of deep dish, and renew the fire upon the whole, under which the bread bakes to as great perfection as in any European oven." Be aware that this method requires a tempered, low fired ceramic dish of the type produced from prehistoric times by southeastern American Indian groups. Eighteenth-century European type earthenware will not withstand direct contact with hot coals. However, you may emulate this impromptu oven using an overturned iron pot.[1]

☙ Dutch Oven Baking

The Dutch oven or bake kettle consists of a three legged iron pot topped by a flat lid with a handle on top. A rim around the lid holds coals for adjusting heat to the top. Dimensions vary, but twelve or fourteen inches diameter is a common and useful size. When a deeper oven is needed for larger, longer cooking dishes, a Dutch oven lid may be paired with a deeper iron kettle. Or your ingenuity and the equipment at hand may inspire you to create an oven for baking an item that does not fit into your Dutch oven.

The art of hearth baking rests in the cook's imagining just what is going on in and out of the oven. How hot are top, bottom, and sides? Where is the food in relation to the heat? How may the heat be adjusted? The cook's level of mindfulness of these variables is the art of Dutch oven baking. This art develops through experimentation and experience.

While skills with the fire and the Dutch oven can only be learned through observation and trial, we can share a few hints to get the beginning hearth cook started. You will find that every hearth cook has a rather personal technique and each may declare her or his method the best. And it is true, many variations work just fine. You will develop your own tricks. Historical cooks must have had individual favorite methods as well. Consider these steps:

Allow your fire to develop a good bed of coals.

Preheat your oven by placing both top and bottom next to the fire with the interior surface of pot away from the fire. While a thorough heating is wanted, take care the iron does not overheat. Much smoke indicates the precious *seasoning* (baked on, protective coating of fat) is burning off. Beyond that, the iron itself deteriorates with excessive heat. This explains damage you may have noticed to feet of mistreated old pots.

Foods may be cooked directly in the Dutch oven pot or in an earthenware dish or tin pan placed in the oven. You may put a trivet, a pair of S-hooks, or green sticks in the bottom of the pot if needed to position a dish or pan midway between top and bottom.

Pull out a layer of coals on hearth or ground near the fire. Set preheated pot on coals. Put in food. Place lid, and shovel coals onto top.

If your food rests directly on the pot bottom, you may balance the heat by having fewer coals beneath the pot and more coals on top. In other cases you may need less heat on the lid to avoid burning the top of a pie or cake. Rotate the pot several times during cooking to provide even heat to the sides.

One advantage to baking in a Dutch oven is the ability to separately control heat on top, bottom, and sides. This is where not only skill but art enters the picture. With experience the cook develops a sense of where the heat is and where more is needed. You may find baking in a ceramic or tin pan in the Dutch oven allows more control of the process. Practice will bring out your special tricks for turning out perfect cakes and pies.

When developing the mindset for hearth baking, begin with little cakes or gingerbreads, for these cook quickly with a single heating of the oven. Then advance to pies, breads, or cakes that will require replenishing coals to maintain even heat on all surfaces.

✍ Cakes, Great and Small

"Put Currants in Some, Carroway Seeds in Some, and Some Plain as you Please"

Pre-1744 Virginia manuscript cookbook, 87.

A receipt for *cake* may turn out either a cookie, a candy, or what we would still today consider a cake. Large cakes were often variations on the basic pound cake. Plum cake was typically a pound cake with a couple pounds of dried fruits added. Caraway seeds were also added to pound type cakes.

Another family of cakes depended on yeast. Today we would consider these sweet breads. To further confuse the subject, varieties of plum cakes and of seed cakes are found among both pound cake and sweet yeast bread receipts. Many sources included one of each type. For example Mrs. Johnson conveniently provided basic recipes that may become either plum or seed cake when "you put what Currants, or Carraway-Seeds, into it you think proper."[2]

Plum cakes and seed cakes—of either yeast bread or pound cake type— properly reside in Chapter 8 among Special Occasions receipts. A large cake is difficult to bake in an iron pot at the hearth. Such cakes were more common in homes with a bake oven and in towns with a bakery. Grand cakes were likely to have been created by a professional baker.

Seed cakes were traditional for agricultural celebrations. Plum cakes were particularly popular at weddings, baptisms, Christmas and such festive occasions. Either sort of cake might have been kept on hand to offer to guests.

An earlier type of cake depended on bread crumbs rather than flour. These may be thought of as dry bread pudding as much as cake. A cherry cake of this sort was discovered among German receipts in the Schmidt manuscript.

A Good Cherry Cake [translation]

Take 2 pounds of cherries and half a pound of butter and stir it until it becomes white. Then take 12 eggs and stir in one after the other. Then stir in 1 ½ quarters of finely pounded sugar [6 ounces or ¾ cup] and a quarter [4 ounces] of fine pounded almonds. Add also ¼ ounce of cloves and ¼ ounce of cinnamon. Cut the peels of a lemon into little pieces. Take about 4 ounces of bread crumbs and moisten them with wine, then stir everything together for about half an hour. Then butter the baking tin and also put some flour on it. Then fill in the dough and let it bake slowly in the oven.

Schmidt household book, 75
(translated from the German).

The resulting cake is an interesting bit of edible history. Half this receipt yields a good sized cake. Although this cherry cake is tasty and historically appropriate, you may decide that such dear ingredients as fresh cherries and almond flour may be better used otherwise.

✍ Little Cakes

The name *cookie* was seldom encountered in early sources. Small, cookie type cakes were ancestral to today's sugar cookies, shortbread, gingerbread, lady fingers, or meringues.

Most recipe collections included one or more recipes for simple small cakes, often simply named "little cakes." One imagines these as relatively quick and easy treats when time was short, perhaps upon arrival of unexpected guests. All were special as they required sugar with butter and/or eggs.

One receipt from an early Virginia source advised: "You must put Currants in Some . . . Carroway Seeds in Some, and Some Plain as you Please." Thus we may produce the three most common sorts of "little cakes," with currants, with caraway, or plain, from any basic receipt. Individual preference will dictate the flavorings. Select from rose water, mace, and/or a dash of cloves, or allow the subtle, rich essence of butter, sugar, and egg to shine through.

Receipts for "little cakes" display the variety possible through varying proportions of basic ingredients: flour and sugar with butter and/or eggs. The recreated open hearth cook will do well to select a personal favorite tea cake receipt, just as his or her ancestors did. The three receipts below became favorites from many cakes tested. Each is from an early southern manuscript. Eliza Lucas Pinckney's "little cakes" are typical, as they are easily assembled from few ingredients:

To make little cakes for tea [*attributed to a "Mrs. Middleton"*]

Of butter, flower, sugar, a quarter of a pound of each and as much yolk of Egg as will mix it in to a stiff paste make them into round cakes and bake them on tinns about the size of half a crown. Put some carraway seeds in them

Pinckney household book.

Eliza Lucas Pinckney's Little Cakes for Tea (Interpretation)

- ¼ pound butter
- 1 scant cup flour
- ½ cup sugar
- 1 egg yolk
- 1 teaspoon caraway seeds

For cakes "the size of half a crown" (approximately 1 ¼ inch) form dough into small marble sized balls and press flat. Alternately, dough may be rolled and cut in shapes.

Silver Teapot. Eliza Lucas Pinckney. South Carolina lowcountry, 1752–53. Maker: Thomas Whipham, London. Courtesy of the Charleston Museum, Charleston, South Carolina.

Such little cakes persisted in popularity. We find the same receipt a century later in Sarah Rutledge's *Carolina Housewife*. Caraway seeds are tasty and quite fashionable for the period, although these little cakes are also marvelous without the seeds. Just imagine how elegant these little cakes became when served with tea from Eliza Pinckney's silver tea pot.

A German housewife brought a rather differently textured sort of simple cakes to coastal Georgia. Her egg rich "My basic cookies" contain little sugar and therefore bake up delightfully delicate and fragile.

My basic cookies

Take a pound of butter and a pound of flour, 6 egg yellows, 6 spoons of sugar. You don't have to work long with the dough, just make the flour disappear and then press it onto baking tins. Otherwise it will not rise.

Schmidt household book, 5 (translated from the German).

From Virginia we get another delicious little cake, related to the above receipts although more flavorful and dotted with currants rather than caraway.In another, almost identical receipt "To make Little Cakes," the unidentified author doubled the sugar and increased the rose water to three spoonfuls. The stronger rose flavor is lovely; on the other hand, the additional sugar produced a harder cookie.[3]

To Make Little Cakes

Take 1 ½ lb flower & ½ lb white Sugar 1 lb Currants mix them well together Then take Six Eggs 1 lb of Butter 2 Spoonfulls of Rose watter: a little Cloves and mace beaten Work them together till it is like a Custard: then put to them ye flower & Sugar Currants & work them together little balls & lay them upon tin plats & bake them in a Gentle Oven

> Unidentified cookbook, c. 1700, Harbury, *Virginia's Cooking Dynasty*, 208.

Little Cakes, Virginia c. 1700 (Interpretation, one-third receipt)

Work together:

> 2 eggs
> 6 ounces butter
> 2 (or 3) teaspoons rose water
> ¼ teaspoon mace and a dash of cloves

Add:

> 1 ¾ cup flour
> ⅓ cup sugar
> ¾ cup currants

Form into little balls and bake.

Another anonymous lowcountry South Carolina lady made "Little Cakes," more like Hannah Glasse's "Another Sort of Little Cakes," that turn out crumbly dough that must be firmly pressed to form little cakes, almost like playing with wet sand. They cook up into tasty little balls, nice while fresh from the oven, but tooth breakers when cold. We prefer the South Carolina, Georgia, and Virginia receipts presented here.[4]

Our ancestors' little cakes were not today's sugar cookies and gingerbreads. Chemical leavening agents had not appeared on the scene. Our over stimulated taste buds delight in the clear flavors of these heirloom baked goods.

✍ Gingerbreads

Gingerbreads took many forms and were widely enjoyed. In the North Carolina Moravian settlements, ginger cakes were sold in shops, and on occasion were taken to Salisbury to sell during Court Days. Although William Byrd rarely deviated from his usual Spartan breakfast of milk, he once noted beginning the day with gingerbread and tea. On a visit to Williamsburg in 1711 he enjoyed gingerbread often. Once, while spending a day reviewing troops with the governor, they "ate gingerbread all day long."[5]

The "Ginger bread Cakes" below may have been penned by one of William Byrd's neighbors. A receipt similar to these c.1700 ginger cakes showed up in Glasse's *Art of Cookery* in several editions through the century. The North Carolina Cameron method from over a century later is identical but for the substitution of egg for cream. The choice might have depended on whether you had a milk cow or a laying hen. The resulting cakes are nearly indistinguishable in flavor and differ only slightly in texture. Both are lovely and both doughs work well. Ginger cakes may be rolled thick or thin, cut into shapes, or stamped with a cake mold.[6]

Ginger bread Cakes

Take 3 pd. of flower a pd. of sugar & a pd. of butter rubb'd in very fine an ounce of ginger & a greated nutmeg mix it with a pd. of treacle then & a quarter of a pint of cream warm'd together then make up yor. bread stiff roul then out them in little cakes & bake them in a slack oven.

Unidentified cookbook, c. 1700, Harbury, *Virginia's Cooking Dynasty*, 246.

Ginger Bread

To 3 quarts of fine flour, well dried add 1 lb butter, 1 lb brown sugar, 1 Nutmeg beat fine, 10 races Ginger beaten, 4 Eggs and as much treacle, as will suit the whole, work it into Dough, till it will roll out fine and smooth, then shape your Gingerbread according to fancy, and bake them in a quick Oven.

Cameron, "Friend to the Memory," 3.

Ginger Bread (*Interpretation from Cameron and Unidentified c. 1700 manuscripts, one-fourth receipt*)

- ¼ pound butter
- ½ cup brown sugar
- 1 egg or 2 Tablespoonfuls cream
- 3 cups flour
- ¼ teaspoonful nutmeg
- 2 Tablespoonfuls ginger (or 1 ½ teaspoons cloves for Clove Cakes)
- Enough treacle (cane sugar syrup) to mix dough (½ to ¾ cup)

Roll out (thin or thick as desired) and cut into shapes or stamp with cake print. Bake.

Among the multitude of gingerbread receipts, ginger was often joined by other spices: cinnamon, mace, nutmeg, allspice, or cloves. The Alston manuscript proposed "Clove Cake," identical to the above ginger bread except for the spice. This South Carolina variation replaced two tablespoonsful ginger with one-half tablespoonful (one and one-half teaspoons) cloves, for an interesting difference.

Cake Mold. Salem, North Carolina, c. 1800. John Blum, carver. Collection of the Wachovia Historical Society, photograph courtesy of Old Salem Museums & Gardens.

Another backcountry North Carolina gingerbread results in an interestingly flavored and differently textured cake. This receipt yields a batter or sticky dough and so results in thin cakes or soft cookies. The flavoring combination of rose water and brandy with ginger was echoed in Rutledge's *The Carolina Housewife* ginger pound cake, although the two receipts were otherwise dissimilar. Rutledge also included a Sugar Ginger Bread similar to the following from an early North Carolina Moravian.[7]

Sugar Gingerbread

1 & ½ lb Sugar—2 lbs Flour—¾ lb Butter—9 Eggs—Cup Rose Water—Do Brandy—Do Ginger

Schober commonplace book.

The above proportions seemed unworkable, but we abided by the receipt. The flavor was exceptional; however, the gingerbread turned out a little "sad" (moist in the center). Is it possible Mrs. Schober was measuring seasonings with a tea cup rather than a measuring cup? Going with the possibility that her cup held less than a standard cup, perhaps 5 or 6 ounces (a scant ¾ cup), the resulting gingerbread has a better texture. Perhaps we crossed the line from interpretation into adaptation? This gingerbread is unusual, but too luscious to omit.

Sugar Gingerbread [*Loose interpretation based on Schober, one-third recipe*]

¼ pound butter

1 cup sugar

3 eggs

2 ⅔ cups flour

A scant ¼ cup each rose water, brandy, and ground ginger.

Bake as drop cakes or as 3 or 4 layers of six-inch diameter.

Gingerbreads of all types were enhanced with fresh, dried, or candied orange or lemon peel, candied ginger or citron, caraway or coriander seeds. An interesting combination of orange peel and caraway flavored Scots receipts for "Dutch Ginger-bread" and "Fine gingerbread." An American version recommended using one or the other, not both: "You may leave out the Sweet Meats if you please and put in . . . Coriander or Carraway Seeds."[8]

Although eighteenth-century gingerbreads took many forms, as a group they were distinctly different from both their ancestors and descendants.

Earthenware Teapot (archaeological reconstruction). Bethabara, North Carolina, c. 1755–1771. Attributed to Moravian potter Gottfried Aust. Courtesy of the Museum of Early Southern Decorative Arts (MESDA) at Old Salem.

Gingerbreads seem to have been less common and quite different before this time. Seventeenth-century cookery books described gingerbreads based on ground almond or bread crumbs rather than flour.[9]

The close of the eighteenth century brought a revolution in cake baking. With the advent of chemical leavenings—pearlash, saluratus, and then soda and baking powder—the textures of cakes and cookies changed, and their tastes as well. Of twelve ginger cakes in the 1872 *Southern Practical Cookery* eleven contained soda. One traditional receipt remained; "Ginger Nuts" was basic rolled and cut gingerbread that a southern housewife from a century before would have recognized.[10]

✍ Macaroons

Among German language entries in the Schmidt manuscript are several little *cakes* that are actually macaroons flavored with cinnamon, nutmeg, lemon peel, and more. Von Rumohr's antipathy toward such lovely German sweets was curious. He warned, "Whole communities have been known to inflict the most serious damage to their entire digestive systems by the consumption of almond pastries and cakes." We beg to differ.[11]

Macaroons were of almond. Not until well into the nineteenth century was the distinction *almond* or *coconut* necessary. Receipts were many but varied little. Although we planned to repeat none of the material gathered into *The Backcountry Housewife*, the Stockton receipt for macaroons is one of the clearest and includes most common elements. The unidentified c. 1700 manuscript method for "Mackaroons" was similar.[12]

To make macaroons

Take a pound Almonds scald and blanch them throw them into water drain them and wipe them pound them in a mortar moistening them with orange flower or rose water or the white of a beaten egg—least they should turn to oil then take an equal quantity of fine sugar with three or four other whites of eggs—beat all well together drop them on a sheet of paper and bake them on a slow fire

Stockton receipt book, 47.

Comparing a bevy of macaroons yielded few differences. Equal quantities of sugar and almond were typical; another group of authors advised only three quarters pound sugar to each pound nuts. Four or five egg whites was a typical proportion for one pound almond flour, although some receipts called for as few as three or as many as eight. Bake on a greased pan, on paper, or on special flour paste wafers.[13]

Although you may find almond flour commercially available, the method outlined in the macaroon receipt above yields a more interesting result.

Pounded Almonds, Almond Meal or Flour (Interpretation)

Blanch shelled raw almonds for several minutes in boiling water or until the
    skins will slip from the nuts.

Drain the nuts and remove the skins.

Spread the blanched almonds to dry several hours or overnight.

Pound nuts, a few at a time, with mortar and pestle, paying attention to the
    consistency.

When the pounded almonds begin to appear oily or clump together, a few drops
    of rose water or orange flower water will rather magically separate the mass
    into almond meal.

☙ Naples Biscuit

As numerous little cakes and gingerbreads are easily made and quite delicious,
one wonders why cakes of the Naples biscuits family were so beloved for centuries. These small sponge cakes are labor intensive and tricky to make. That
may explain their appeal. Perhaps the Naples biscuit, and its descendant the
lady finger, were status symbols on the tea table.

Light biscuits (small cakes) of egg, flour, and sugar with no shortening have
a complex genealogy. They came by a variety of names: Naples, Savoy, Drop,
Sponge, and Common Biscuits. To *The French Cook* of 1653 it was simply Biscuit. Most of us today would call them lady fingers, although that name did
not appear in early sources. By 1872 we find Lady Fingers in *Southern Practical
Cookery*.[14]

Naples biscuits were employed as thickening in puddings or in construct-
ing desserts such as the trifle. It is therefore curious that some basic cookery
books did not give a receipt for these little cakes yet listed Naples biscuits as an
ingredient in a variety of preparations. When a receipt simply calls for biscuit
one may puzzle whether this little sponge cake or the basic cracker like biscuit
is required

Since these delicate cakes are a bit tricky to make at the hearth, one suspects
they were an item for affluent households and may have been purchased from
a professional baker. Karen Hess theorized Naples biscuits may have been imported. Evidence suggests some early American households were producing
them at home. Two early nineteenth-century North Carolinians jotted down
brief formulas. Anna Paulina Schober wrote "14 ozs Flour—12 ozs Sugar—6
Eggs—Carraway comfits over them if you please—Naples Biscuit." The Cameron family receipt was quite different: "Ten Eggs, the wt of 9 in sugar & six
in flour, one yolk may be left out." Neither of those backcountry housewives
bothered to detail a method. The trick was said to be in beating the eggs until
very light, gently adding in dry ingredients, and getting the biscuits into the
oven quickly.[15]

Naples Bisquits

Take 12 Eggs both yolks and whites, let them be well beaten and Strain'd, then beat them with a whisk until They are light one pound of sugar, one pound fine Wheat flour, butter your pans and fill them but half full, a quarter of an hour will bake them

> Pre-1744 Virginia cookbook, 90.

It is reasonable to assume a post-1744 date for the above receipt, for it was added to the manuscript in a third handwriting style, following recipes attributed to a Jane Randolph with the date 1744.

The Naples Bisquits receipt concluded "lay them on pewter dishes till they are Cold and then put them into the Oven again till they are dry." Other authors omitted the final drying.

Caution: Use of pewter is not recommended near the fire or oven. Pewter has a low melting point and should not be heated. We have witnessed bouncing drops of pewter in a spider from a half melted spoon as an inexperienced and greatly embarrassed hearth cook sautéed onions. A pewter spoon may even soften and bend when used to serve hot food. The above receipt may have assumed the cook would switch the Naples biscuits to a pan for drying in the oven, or perhaps a barely warm oven was understood. Simply placing cakes on pewter to cool should offer little danger; however, be cautious of moist and acid foods in contact with old pewter, as low quality antique pewter contained lead.

The majority of Naples biscuits receipts agreed on equal weights of flour and sugar. Most other methods involved more sugar than flour; the Schober receipt was an exception. Number of eggs varied widely. Six, eight, ten, or twelve eggs were suggested to mix up one pound each of flour and sugar. By the twentieth century the proportion of egg was much greater.

The French Cook's proportions were also typical through centuries. Naples biscuits in the unidentified c. 1700 Virginia cookbook, the nineteenth-century Cameron manuscript and *The Kentucky Housewife* followed this ratio of sugar to flour but with varying amounts of egg. The Virginia receipt called for only six eggs, the French eight, the Kentucky ten, the North Carolina Cameron receipt a dozen or more.[16]

How to make bisket

Take eight eggs, one pound sugar into powder, with three quarters of a pound of flowre. Mix all together, and thus it will be neither too soft nor too hard.

> La Varenne, *French Cook*, 240.

Several receipts added seasonings. For appropriate period flavor you may choose from rose water, orange peel, peach kernels, white wine or brandy, nutmeg, caraway or coriander.

Virginian Mary Randolph described the proper pans for Naples biscuits as "long pans, four inches wide, with divisions; so that each cake, when done will be four inches long, and one and a half wide." Authors directing to bake "in molds" were likely recommending these specialized pans. A finger shape was the norm, even when baking on a flat pan. It seems this distinctive shape was well known. In 1699 *Acetaria* John Evelyn noted one of his seasoning mixes was to be formed "in shape of Naples-Biscuit" which revealed two facts: the shape was commonly known and was distinct from other cakes. William Byrd casually mentioned a gift of Naples biscuit in his "Secret History," again suggesting common knowledge but also novelty.[17]

As late as 1839 *The Kentucky Housewife*, Lettice Bryan, detailed a hearth option: baking Naples biscuit in muffin rings in a Dutch oven. As usual, we can count on her to detail the method.

Naples Biscuit

Beat ten eggs as light as possible, first separating the whites from the yolks; and after they are beaten, mix them together again. Add one pound of powdered sugar, a glass of white wine, and two powdered nutmegs. Beat the whole very well, and then stir in lightly and gradually three quarters of a pound of fine flour. Stir it no more than is really necessary to mix it well, as much stirring will make the biscuit tough. Place some muffin rings on the bottom of a clean, hot oven, having them first rubbed lightly with butter to prevent the biscuit sticking to them; put in your batter by spoonfuls, filling the rings about half full, and bake them with a brisk heat.

Bryan, *Kentucky Housewife*, 290–91.

In seventeenth-century England, Naples biscuit had been another thing altogether, an almond and pine nut macaroon rather than a lady finger. "Take of the same stuff the Mackaroons are made of [egg white, sugar, pounded almond], and put to it an ounce of pine-apple-seeds [pine nuts] . . . for that is all the difference between Mackaroons and the Naples Bisket." Although biscuits and almond macaroons were quite different, their uses overlapped.[18]

✺ Naples Biscuits and Macaroons used in puddings and more

Naples biscuits and macaroons are quite nice on their own. Employing these special cakes to thicken desserts seems improvident but delicious. Nevertheless, that was the practice.

Naples biscuits were widely known and employed as thickener. Among English language entries in the Schmidt manuscript receipt book was a basic pudding, thickened with Naples biscuit and boiled in a ceramic bowl. I judge the pudding and bowl were to be tied up in a cloth as in similar receipts. This pudding may be simply boiled in a buttered cloth without the bowl. Refer to Chapter 3 for details of tying a pudding in cloth for boiling, with or without a bowl.

Naple Biscuit Pudding

Take a Pint of Milk, boil it and pour it over as much Naple Biscuit as will make it thick, then beat up the yolks of 4 Eggs and half the whites, 1 spoonfull of flour, 2 Oz of powder Sugar, a little Orange flowr water, some grated Nutmeg, add them all together, and boil it an hour in a China Bason, well butter the inside of it first. Beat up some butter, sugar, and sack for sauce.

Schmidt household book, 80.

Although the quantity of biscuit is vague, the other ingredients will produce custard however few or many Naples biscuits are used. About two cups crumbled biscuit is good. Wolley's almond pudding was quite similar but for a quarter pound of pounded almonds in place of Schmidt's spoonful of flour. She noted "you may boil it, or bake it, or put it into Skins." Kettilby's "Orange Pudding for Skins" was thick with Naples biscuit, pounded almonds, and bread, bound with egg and lard, stuffed into skins (intestines) and boiled.[19]

Scots author Elizabeth Cleland called for "Spunge Biscuits" as base of a trifle. Englishwoman Hannah Glasse's trifle begins: "Cover the bottom of your dish or bowl with Naples biscuits broke in pieces, mackeroons broke in halves, and ratafia cakes." In one nineteenth-century variation a sponge cake was hollowed to contain the custard, jelly, and perhaps fruit. Sliced sponge cake or other cake became a substitute for the Naples biscuits. The Stockton receipt below is a good basic method that traveled to America. Naples biscuits or sponge cake would be just as successful as the macaroons. Cover the bottom of your dish with the biscuits and proceed as directed with wine, custard, and whipped cream. Overnight soaking will not be necessary as biscuit is more absorbent than almond macaroon.[20]

Trifle

Half a pound of macaroons [or Naples biscuit], place them in the dish intended to serve it in, soak them one night in as much sweet wine as will just cover them, then press gently with back of a spoon, cover them with a thin boiled custard &

over that a whipt syllabub, garnish it with currant jelly raspberry jam or any other sweetmeat.

Stockton receipt book, 4.

Glasse's suggested garnish of flowers along with jelly sounds even prettier. Violets and rose petals come to mind.

✍ Breads

A small loaf can be baked in a Dutch oven; however, sufficient bread for a household required a bake oven or a nearby bakery. Loaf bread receipts are left for those of you with bake ovens.

Judging from travelers' journals, the more commonly eaten breads were of corn meal, baked on an iron sheet or griddle, on a board propped beside the fire, in a Dutch oven, or even on a hot stone covered with ashes and coals.

The same methods work for small breads of wheat and other grains. Early biscuit and muffin receipts are likely to surprise you.

✍ Biscuits

Biscuits of two centuries ago were nothing like today's beloved fluffy or flakey quick bread. An eighteenth-century *biscuit* was a hard cracker, a mildly sweet yeast biscuit, or the little sponge cake made light with egg (Naples biscuit). The basic biscuit or cracker was simply flour made up with a little butter and either milk or water. The dough was beaten with a rolling pin or other instrument to add a bit of lightness.

Hard Biscuits

Warm two ounces of butter in as much skimmed milk as will make a pound of flour into a very stiff past, beat it with a rolling pin, and work it very smooth. Roll it thin, and cut it into round biscuits; prick them full of holes with a fork. About six minutes will bake them.

Rundell, *New System of Domestic Cookery*, 247.

These were known as hard biscuit, ships biscuit, or simply biscuit, until the end of the nineteenth century when they gained the descriptive name *beaten* biscuits. Hard biscuit was a convenient travel food or provision for soldiers or sailors, useful for thickening sauces and soups at home or on the road.[21]

A delicious family of early biscuits were made tender with yeast. These spanned the eighteenth century under evolving names. "Tavern," "Wine," and "Dutch" biscuits and "Biscuit Bread" were begun from scratch with flour, butter, liquid (milk or water), and yeast plus a little sugar. The early Tavern Biskett was fragrant with subtle flavor from sack or rose water; Dutch biscuit contained caraway. Later receipts survive from Virginia and both Carolinas. The

Cameron manuscript receipt for "Miss Butler's biscuit," *The Virginia House-wife's* "Nice" and *The Carolina Housewife's* identical "Very Light" Biscuits were simply risen bread dough with a little butter kneaded in, cut into thick or thin biscuits and baked.[22]

To make Tavern Biskett

To one Gallon of fine Flower one pound Fresh Butter, Rub'd Dry in the Flower, one pound fine Sugar half a pint good Yeast mix 2 or 3 Spoonsfull of Sack or Rose Water, make it into a stiff past, with Milk and Water make the Biskett thin and Bake them well. . . . Rise the Yeast.

Pre-1744 Virginia cookbook, 90 (added later, by another hand).

Tavern biscuit [Interpretation, one-fourth receipt]

Rub one fourth pound butter into four cups flour until no lumps remain.
Stir in one half cup sugar.
Add one cup warm milk and/or water with one package yeast dissolved in
    two tablespoonfuls warm water.
Flavor with two teaspoonfuls sack or rose water, if desired.
Add more liquid as needed to form workable dough.
Allow to rise, "Knead it quickly up, and let it repose an hour."[23]
Roll thin, cut out biscuits, and bake.

This may well have been the sort of biscuits served to celebrate General Oglethorpe's birthday in Georgia in 1737. Local officials and inhabitants gathered at a fort "where, some bottles of wine and some biscuit being prepared, about noon His Majesty's health and the Royal family's were drank under a discharge of thirteen guns."[24]

✍ The Yeast Challenge

Yeasts are everywhere. These little plants possess different flavors and differing hardiness. Our ancestors knew how to capture and nourish yeasts, and when they found one they really liked, they employed various tricks to propagate it. Yeasts are basic to brewing as well as baking. In fact yeast for bread was typically a byproduct of brewing or the preliminary steps of distilling.

When experimenting with brandy and whiskey making at a living history farm, a group of historical interpreters produced some interesting breads from the fermenting fruit pomace and corn mash. On one particular occasion we were distilling apple brandy, and of course baking. I scooped a jug of the fragrant bubbly apple pulp, carried it to the warm dark log kitchen, and set about my bread making. Several hours later the fragrant round of well risen dough was baking in a Dutch oven. At this point an especially curious visitor who had been wandering back through the cabin all afternoon to check the bread's progress, asked to take the remaining yeast out onto the porch to examine better in the sunlight. It was then we discovered what no one had noticed earlier. The pomace was alive with more than healthy yeast. The pulp was wiggly with maggots.

The ending of that story is the bread turned out nicely. Although I forewarned the historical interpreters who sat down to dinner at the end of that busy day, those of us who tasted the bread pronounced it delicious. The legend of the maggoty bread persists.

Beyond that adventure, fellow open hearth cooks and I have experimented with capturing yeasts in a variety of ways and with mixed success. We have chopped apple peelings and cores; mashed overripe peaches; and prepared Harriot Horry's potato, hops, and brown sugar medium. Each was set aside from several days to a week, until bubbling with a yeasty smell. With a little pampering some of these yeasts produced a decent loaf. A few truly delicious strains of yeast have resulted; some were "off" flavored; and many were uninteresting. We have definitely not mastered this aspect of eighteenth-century foodways and consider it as much magic as science. There is much more to experience. We challenge you to capture, nourish, and propagate your own particular pet yeasts.

Period cookery books typically include one or more recipes for yeast. These are mainly recipes for a medium in which to propagate a favorite yeast that had been captured or acquired from a brewer or baker. A cook who baked often could simply save a lump of dough buried in flour, ready to dissolve in warm water and feed before beginning the next week's baking.

Baking yeast breads or cakes from historic recipes generally forces today's cook to adapt rather than simply interpret. Yeast presents a problem that most of us address by adapting to modern yeasts. When we substitute today's dry yeast for yesterday's yeast or barm, our tavern biscuits, muffins, and seed cakes can never be quite like the ancestral baked goods.

✒ Corn Breads

The simplest corn cake (ash cake, journey cake, johnny cake, hoe cake, Indian corn bread, bannock, or griddle bread) was mixed from cornmeal and water or simply made from leftover mush. A little salt or fat made it better. More tempting corn breads contained eggs, milk, butter, and perhaps molasses or maple sugar. Flour mixed with the cornmeal was a refinement. A little mashed sweet potato or pumpkin was also considered an improvement.[25]

There is great variability among corn bread batters, in fact one suspects the experienced cook estimated quantities and used no exact receipt for these everyday breads. Some formal receipts for corn breads appeared in early American cook books. Most were rather sophisticated; however, schoolboy William Blackford, recorded two simple corn breads reminiscent of a century before. The fact that the Johnny Cake requires additional water and "Flappers" a little less milk causes one to suspect that these receipts may have been collected from a family cook who tended to simply mix to a desired consistency.

Johnny Cake

Mix a quart of corn meal, and a pint of water in a pan, to a batter, and add a small teaspoonful of salt. Beat until it becomes quite light. Then spread it thickly and evenly on a stout piece of board, and set upright before the fire and bake well. Cut into squares, split and butter them hot, and send them to table.

Blackford, "Recipes in the Culinary Arts," 38.

Experience revealed that additional water is required to mix this quantity of meal into a workable batter; use about three cups of hot water for a quart of meal. This rudimentary corn bread does indeed bake well on a dry board. By this method the cake bakes from one side only.

Johnny cakes also cook handily as griddle cakes where they can be turned to brown on both sides. One might argue that corn cakes then become batter cakes, pancakes, slapjacks, or flapjacks. In contrast to the heavy and hearty Johnny Cake the following receipt yields thin, delicate pancakes.

"Indian Flappers"

Mix one pint of flour, a quart of meal, and a little salt. Beat 8 eggs very light and stir them by degrees into two quarts of milk in turn with the meal. They can be made in a very short time and should be baked as soon as mixed on a hot griddle, allow a large ladlefull of batter to each cake and make them all of the same size. Send them to table, hot, buttered and cut in half.

N.B. The proportions of course can be lessened if desirable.

Blackford, "Recipes in the Culinary Arts," 39.

The question then becomes when is a griddle bread a pancake and when is it a muffin? Any of these American quick breads might have been made of corn, wheat, or rice, as they were made of oats, wheat, or barley in European homelands. At the beginning of the nineteenth century, naturalist F. A. Michaux found a log "public house" in the Pennsylvania backcountry "tolerably well supplied with provisions for the country, as they served us up for dinner slices of ham and venison fried on the hearth, with a kind of muffins made of flour, which they baked before the fire upon a little board."[26]

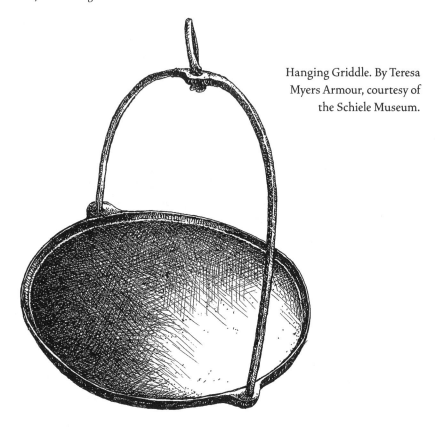

Hanging Griddle. By Teresa Myers Armour, courtesy of the Schiele Museum.

✎ Muffins

In 1837 Mecklenburg County, North Carolina, Sarah Few Davidson and guests arrived home one evening to find supper ready, and so they partook of "one cup of hot coffee—muffins &c. &c." These chance remarks set me wondering about *muffins*. (And what was the *etcetera* served with coffee and muffins at the Davidson plantation?)[27]

As we might expect, muffins of two centuries ago were nothing like today's outrageous cake like muffins that might appropriately serve several people rather than an individual. Although Jane Randolph entered muffins in her 1743 manuscript and Hannah Glasse in 1747 gave a method "To make Muffings and Oat-Cakes" it seems that the name *muffin* was not common until the turn of the century. Michaux was familiar with them in 1801, while Miss Davidson considered muffins worthy of note in her 1837 journal although she rarely mentioned food otherwise.[28]

Most nineteenth-century personal collections and cookery publications contained at least one receipt for muffins. *The Carolina Housewife* furnished two mainstream receipts, corn muffins as well as wheat muffins, both with yeast. In addition, her rice muffins, egg muffins, and corn ring cakes illustrated the link between ancestral griddle cakes and the new yeasty versions.[29]

The most basic of muffins was found among Cameron family receipts, akin to Hannah Glasse's and Jane Randolph's simple flour, yeast, and warm water mixtures. A thick batter or sticky dough is the wanted "tolerably stiff" texture.

Muffins

2 spoonsful of yeast, a little salt, about 3 half pints water, & sufficient flour to make it tolerably stiff.

> Cameron, "Friend to the Memory," 10.

This amount of water will require about eight cups of flour with a packet of yeast softened in two tablespoons warm water. Half quantities will produce a good batch of muffins. *The Carolina Housewife* described the proper consistency, "as much flour as will make it thick enough for a spoon to stand" and added, "To be baked in rings." Her receipt was richer than the above, as were most.[30]

Schober's early nineteenth-century version from the North Carolina backcountry was typical, although her cooking instructions were atypical. Cooking on the hearth harkened back to earlier days. Related muffin receipts instructed the cook to bake the muffins on a griddle, usually in tin rings. An Avery family receipt is similar to Schober's with the exception of doubling the eggs and adding a little sugar and salt. The Avery manuscript recommended "make into a stiff batter at bedtime & set to rise for breakfast" as Mary Randolph also suggested. The yeast will dictate the time necessary for the batter to become light. These receipts result in pleasing muffins, a step above the basic.[31]

Muffins

Mix two pounds of flower with two eggs, two ounces of butter, melted in a pint of milk & four or five spoonfuls of yeast, beat it thoroughly & set it to rise 3 [or] 4 hours. Bake on a hot hearth in flat cakes. When done on one side turn them over.

> Schober commonplace book.

Muffins (Interpretation from Schober and Avery, one-half receipt)

> 4 cups flour
> 1 ounce butter melted in 1 cup warm milk
> ½ or 1 packet yeast in 2 tablespoons warm water
> 1 (or 2) egg
> (Optional: a little salt and sugar)

Mix thoroughly, then allow to rise

Bake on a griddle in metal rings, or on a hot hearth in flat cakes, turning to
  brown on both sides.

Several popular authors contributed details for baking muffins. Eliza Leslie
directed, when the dough is light "grease your baking-iron, and your muffin
rings. Set the rings on the iron, and pour batter into them. Bake them a light
brown." A griddle was the usual baking iron. Glasse's flat sheet of iron served
the purpose, especially for travelers. Dods noted that muffins "at a pinch may
be baked on the Scotch girdle [*sic*], or in a thick-bottomed frying-pan, or the
cottage-oven pot." Mary Randolph reminded the cook to "put it on the griddle
in a round form, and bake nicely, turning them frequently till done."[32]

Quite a few authors cautioned, as Glasse did, "with your Hand pull them
open, and they will be like a Honey-Comb . . . but don't touch them with a
Knife, either to spread [butter] or cut them open, if you do they will be as heavy
as Lead." This would be the cinching clue, if you have not already deduced:
these early muffins were the breads we today call English muffins.[33]

✍ The Pastry Art, a Delicate Touch

We gather insight into pastry making from "Of Apple-Pyes: A poem, by Mr.
Welsted" as included in the English *Country Housewife's Family Companion*.[34]

> Dear Nelly, learn with care the pastry art,
> And mind the easy precepts I impart;
> Draw out your dough elaborately thin,
> And cease not to fatigue your rolling-pin:
> Of eggs and butter, see you mix enough:
> For then the paste will swell into a puff,
> Which will in crumbling sound your praise report,
> And eat, as housewives speak, exceeding short:

Three fundamental ingredients—flour, fat, and water—yield everything from
a sturdy pie casing to lovely flaky puff pastry. Proportions vary, as does technique.

There are many eighteenth-century pastry receipts. Some depended on
drippings, lard, or suet. Some were beaten, as one might pound hard biscuit
or cracker dough. Another family of pastries, for "coffins" or "raised" crusts,
was mixed with hot fat and liquid. The filling for which the pastry was intended prescribed the fat to be used. Alternately, any fat at hand could produce
a pie crust in a pinch. Many receipts await further exploration. We have been
delighted with results from the rich and flavorful varieties included here.

Today's year round abundance of butter, eggs, and cream allows us to adopt
extraordinary pastry as an ordinary choice. Nevertheless, bear in mind the

historical context. In earlier days such extravagance was limited by seasonal availability and prosperity of the household.

A meander through historical cookery books revealed an eighteenth-century fondness for the texture and taste differences achieved from including egg in pastry. Another lavish touch involved milk or cream in place of water, perhaps with brandy, wine, or even rose water. We were interested to find only a few receipts suggesting salt.

We selected groups of similar receipts to test. Each of the new favorite pastry methods included here were common to at least three early sources. This study centered on general purpose crusts, typical of the time, but a step above the ordinary. Family and friends declared experimentation with early pastries their favorite facet of this project.

✒ A Crust above the Ordinary

For a simple crust you may enjoy the receipt touted by von Rumohr as borrowed from the French, those "undisputed experts when it comes to making firm pastry for cold pies"; by English authors, Glasse and Johnson, for a general "cold crust"; and by C. Carter who added a little sugar for "Tart Paste for Patty-pan Tarts." Two of the receipts called for whole egg, two for egg yolk only.[35]

A Cold Crust

To three Pounds of Flour, rub in a Pound and half of Butter, break in two Eggs, and make it up with cold Water.

> Glasse, *Art of Cookery* (1747), 75 & Johnson,
> *Every Young Woman's Companion*, 102.

Glasse and Johnson's Cold Crust (*Interpretation, one-sixth receipt*)

To a scant 2 cups flour, rub or cut in 4 ounces butter.
Mix in about one-third whole egg or about three-quarters of a yolk (estimate).
Add cold water as needed to mix into a workable pastry.

✒ A Rich, Delicate, Crumbly Pastry

The above method produces a nice crust without the egg flavor of the following richer pastry. However, "Crust for Custards" has a particularly appealing delicate crumbly texture.

To make a Crust for Custards

To half a Pound of flour add six Ounces of Butter, three Spoonfuls of Cream, and the Yolks of two Eggs; mix these well together, and let them stand for about a Quarter of an Hour; after that, work it up and down well, and roll it as thin as you please.

Johnson, *Every Young Woman's Companion,* 103

& Glasse, *Art of Cookery* (1747), 76.

This pastry is nice with many sorts of fillings, not only custards. A similar receipt in the Virginia pre-1744 manuscript "To make thin past Crust" was meant for fruit tarts. It appeared among Ashfield family receipts as the proper crust for cheese cakes.[36]

Von Rumohr proposed a whole egg rather than two yolks with the above proportions of flour and butter. He added sugar and a little brandy for flavor. His method was quite different, however, using a puff paste layering technique.[37]

✍ A Puff Pastry

The simplest, and quite lovely, puff pastries were made with only flour, butter, and water. The ingredients are the same as in other crusts, but the order and method of combining ingredients differs. For puff paste only a fraction of the butter is cut into the flour before mixing with liquid. The remaining butter is incorporated though repeatedly rolling out the pastry, dotting with butter, sprinkling with flour, folding into thirds, and rolling again until all the butter is used. For another efficient technique "roll out the Paste, and stick it all over with Butter, shake Flour on it, then roll it like a Collar, double it up at both Ends, that they meet in the Middle" and repeat several times.[38]

To make Puff-Paste.

To a peck of flour you must have three quarters the weight in butter; dry your flour well, and lay it on a table; make a hole, and put in it a dozen whites of eggs well beaten, but first break into it a third part of your butter; then with water make up your paste, then roll it out, and by degrees put in the rest of the butter.

Smith, *Compleat Housewife,* 165.

What a notable example of why one should read a receipt all through before beginning. One third of the butter should be cut into the flour, before adding egg white and water. We would seldom be beginning with a peck of flour. Cutting Smith's proportions yields a more manageable batch of pastry:

E. Smith's Puff-Paste (Interpretation, one-sixteenth recipe)

Cut or rub 2 ounces butter into 2 cups flour.
Stir in a small egg white mixed with ¼ cup cold water. Add more water if needed.
Roll thin. Dot with bits of butter, sprinkle with flour, and fold in thirds.

Repeat several times until 4 additional ounces of butter have been layered into
the paste.

Various receipts recommended from three to as many as a dozen repeats of
the roll-butter-flour-fold process, building flaky layers into the pastry. Some
omitted the egg white. Other authors doubled the egg white or included more
butter. The more butter, the richer the crust. The Cameron manuscript suggested layering twice as much butter into the paste.[39]

✍ A Particularly Good Crust

Not everyone liked the consistency and taste of an egg paste. Englishman
Richard Bradley was especially critical. "There are many sorts of Paste made,
and among them, are some which are made with Eggs, according to the old
fashion; but these are always hard . . . they will fly and crackle in the Mouth,
but they will taste like Sticks." He suggested leaving out the eggs "and your
Paste will melt in the Mouth, and be agreeable to the Taste." Although the
egg pastries are very nice, I agree that the following eggless recipe is particularly good:

Or, to make a good crust,

you may use cold milk instead of cold water, with an addition of as much brandy
as an egg-shell will hold [approximately 3 Tablespoonfuls], and fine sugar, with
two pounds of butter, and three pounds of flower for pyes, tarts, &c.

Ellis, Country Housewife's Family Companion, 91.

Similar receipts differed mainly in quantity of butter. Combining three mid-
eighteenth-century receipts and cutting down proportions yielded the following exceptionally good crust:[40]

Good Crust (Interpretation and combination from Ellis, Bradley, and S. Carter)

Rub in 4 (or as much as 6) ounces cold butter
Into a scant 2 cups flour and 2 (or 3) Tablespoonfuls sugar.
Make into paste with ¼ cup cold milk (more if needed) and up to 1 T. brandy.
Stir just until mixed.

Several secrets for producing tender pastry emerged: Rub cold butter into
flour with cool fingers or cut butter into flour with knives or a pastry blender
until the mixture resembles coarse corn meal. When adding liquid stir just
until paste comes together. Handle the paste as little as possible after liquid
is added. The art to pastry making is a delicate touch. Martha Washington's

ancestral cookery book advised: "nor work it over much, nor heat it with yʳ hand."[41]

When first testing the "Good Crust" receipt, the only brandy on hand was rose brandy. Wow! That was delicious pastry indeed. Perhaps you will find yourself compelled to make that same substitution. Actually, rose scented pastry is not without precedent. *Martha Washington's Booke* suggested sack and rose water in a sweet paste.

᪲ Pastry Styles and Adornments

Then as today, a pie may have one crust or two. When making a pie we generally assume a bottom crust. While that is most often the correct assumption, there are interesting exceptions. From studying scores of early receipts several unique period traits surfaced.

Meat, vegetable, and fruit pies commonly had two crusts. After baking, the pastry lid might be lifted to introduce a *lear* (sauce). Otherwise, the lid was left intact until serving, as today. Alternately one might "cut the lid in pieces and stick it in the meat round the pie."

Use of top crust only may not have been unusual. Quite a few receipts clearly propose the option of an upper crust alone, some with a decorative rim. Dods notes for a gooseberry pie, "Line the dish or merely border it with paste," fill, then cover the pie; while for an apple pie she suggests a strip of pastry around the edge and a cover decorated with leaves and flowers, This opens a welcomed historical option for the cook who, like me, prefers the crisp lid to the moist pastry bottom.[42]

Custard type pies provide interesting options. Although today we think of custard, quiche, pumpkin, and such pies as open faced, early cooks at times added a pastry lid or cross bars.

Another novel and useful technique surfaced among pie and baked pudding receipts. Edging a pie with pastry seemed at first just another case of confusing wording. After encountering multiple instances the question arose: Did they really mean only a rim of pastry, with no side or bottom pastry? That would prevent a lot of spills and overruns, wouldn't it? Consider documentary bits that indicate this practice:

Kettilby (1734) directed, "Garnish the Brim of your Dish with Paste, and lay Slips cross the Top" for spinach pudding and almond pudding."[43]

In 1796 Glasse gave specific pastry styles for different puddings. She was often very precise as to if, how, and where to use paste for baked puddings, from simply "butter your dish" or "puff-paste all round the dish at the bottom" or "lay it all over the dish and round the rim," to only "put a puff-paste round the rim."[44]

Rundell (1810) stated, "A paste round the edge makes all puddings look better, but is not necessary."[45]

According to Dods (1829), "A baked pudding for company has often a paste-border."[46]

Such intriguing hints did not prove the practice of a mere rim of pastry. Thus, we turned to *The Kentucky Housewife* (1839) for detail. Her careful instructions are convincing. "Dishes for baking pudding should be sufficiently deep, and provided with a broad, flat rim, on which to lay a paste, or garnish for the pudding." She expanded this idea in many of her pudding receipts. In each case the pudding mixture was to be poured into a buttered dish with a broad, flat rim. For an almond pudding "lay round it, on the edge of the dish, a thin narrow slip of puff paste, having one edge neatly serated, notched or crimped." The finishing touch for her rice pudding was to cut the paste "into small scalloped leaves, with little tin cutters; concatenate them together, so as to form a wreath, lay it round the pudding, on the edge of the dish." And equally ornamental, "cut it into three long strips, about three quarters of an inch wide; roll them . . . until they become round; plat them together, and lay it round the pudding on the edge of the dish."[47]

While we may not go to the trouble to mix up a batch of paste just to edge a single pudding or pie, when preparing several pies such a touch would be practical. This does not suggest that a particular dish required a particular ornament. As early cooks had individual styles, so we can feel free to develop our own favorite pie and pudding presentations.

Of course we may simply bake a pudding in a buttered dish or a pastry shell as usual, with or without a top. Either a solid lid or lattice is historically appropriate. On occasion we can go wild with pastry embellishments, as our ancestors did.

✍ Fancies and Conceits: *Crinkumcranks*

> Hence we proceed the outward parts to trim,
> with crinkumcranks adorn the polish'd rim,
> and each fresh pye the pleas'd spectator greets
> With virgin fancies and with new conceits.[48]

The OED defines *crinkum-crankum* as "a word applied playfully to anything full of twists and turns, or intricately or fancifully elaborated." But do not nickname your pastry fancies *crinkum*, a term for venereal disease. Twisted or braided paste and a wreath of pastry leaves certainly qualify as crinkumcranks to adorn the rim of a pie, with or without a bottom crust or a lid. Even for a regular two crust pie one might "garnish ye brim of ye dish."[49]

Just what other "fancies" and "conceits" were likely to show up in pastry? Searching stacks of cookery sources revealed answers, and more questions. Many mentions of floral ornaments and decorative borders suggested that we may look to the general vocabulary of period design for inspiration. Foliage, flowers, birds, hearts, swags, and geometric devices were popular in everything from furniture and needlework to tombstones and doodling in school books. It is reasonable to imagine the early cook employed the same popular motifs when creating a pie.[50]

Fancies, conceits, and crinkumcranks drawn from period receipts provide an extensive album from which to choose. Among "pretty Conceits made in Paste" were tulips or other flowers; leaves, especially vine (grape) leaves; stars, knots, ciphers, twists, or braids; or "whatever form you please." Raffald proposed pastry birds to identify the contents of "Goose Pie," which contained, in addition to the goose, a turkey, ducks, woodcocks, and even a hare. The various pastry embellishments were cut freehand, or with a tin cutter. Markham described laying paper patterns on the paste and proceeding to "cut in divers proportions, as beasts, birds, [coats of] arms, knots, flowers."[51]

With so many options for pastry and its adornment, we may each develop our personal styles, yet operate within the eighteenth-century norm. The ancestral pie might have contained almost anything—perhaps even the "four and twenty blackbirds" remembered from a nursery rhyme. One outrageous mid-seventeenth-century "extraordinary Pie" directed baking a two crust pie filled with flour. When done, the cook was to remove the flour filling in order to "put in live birds, or a snake, which will seem strange to the beholders, which cut up the pie at the Table. This is only for a Wedding to pass away the time." That pie would unquestionably liven up a wedding feast. I have discovered no instance of live animals actually enclosed in a pie.[52]

To Fill a Pie . . . with Imagination and Good Judgment

A cook can really use anything he can think of to fill a pie and can use his creations to demonstrate imagination and good judgment.

Von Rumohr, *Essence of Cookery* (1822), 113.

Meat Pies

One might classify meat pies from simple to grand to impossible. Battallia Pye, with its outrageous collection of ingredients, is definitely an extreme. Even if these components were available today, I suspect few among us would be tempted to reproduce this dish.

Battalia Pye

Take 4 small Chickens 4 squab pidgeons 4 sucking rabbits cut them in pieces &
seasons them with savory spice lay them in ye. pye with 4 sweetbreads sliced & as
many sheeps tongues 2 shiverd Pallats 2 pare of lamstons 20 or 30 cocks-combs
with savory balls & oysters lay on butter & close ye. pye when bakd pour in a Lear

Unidentified cookbook, c. 1700, Harbury,
Virginia's Cooking Dynasty, 236.

This astonishing pie would obviously not fit into an ordinary pie dish or Dutch
oven. The Battallia pie was likely meant to be contained in a *coffin*, a free standing box of sturdy pastry, and baked in an oven. Although we will not be including sheep tongues, thymus glands, or lamb testicles in our meat pies, there are
other interesting period touches that create a luscious pie.

The more interesting the ingredients, the more interesting the pie. Meats
were combined with small quantities of seasonal or preserved vegetables or
fruits and lots of butter, marrow, or suet. Earlier meat pie receipts more often than not included currants, raisins, citron, candied citrus peels, and other
sweetmeats as well as sugar and spices. Later meat pies were enlarged with
onions, boiled egg yolks, forcemeat balls, mushrooms, or artichoke bottoms.
During the eighteenth century, we find both sweet and savory meat pies.

Savory meat pies were popular in all levels of society. A pot pie of pork,
perhaps with fowl or other meats was a typical celebratory dish in the early
southern backsettlements. The common name *sea pie* arose from its usual ingredient, not fish but salt pork which was generally available and kept well on
a sea voyage.[53]

On the other hand, complex sweet and fruity meat pies were meant as side
dishes on an opulent dinner table, not as the main dish. The mincemeat pie of
today's holiday dinners is a member of this culinary family. A meat pie, either
savory or sweet, might have graced a holiday dinner table of any social class, or
served as a year round supper dish among the gentry.

German author Rumohr criticized the French for their practice of making
pies from leftover cooked meats. He believed meat should be put raw into a
pie so that none of the juices would be lost. I side with the French on this
matter. Stewed, fricasseed, or roasted meats can become a luscious pie. The
cook then need only attend to proper baking of the crust and other ingredients
with assurance the meat is thoroughly done. On the other hand, quick cooking meats, such as fish and shellfish do not require precooking. Fowl, rabbit, or
such meats may be precooked or may enter the pie raw if cut into pieces. One
beauty of baking in a Dutch oven is the ability to separately adjust the heats of

"Recipes in the Culinary Art," Blackford Family Papers. Southern Historical Collection, Wilson Library, the University of North Carolina at Chapel Hill.

lid and pan by rearranging coals above or below. The pie filling may be baked until nearly done before the upper crust is allowed to brown.[54]

Compare and contrast the following chicken pie methods, from early and later periods, ranging from complex to simple. None is the chicken pie of our modern experience. The first receipt illustrates the sort of pie that might have been found on a Virginia plantation table, rather than a pie we might choose to replicate. Most of us would have difficulty procuring chickens with their heads on as well as a disinclination to add cocks combs and sweetbreads.[55]

Chicken Pye

Take young Chickens set them in half Milk and Water and Strip their skins of them butter your Dish and put puff past round it and in the bottom then lay a layer of butter and a layer of all sorts of Sweet Meats then Truss up your Chickens with their heads on Season them with Cloves Mace and Nutmeg Salt and a little good Suger then rowle up the Seasoning in a peice of butter and put in their bellyes and lay them in the pye with a good layer of butter over them and Sweet Meats then lay on the led being made of Puff Past . . . To make it Savorey Cut in some Mashoroms instead of Sweet meats with harty Choake botto[ms] Cocks Combs and Pallets veale Sweet breads. . . . [also force meat balls, "some long and some round," of marrow, chicken, thyme and savory, bread crumbs, egg yolk, and spinach]. . . . Harty choake Pye is the Same way your Chicken Pye only Add some Yolks of hard Eggs cut in quarters.

Pre-1744 Virginia cookbook, 53–54.

A cock's comb was just that, the comb trimmed from the rooster's head. According to French cook Ude, an amusing substitute in any dish calling for cock's combs may be created by cutting a slice of tongue or a little toast in the shape of the comb.[56]

A second Virginia manuscript included two chicken pie receipts, one sweet with preserved fruits related to the above and the following savory method for "Hen Pye" with forcemeat balls and boiled egg yolks.

A Hen Pye

Cut it in pices season & lay it in ye pye lay in balls yolks of hard eggs butter & close ye. pye when tis baked pour in a lear [sauce] thickened with eggs.

Unidentified cookbook, c. 1700, Harbury,
Virginia's Cooking Dynasty, 234.

William Byrd recorded having chicken pie for dinner and supper and even served to guests at breakfast, although he began his day as usual with only milk. We are left to wonder which sort of chicken pie Byrd's cook prepared.

Both of the above receipts were drawn from manuscript cookery books of Tidewater Virginia households.[57]

Concluding directions for a savory chicken pie, the Scottish Mrs. Dods observed, "this pie, and all pies, may be made plainer at the discretion of the cook." This note reminds us that, in any century, one expects cookery books to include more extreme dishes than everyday fare.[58]

A mid-century version is straightforward and appealing. This is a pie that we may thoroughly enjoy reproducing with any sort of small bird. Since it seems to have only a top crust, we can manage the Dutch oven with steady heat below to stew the bird thoroughly inside the pie. The lid can remain cooler until near the end of cooking when coals may be shoveled on top to bake the pastry. The palate of flavors in Raffald's chicken pie is quite nice.

A savoury chicken Pie

Let your chickens be small, season them with mace, pepper and salt, put a lump of butter into every one of them. Lay them in the dish with the breasts up and lay a thin slice of bacon over them, it will give them a pleasant flavour. Then put in a pint of strong gravy and make a good puff paste, lid it and bake it in a moderate oven. French cooks generally put morels and yolks of eggs chopped small.

Raffald, *Experienced English Housekeeper*, 75.

To ensure doneness and for ease of serving, cut the chicken into pieces. This method should work admirably for quail or other small birds. Since your pie will likely be much smaller than Raffald's, less liquid will be needed. Actually we have found butter, bacon, and natural juices provide adequate moisture with little or no gravy. If you do not have gravy or broth, water will do. *The French Cook*, Ude, suggested a few drops of white wine in water as a substitute for broth.

From the end of the eighteenth century we get another basic chicken pie. Of course the size of your dish and your oven will determine the size of your pie. We are certainly more likely to use one chicken rather than six. Half a modern chicken with two ounces butter fills a pie dish suitable for the average Dutch oven. Cut the larger joints of chicken into several pieces. Simmons' pie included the *inwards* (liver, gizzard, heart).

A Chicken Pie

Pick and clean six chickens . . . joint the birds, salt and pepper the pieces and inwards. Roll one inch thick paste . . . cover a deep dish, and double at the rim or edge of the dish, put thereto a layer of chickens and a layer of thin slices of butter, till the chickens and one and a half pound butter are expended [or one quarter pound butter per chicken], which cover with a thick paste; bake one and a half hour.

Or if your oven be poor, parboil the chickens with half a pound of butter, and put the pieces with the remaining one pound of butter and half the gravy into the paste, and while boiling, thicken the residue of the gravy, and when the pie is drawn, open the crust, and add the gravy.

Simmons, *American Cookery*, 58.

The note to parboil the chicken "if your oven be poor" is good advice. When the chicken has been boiled, a little of its broth may be put into the pie with the requisite amount of butter. Remaining broth may be reduced and thickened for pouring into the pie after baking, if desired.

And, while on the subject of "inwards," giblet pie was not at the top of the list to explore for this study; however, William Byrd and his neighbors insisted. Remembering that Byrd prided himself on eating only one dish at a meal, I was intrigued to note his choosing goose giblets or giblet pie, even on one occasion when dining at the Governor's. One imagines the governor's table offering many other tempting dishes. Further investigation disclosed two of the Byrds' Virginia neighbors offered versions of the same receipt.[59]

Giblett Pye

Take your Gibletts and Scald them then put them over the fire and Stew them very Tender and Season them with Salt and pepper pritty high with a bunch of Sweet herbes and an Onion and Just Water enough to cover them then let them stand to be cold take them out of the liquor then putt them into your petty pan with good Puff past round it and put in what quantity of Butter you think fitten with the Yolks of hard Eggs and lay over it forst meat balls and when you have lided your pye leave a hole a Top and Just as it goes into the Oven put in half the liquor that your Gibletts was stew'd in then shake it and Sarve it in

Pre-1744 Virginia cookbook, 56.

This Virginia giblet pie was simpler than any variation found in published cookery books. Goose, duck, or chicken giblets (liver, gizzard, heart, pinions, feet, neck, even cleaned intestine) were used. A beef, veal, or mutton steak might have been put into the pie under the giblets, or sliced potato added. Two Scots versions placed a distinctive pudding in the middle of the pie. The pudding contained goose blood along with suet and other expected ingredients, enclosed in the skin of the neck of the goose.[60]

Pigeons, duck, turkey, and other wild and tame fowl were prepared in similar ways. Other meat pies offered the same wide range of possibilities as seen in chicken pie receipts. It is hard to imagine an oyster or herring pie with currants, dates, spices, and sugar, isn't it? Apparently seventeenth-century English diners considered such combinations pleasing. Just as with chicken pies, simple and more savory combinations of other meats became the norm in subsequent centuries.[61]

Every imaginable cut of brawn (muscle meats), as well as some unimaginable parts of the animal, showed up in pie receipts. Kidneys, sweetbreads, and calves head have generally lost their place on our southern tables. Liver, giblets, tongue, and even pigs feet and chitterlings are still enjoyed by some.

Besides chicken, giblet, and pork pies, William Byrd recorded dining on pies of mutton, turkey, venison, pigeon, and blue wing teal (duck). Collected here is a sampling of simple and typical pies that illustrate interesting possibilities. Beginning with these examples, you may create your own specialty.

Beef Steak Pie

Cut nice steaks and stew them till half done, put a puff paste in the dish, lay in the steaks with a few slices of boiled ham, season the gravy [broth from stewing the steaks] very high, pour it in the dish, put on a lid of paste and bake it.

M. Randolph, Virginia Housewife, 45.

To make a Hare Pie

Cut your Hare in Pieces, break the Bones, and season it to your Taste, with Pepper, Salt, Cloves and Mace; lay it in your Dish with Slices of Butter and Lemon Juice: Cover it with Puff Paste.

Cleland, New and Easy Method, 82.

A Lamb Pye

Cut an hind quarter of Lamb into thin slices season in with savory spice lay them in ye. pye with an hard lettuce & artichoke bottoms ye. tops of an hundred of asparagus lay on butter & Close ye. pye when tis bakd, pour it a Lear

Unidentified cookbook, c. 1700, Harbury, Virginia's Cooking Dynasty, 234.

"A Lear for Savory Pies" in the c. 1700 Virginia manuscript was a blend of claret, gravy, oyster liquor, anchovy, sweet herbs, onion, and butter, with no quantities given. Since using both pickled oyster liquor and anchovy seems redundant, we may create a lear from wine, anchovy, herbs, onion, and butter, adding broth if more liquid seems needed.

Meat and butter alone filled the simplest of English receipts for mutton steak pie. A sauce (lear) of boiled parsley, white wine, vinegar, butter, and sugar might have been poured into the pie before serving. The following savory pie would require no added sauce.

To make a Mutton Pie

Cut a Loin or Neck of Mutton in steaks, and season it with Pepper and Salt, and Nutmeg, then lay it in your Pie upon Butter; then fill up your Pie with Apples sliced thin, and a few great Onions sliced thin, then put in more Butter, and close it and bake it, and serve it in hot.

Wolley, Queen-like Closet, 172.

Taken together these receipts chart a basic formula for meat pies. Seasoned meat was layered with butter in a dish, covered with paste and baked. If the meat was precooked, a little liquid might be added. A mixture of meats was relished in pies as in soups and stews. Keep in mind, we may feel free to use anything we can think of to fill a pie as long as we work within an historical mindset. Remember von Rumohr's admonition to "demonstrate imagination and good judgment."

A Simple Meat Pie in the Eighteenth-century Mode (Composite interpretation)

Choose any meat or a combination of several. Meat may be put in raw or cooked. Small pieces or thin slices will cook more easily, although whole birds were enclosed in pies. Stewed meats or hashes are excellent for pies.

Line the dish with paste (or simply butter the dish).

Layer meat with butter, as you "think fitten."

Seasonings: Choose from salt, pepper, mace, nutmeg, cloves, sage, rosemary, thyme, parsley.

Cover with paste and bake.

Options:

If more liquid is desired include a little broth, gravy, wine, vinegar, or water; or after baking, pour sauce (lear) or gravy into pie just before serving.

For a savory pie: include onion, apple, sweet or Irish potato, mushrooms, capers, artichoke bottoms, boiled egg yolks, forcemeat balls, even asparagus, lettuce, or cucumber.

For a sweet pie: include sweetmeats (currants and other dried or candied fruits).

Meat pies were common on a dinner table or as the traditional centerpiece for a rural celebration. See Chapter 8 for tempting seafood pies and the harvest pot pie. Pies were also employed to use up leftover bits. Pie was served for supper or even breakfast. "The remainder of it from dinner, being eaten with milk in the evening."[62]

✒ Vegetable Pies

You are likely to be pleasantly surprised with "Herb Pie for Lent." Many of us lack familiarity with groats (cut or coarsely ground oats) for anything but a breakfast cereal. This hearty grain is much more flavorful than rice. Groats with onion is delicious by itself; but add chopped greens, butter, and some apple and it becomes a vegetarian dish fit for company. Cook it in a crust as directed or simply in a buttered dish. As usual, you will probably want to cut these proportions to one half or even one fourth.

Herb Pie for Lent

Take lettuce, leeks, spinach, beets [greens] and parsley, of each a handful. Give them a boil, then chop them small, and have ready boiled in a cloth one quart of groats with two or three onions in them. Put them in a frying pan with the herbs and a good deal of salt, a pound of butter and a few apples cut thin. Stew them a few minutes over the fire, fill your dish or raised crust with it, one hour will bake it. Then serve it up.

Raffald, *Experienced English Housekeeper*, 76.

Another favorite dish from the eighteenth into the twenty-first century is Hannah Glasse's onion pie. (See receipt in Chapter 1.) That savory pie of onions, apples, potatoes, and eggs is ever so simple yet deliciously different. Glasse's artichoke bottom pie was made elaborate with truffles and morels. She also gave a potato and egg pie with a different seasoning touch.[63]

A Potatoe Pye

Boil three Pounds of Potatoes, and peel them, make a good Crust, and lay in your Dish; lay at the Bottom half a Pound of Butter, then lay in your Potatoes, throw over them three Tea Spoonfuls of Salt, and a small Nutmeg grated all over, six Eggs boiled hard and chopped fine, throw all over, a Tea Spoonful of Pepper strewed all over, then half a Pint of White Wine. Cover your Pye, and bake it half an Hour, or till the Crust is enough.

Glasse, *Art of Cookery* (1747), 113–14.

A mid-eighteenth-century Scots author proposed a pie of sliced apples and half boiled potatoes layered with sugar, cinnamon, lemon peel, and butter. An onion and apple pie was described as an English country dish. These odd pies are surprisingly good. Little sugar is needed since both apples and onions are naturally sweet. Their sweetness or tartness dictates the amount of sweetening desired.[64]

Onion Pye made by labouring Mens Wives

They mix chopt apples and onions in equal quantities, and with some sugar put them into dough-crust and bake them: This by some is thought to make as good a pie as pumpkins do.

Ellis, *Country Housewife's Family Companion*, 315.

This Onion Pye is quite interesting to concoct in historical context. It may or may not become your twenty-first-century favorite. At any rate, it is worth a try. It is puzzling that this English cookbook author compared onion and apple pie to pumpkin pie until one realizes that pumpkin and apples were also commonly combined in pies.

✍ As American as Apple Pie?

Certainly, apples or pippins were much enjoyed by all sorts of early Americans. Peter Kalm observed that apples were commonly used by farm families "for pies, tarts and the like" as well as cider and brandy. Wealthy Virginia plantation owner William Byrd enjoyed apple pie as well as roast apples, apple puddings, and dumplings at breakfast, dinner, or supper.[65]

However, English cookery sources offered a wide assortment of apple receipts including several sorts of pies, dumplings, and puddings. For example *The English Housewife* of 1635 gave five options for preparing an apple pie or tart. The poem "Óf Apple-Pyes" lends insight into special touches for raising a simple apple pie above the ordinary:[66]

> Rang'd in thick order let your quincies lie;
> They give a charming relish to the pye:
> If you are wise, you'll not brown sugar slight,
> The browner (if I form my judgment right)
> A tincture of a bright vermil' will shed
> And stain the pippin, like the quince, with red.
> When this is done, there will be wanting still
> The just reserve of cloves, and candy'd peel;
> Nor can I blame you, if a drop you take
> Of orange water, for perfuming sake;
> But here the nicety of art is such,
> There must not be too little, nor too much;
> If with discretion you these costs employ,
> They quicken appetite, if not they cloy.[67]

One family of pies, "apple pudding," is apple lemon custard baked in a crust. Another is more akin to the apple pie we know best. Often we are directed to stew the apples before putting them into the crust. Those receipts starting with sliced raw apples are more familiar to contemporary American apple pie makers. Susannah Carter, writing for Americans, copied Hannah Glasse's English method word for word. This receipt is typical.[68]

An Apple [or Pear] Pie

Make a good Puff-paste Crust, lay some round the Sides of the Dish, pare and quarter your Apples, and take out the Cores, lay a Row of Apples thick, throw in half your Sugar you design for your Pye, mince a little Lemon-peel fine, throw over, and squeeze a little Lemon over them, then a few Cloves, here and there one, then the rest of your Apples and the rest of your Sugar. You must sweeten to your Palate, and squeeze a little more Lemon; boil the Peeling of the Apples, and the Cores in some fair Water with a Blade of Mace, till it is very good; strain it and boil the Syrup with a little Sugar, till there is but very little and good, pour it into your Pye, put on your Upper-crust and bake it. You may put in a little Quince and Marmalade, if you please.

   You may butter them when they come out of the Oven; or beat up the Yolks of two Eggs, and half a Pint of Cream, with a little Nutmeg, sweetened with Sugar; [In the 1796 edition Glasse added: "put it over a slow fire and keep stirring it till it just boils up"] and take off the Lid, and pour in the Cream. Cut the Crust in little three-corner Pieces, and stick about the Pye, and send it to Table [cold].

Glasse, Art of Cookery (1747), 114; & S. Carter,
Frugal Colonial Housewife, 99.

Today, most Americans would add butter and enjoy the pie hot. The British tradition of custard with fruit pies still holds sway elsewhere. The custard included above is standard. Pour into the pie as directed, or cool separately and spoon custard over pie when serving. In the latter case, we custard lovers might want to double the above quantities. Quaking pudding is lovely served alongside a fruit pie, in place of custard sauce. The apple pie receipt further noted: "Thus make a pear pie, but do not put in any quince."

   Period sources disagreed about whether apples should be sliced, chopped, or quartered for pie. Boiling the peels and core to extract the last bit of flavor from the apple is thrifty but adds labor to the pie making. Simply leaving the peel on the apple is a good and historically appropriate alternative. Ellis wrote of super thrifty English farms where even the cores were chopped into the pies.[69]

   Of course apples differ markedly in flavor and texture. Track down some heirloom varieties and have a tasting party. Many of the apples common even a century ago were quite different from today's apples. When available apples are not as flavorful as you wish, follow Lydia Child's suggestion: "If your apples lack spirit, grate in a whole lemon."[70]

   The magic ingredient in apple receipts was lemon. Cinnamon is delicious, but ho-hum. Yes, cinnamon was also used with apples back then, alternately cloves, mace, or nutmeg. Rose water was a nice occasional touch. Lemon,

Pie of Heirloom Apples (Russet or Rusty Coat). Author photograph.

however, was ubiquitous. Your everyday apple pie will just sing with the juice and grated peel of about half a lemon or a bit of candied lemon or orange peel. A dash of spice may join the lemon if you choose. Try a little rose water for a change.[71]

While apples were enjoyed through a long season, perishable soft fruits such as peaches, cherries, and berries were celebrated as they ripened. In July 1795 Piedmont North Carolina traveler John Brown was delighted with "Ripe Peaches and Peach py which was soon in the season." *American Cookery* tells us "Every species of fruit such as peas [peaches or pears?], plums, raspberries, black berries may be only sweetened, without spices—and baked in paste." Winter tarts were made of fruit marmalades or preserves.[72]

From Glasse's Bread and Butter Pudding and Apple Pie we draw a basic custard receipt to fit many purposes. Serve warm or chill and spoon over whatever dish seems to want a custard sauce or lear.

Basic Custard (Interpretation)

    1 pint milk or cream
    4 egg yolks or whole eggs
    ¼ cup sugar

(optional) a little nutmeg
(optional) 1 teaspoonful rose water or orange flower water
Pour into dish calling for raw custard, or cook slowly for use as a sauce.
Slowly bring just to the boiling point, to avoid curdling. The slower, but more fail
    safe method is to combine custard ingredients in an earthenware jug, set into
    a pan of boiling water, stir until thickened.[73]

And while on the subject of custard, let us not neglect the popular bread and
butter pudding. This simple custard based dish hardly needs a receipt; nevertheless, there are many, with few differences among them. The trusted 1747
English author, Hannah Glasse, left a detailed description with extra bits of
information.[74]

A Bread and Butter Pudding

Take a Penny-loaf, and cut it into thin Slices of Bread and Butter, as you do for
Tea. Butter your Dish as you cut them, lay Slices all over the Dish, then strew a
few Currans, clean washed and picked, then a Row of Bread and Butter, then
a few Currans and so on, till all your Bread and Butter is in; then take a Pint of
Milk, beat up four Eggs, a little Salt, half a Nutmeg grated, mix all together with
Sugar to your Taste [¼ cup]. Pour this over the Bread, and bake it half an Hour.
A Puff-paste under does best. You may put in two Spoonfuls of Rose-water.

Glasse, *Art of Cookery* (1747), 111.

Only two of multiple sources suggested a paste underneath; a crust seems redundant for there is a layer of bread at the bottom. An 1830 source directed
"put a paste around the edge of the dish" after assembling the bread pudding.
The flavorings varied from none to rose water, orange flower water, nutmeg,
citron, orange or lemon (peel, fresh or candied). Allowing the dish to set an
hour or longer before baking, while the bread absorbs custard, is a good idea.[75]

Another question arises: were the currants fresh or dried? We might assume dried, for that is the form we generally have today. The directions to
wash and pick may simply indicate that an early cook's dried currants needed
to be examined and picked over. The dried currants are certainly delicious,
especially so when joined with a few bits of candied orange and lemon
peel.

On the other hand one can imagine bread and butter pudding with fresh
fruits. Trials with fresh blueberries turned out very nicely. Other berries or
chopped fruits should work out as well.

For a rather different pudding *The Kentucky Housewife* (1838) told readers to
layer buttered bread with stewed sweetened gooseberries before pouring on

raw custard. Her receipt closed with the note: "A bread and butter pudding may be made in the same manner with any kind of nice stewed fruit." [76]

Raffald titled such a bread and custard dish "Sippet Pudding." In place of butter, she layered marrow or suet with the bread and currants.[77]

Moving on to an even easier and equally delicious idea for using old bread, the "Charlotte." Scotswoman, Dods, identified the Charlotte as a French fruit pudding "much admired on the continent, and particularly in France, where the solid, lumpy, and doughy English pudding and fat pie or tart crust, are not so much esteemed as they are at home."[78]

Two dissimilar types of charlotte showed in nineteenth-century southern cookery books. *The Carolina Housewife* included two Charlotte Russe receipts. These showy dishes involved lining a mold with cake, filling with a cream, flummery, or jelly; then chilling or freezing; finally unmolding to serve. *The Kentucky Housewife* considered "A Plain Charlotte" to be more like a trifle of pound cake spread with preserves, filled with egg cream (custard), and crowned with meringue.

Of more interest to our investigation is a simpler type of charlotte, in which a bread lined dish or mold is filled with stewed or fresh fruit and then baked. Simple and delicious. The fruit charlotte may have evolved (or did it descend?) from the bread and butter pudding. Maria Rundell agreed with Harriot Horry in simply slicing raw apple into the charlotte while Mary Randolph deemed stewed fruit better.[79]

Charlotte à la façon de Mr. Short

Rub some butter over the pan first.—Then cover the inside of the pan with thin slices of stale bread well buttered. Next shake a little brown sugar all over the bread. Now begin with the apples. Cover the bread and sugar which was first laid over the pan, with apples sliced thin, then shake a handful of brown sugar over the apples, then a handful of two of grated bread all over the sugar, then small bits of butter all over the grated bread. Then shake either powdered Cinnamon or nutmeg all over the butter. And so you go on beginning again with the apples and finishing with the cinnamon or nutmeg until the pan is full enough to put into the oven. When you find it shrinking in the middle that is a sign of its being done. It requires a great deal of baking and the oven must not be too hot.

Horry, *Colonial Plantation Cookbook*, 136 (in different hand, probably later).

Charlotte

Stew any kind of fruit, and season it in any way you like best; fry some slices of bread in butter, put them, while hot, in the bottom and round the sides of a dish which has been rubbed with butter, put in your fruit, and lay slices of bread on the top; bake it a few minutes, turn it carefully into another dish, sprinkle on some powdered sugar, and glaze it with a salamander.

M. Randolph, Virginia Housewife, 155.

The salamander is a cast iron disk attached to a rod handle. The disk is heated and held above food to brown it. A heavy fireplace shovel can be used similarly: "Take a red hot Iron fire Shoevell and hold over them." We have found that a lightweight shovel will not hold heat enough to function as a salamander.[80]

Charlottes were generally meant to be unmolded before serving as above. You will have fun getting creative with a Charlotte or a Bread and Butter Pudding, using whatever fruit is at hand. "Any kind of preserved or ripe fruit may be used instead of apples. A few thin slices of bread soaked [in milk] and buttered thus make a good crust to a rice or other pudding."[81]

This sort of baked pudding makes an interesting breakfast or supper dish in any century. Creating a charlotte is a sweet kitchen adventure to share with a child.

A pie or pudding might have appeared on the table morning, dinnertime, or evening. Pie leftover from dinner was convenient for breakfast or supper or to offer to travelers. We learn from William Byrd's personal diaries that he regularly chose pie or pudding for dinner or supper and occasionally for breakfast. Personal accounts document pies and puddings on plantation dinner tables and at backcountry gatherings—celebrating seasonal bounty or covering wintertime scarcity.

Whether you are a culinary adventurer mingling the old with the new, a time traveler, or a historical interpreter you are likely to discover new favorite receipts here. Most cakes, breads, puddings, and pies collected in this chapter will be equally successful baked in a modern oven or a Dutch oven at the fireside. A steady fire with continual renewal of a good bed of coals is key to successful baking at the open hearth.

Roasting and broiling require still closer attention to fire management while supervising spit or gridiron. These fireside methods cannot be duplicated in today's kitchen, but may add new style and flavors to the backyard cookout.

CHAPTER 5

At the Fireside

A sensible Scot warned: "bear in mind that next to broiling, roasting is the most difficult of all elementary culinary processes." Roasting and broiling differ from baking as the food is heated on one side only and must be turned for even cooking. Roasting is a slow process while broiling is quicker. The roast is positioned to the side of the fire to receive a constant gentle heat. In contrast, broiling is equivalent to today's grilling; food placed on a gridiron over coals and turned halfway through cooking. In general, bulky cuts of meat should be roasted; thin, small, or quick cooking foodstuffs may be successfully broiled. However, barbecuing is slow broiling of a large joint or whole animal.[1]

These techniques are only learned at the fireside. However, advice from early authors and cooks may help us hone skills and develop personal styles for roasting or broiling. Those two careful authors, Scotswoman Margaret Dods and *The Kentucky Housewife* Lettice Bryan, provided details omitted by earlier writers. Consider their advice.

🖎 Broiling

This mode of dressing, though unsuitable for a large dinner . . . is the way in which the solitary epicure best relishes this luxury.

> Margaret Dods, *Cook and Housewife's Manual* (1829), 170.

Not surprising, today's craze for cooking everything on the grill has ancient beginnings. Broiling was a favored method for steaks, organ meats, small fowl, and fish.

> Broiling is the most delicate manual office the common cook has to perform, and that which requires the most unremitting vigilance. She may turn her back on the stew-pan or the spit, but the gridiron can never be left with impunity. . . . The state of the fire is the primary consideration. It must be clear and radiant, consequently free of smoke. A fire nearly two-thirds burnt is best. . . . The gridiron must be hot through, (which

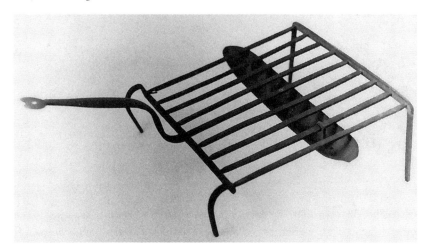

Gridiron. With detachable trough for drippings, c. 1750–1800. Collection of the Museum of Early Southern Decorative Arts, Old Salem Museums & Gardens.

will take five minutes,) before any thing is put on it. It must then be rubbed with a piece of fresh suet, to prevent the meat from being branded, or sticking to the hot bars.[2]

Scotswoman Dods recommended positioning the gridiron three to six inches above the fire. If fat dripped into the fire creating smoke she advised removing or slanting the grill to prevent impairing flavor and appearance of the meat.[3]

The Kentucky Housewife provided additional details for broiling fish. "Place a clean hot gridiron over a bed on clear coals, grease the bars and wipe them with a cloth, and rub them with a little flour to prevent the fish sticking to them." A piece of fresh suet is convenient for greasing the gridiron.[4]

Seventeenth-century, eighteenth-century and nineteenth-century sources offered numerous receipts for broiling (grilling), followed by simmering in flavorful sauce or with sauce poured on. The two receipts below offer different interpretations of method and seasoning. The early *French Cook* left us an especially appealing receipt for broiling fish stuffed with herbs.[5]

Vilain [small freshwater fish] with ragoust [sharp flavored sauce]

After it is dressed, broyl it on the gridiron with a bundle of herbs in the body of it, well seasoned. After it is rosted, pass in the pan [sauté] an onion minced with fresh butter, chippings [breadcrumbs], capers and anchovies, all well seasoned according to your taste, stove all together, and serve.

La Varenne, *French Cook*, 147.

These methods are appropriate for other species of fish as well. Although foods are usually turned for broiling on both sides, the following technique can be useful for certain fish and other delicate foods.

To barbeque Shad

Split the fish down the back & having seasoned it highly with Salt & Cayenne pepper, on the inside, close the incision and let it remain one hour. You will in the next place, raise your Gridiron over Good Hickory coals, on four bricks, and placing the Shad open, upon the Gridiron, with the Skinny Side up, covered completely with a dish; when sufficiently broiled; it should be turned over on the same dish & sent to table. Near ¼ lb butter for a Large Shad. ½ pint of wine melted with the Butter, & poured on hot, when the fish is ready to be sent to table. When cleverly brown the shad is fit to go to table. The shad should not be turned.

Purviance household book.

Receipts for broiling fish, beef, veal, mutton, pork, venison, chicken, small game, and more are repetitive in method. Broiling is as simple as placing the meat on the gridiron and turning when half done. The art is in attention to the fire, the relationship of meat to fire, and avoiding smoke from greasy drippings.

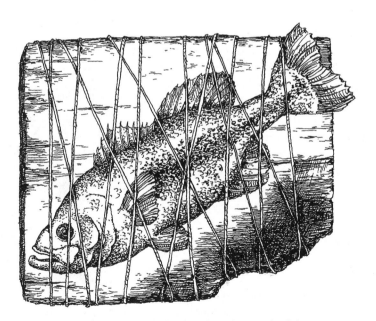

Planked Fish. Planking is another handy technique for fish, somewhere between broiling and roasting. The fish cooks through without turning. By Teresa Myers Armour, courtesy of the Schiele Museum.

Saucing in an eighteenth-century style will give your broiled and roasted foods a period personality. Examples of seasonings appropriate for each meat will be found among receipts for boiled, stewed, and made dishes throughout this collection. See Chapter 7 for additional sauces and accompaniments.

✍ Roasting

To understand the principles of roasting, let's first consider a delectable roasted apple. From a slave cabin, a backwoods household, or a traveler's campsite to the most elegant Williamsburg fireside one might have found an apple roasting. William Byrd recorded supping on roast apples with wine or with toast and cider. When suffering from a sore throat he found comfort in roast apples and milk. Indeed a roasted apple is convenient and thoroughly delicious fare, with caramelized natural sugars much like a baked apple.[6]

The simple roasting of an apple illustrates basic considerations. One sets the apple beside the fire in a spot with even heat of the proper intensity. Variables should be examined in selecting the proper spot relative to the heat radiating from the fire and from warm stone, brick, or iron. For example, an apple resting on a hot hearth or stone is likely to overcook on the bottom. If the apple is positioned too high or too low it will not roast evenly. The apple should be rotated a quarter turn as each side begins to soften. Similar factors must be considered when the apple is roasted on a stick or fork. Think of roasting a marshmallow, perfectly browned on every surface. Surely, that is seldom accomplished but is a notable goal. Aim for the same goal when roasting an apple, a fowl, a sirloin of beef, or a whole pig.

Basic roasting can be accomplished with little or no equipment. However, this method requires the cook's attention. The spit may be as fancy as a wind up jack or as simple as a green stick or a *Gipsy jack* (a string suspended beside the fire). Again, we cannot improve on Mrs. Dods advice:

In roasting

The management of the fire is half the battle. . . . An hour before the roast is put down, make up a fire suited to the size of the joint; let it be clear and glowing, and free of ashes and smoke in front. . . . Place the meat at a

A "Gipsy Jack." Roasting Chicken on a String. By Teresa Myers Armour, courtesy of the Schiele Museum.

due distance, that it may heat through without the outside becoming shriveled and scorched. To prevent this, baste diligently for the first half-hour. The larger the joint the greater must be the distance from the fire . . . A radiant fire, due distance, and frequent basting, can alone ensure a well-roasted joint.

Dods, *Cook and Housewife's Manual*, 92.

The meat should be balanced on the spit and secured, with a dripping pan positioned underneath. Butter or lard may be used for initial basting; as roasting progresses baste with drippings from the pan. Dods suggested a handy basting technique for chickens, "The birds should occasionally be taken off the fire, and rubbed with butter tied in a muslin rag."[7]

The position of either meat or fire should be altered as required. Once or twice during roasting it generally becomes necessary to move the spit away from the fire while fresh coals are raked toward the spit and fuel added to the opposite side of the fire. This protects the roast from smoke and ashes.

Authors writing for professional cooks recommended tying or skewering buttered paper over the roast to allow the interior to cook without burning the exterior. Toward the end of roasting, the paper was to be removed, the spit positioned closer to the fire, and attention paid to basting and browning the roast perfectly. This was certainly advice for an affluent and well staffed kitchen, not likely to have been practiced by most cooks.

More finicky roasting was finished by *frothing*. Just before removing the roast from the spit, the meat was lightly dusted with flour or bread crumbs and basted "bountifully with butter till a rich froth is raised." French author Ude declared this English custom "utterly absurd" as "the froth of the flour and butter adhere to the palate, and have a most abominable taste." He approved the practice only if done early enough for the flour to become nicely browned.[8]

Make of that what you will. Experiment with this fussy technique or simply roast without so much ado. We have had beautiful and delectable results by simply carefully tending the fire and minding the distance of meat from the heat.

Hearth cooking students have been delighted with results achieved following Hannah Wolley's 1672 direction for roasting fresh pork. Since your pork roast is not likely to have skin, you can skip the first step and begin by sticking the meat with rosemary and cloves. If very lean, you may baste with butter. Each cook will balance seasonings according to individual preferences. Taste and adjust seasonings as you mix the sauce.

To rost Pork without the Skin

Take any joint of small Pork, not salted and lay it to the fire till the Skin may be taken off, then take it from the fire and take off the Skin, then stick it with

Rosemary and Cloves, and lay it to the fire again, then salt it and rost it carefully, then make Sauce for it with Claret Wine, white bread sliced thin, a little water, and some beaten Cinamon; boil these well together, then put in some Salt, a little Butter, Vinegar, or Juice of Limon, and a little sugar, when your Pork is rosted enough, then flower it, and lay it into a Dish with the Sauce, and serve it in.

Wolley, Queen-like Closet, 105.

This receipt showed up later, simplified, in the 1759 *A New and Easy Method of Cookery*. In 1824 Virginia, Mary Randolph suggested an even simpler sauce of melted butter with caper vinegar. Any pleasantly flavored vinegar may be substituted.[9]

Although you may find directions and cautions associated with broiling and roasting a bit confusing and even daunting, do not hesitate to try your hand. You are unlikely to ruin your meat, for there is a failsafe backup: A welcome technique discovered in period cookbooks is that of partially roasting a cut of meat prior to stewing. This frees us from worry over a well browned fowl or joint of meat that is underdone. Simply remove from the spit and put into a pot with a little water, broth, or wine, seasonings, and perhaps a few vegetables; then simmer until done. Thus the cook achieves beautifully browned meat in a lovely gravy or sauce. (See Chapter 6 for related receipts.)

All sorts of small birds were roasted, often with a stuffing. Most birds were plucked and drawn before cooking. Woodcocks and snipes were exceptions as these were plucked but not gutted. Hannah Glasse noted, "You are to observe, we never take any Thing out of a Woodcock or Snipe." The drippings from bird and entrails were caught on toasts and the roasted birds served on those toasts. We wonder just why our ancestors considered the entrails of these two particular insect and worm eating birds appealing. William Byrd dined on snipe in Virginia and explorer John Lawson found Carolina snipe plentiful and the woodcock "as dainty meat as any in the world." He noted that Indians also cooked rabbits and other game with the guts in, "after the Woodcock Fashion." While we are unlikely to roast a snipe or woodcock, nor any other animal complete with intestines, this is an interesting bit of our culinary heritage.[10]

To Roast Snipes or Woodcocks

Don't draw them, slit them across, toast some Bread, lay it in a Plate under them, that the Trale may drop in it; When roasted well, lay them on the toasted Bread, and pour beat Butter with Gravy over them: Send them up hot.

Cleland, New and Easy Method, 101.

Boiling, Baking, and Roasting. By Teresa Myers Armour,
courtesy of the Schiele Museum.

Roasting can really be as simple as sticking meat on a spit and cooking it by
the fire, once the cook has gained experience and a sense of timing. Since these
skills cannot come from a book, but only from the fireside, how can one learn?

Go build a fire. Put a chicken on a spit and set it to roasting. Assemble an
hodge-podge of meats and vegetables in your stew pot. This scenario can lead
to several outcomes. Your very first roasted chicken may turn out perfectly and
you will serve it proudly alongside your stewed dish. On the other hand your
chicken may become beautifully browned, but still ooze blood. You then remove it from the spit, add the chicken to the other foods simmering in your
pot, and allow it to complete cooking. In the unlikely case that your roasting
chicken does not turn out to suit you, there is a clever backup plan: You set
the chicken aside to use in a pie tomorrow while nonchalantly serving up your
lovely stewed meat and vegetables. So, let us next explore methods for making
a soup or stew nice enough for guests.

Having examined a philosophy for interpreting early foodways and investigated specific cookery techniques, I hope the reader is eager to explore further. Part III is chock full of additional receipts worthy of replicating in any century and in any sort of kitchen. The open hearth interpreter, the adventurous cook, the "foodie," and the armchair culinary historian should each find food for thought among the following collected receipts and lore. How about hodgepodge or salamagundi for your next dinner party? Perhaps you will treat your family to the charming "Asparagus Forced in French Rolls" or a deliciously simple fish pie. Or tease your friends with chocolate cakes or hedgehog, not at all what their names suggest.

PART III

Collected
Receipts

*Foods of Our Ancestors,
Ancestors of Our Foods*

CHAPTER 6

Soups, Stews, and Made Dishes

A profusion of everything, but in the coarsest and plainest style.

J.F.D. Smyth, *Tour* (1784), 172.

For descriptions of everyday meals we look to journals kept by travelers and newly arrived settlers in the mid-Atlantic and southern colonies. Let's peer into that large pot hanging on the crane in an early American fireplace. Whether in a simple household or opulent plantation kitchen, the everyday meal probably bore little resemblance to dinners described in cookery books.

Every family, besides a little garden for the few vegetables which they cultivate . . . raised corn for roasting ears, pumpkins, squashes, beans and potatoes. These, in the latter part of the summer and fall, were cooked with their pork, venison and bear meat for dinner, and made very wholesome and well tasted dishes.

Doddridge, *Notes on the Settlement*, 88.

Replicating such a "wholesome and well tasted" dinner, will begin with an assemblage of meats and vegetables appropriate to the season and place. Soups and stews could be as plain or as complex as available ingredients and the ingenuity of the cook allowed.

Moravian settlers kept extensive journals. During their first few years in North Carolina (at Bethabara near present day Winston-Salem) they wrote of bounty and of scarcity in different seasons. Their diet included domestic livestock and game animals, Old World vegetables and New. These records illustrate seasonal availability, favored foods, and adjustment to new American foodstuffs. Although the Moravian way of life differed from their neighbors' in many ways, their new American diet of necessity was similar.

[In 1754] Their garden has given them good service; from May 8th to July 5th they had salad every day for dinner, and nearly every evening also. When the salad came to an end they had cucumbers for three weeks, with three or four meals of sugar peas, beans several times, occasionally cabbage, and squashes twice. Their usual and best food is milk and mush and whatever can be made from cornmeal.

[Until Sept 25th] mush for breakfast and supper, and at noon either green beans ... or pumpkins ... out of grease for our mush

[During September they killed cattle, hogs, and bear] After we began butchering we usually had meat for dinner every other day ... With the meat we had potatoes or white turnips, which are very good, or else sequata [squash]. In October we could have milk only once a day; the first part of November only every other day; and now we can have it only every third day. Therefore in the morning we have mush with milk or drippings; at supper mush with drippings, or pumpkins, or squashes; and at noon when we have no meat we use pumpkin or beans.

[In January, 1755] For lack of vegetables we are now eating meat each day for dinner, which agrees with us well, and makes us feel strong for work.[1]

The Moravian settlers had only half enough meat during January 1758. They planned out a menu to make the best of their scarce food: Tuesday "meat and carrots," Wednesday "sausage and dried pumpkins," Thursday "dumplings," Friday "pigs' feet and heads, and turnips," Saturday and Sunday "beans and

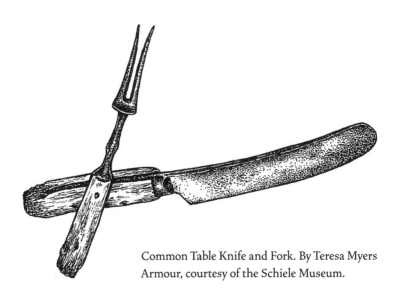

Common Table Knife and Fork. By Teresa Myers Armour, courtesy of the Schiele Museum.

butter," Monday "meat and dried pumpkins," Tuesday "dumplings and radish," Wednesday "meat and turnips," Thursday "dumplings and radish," Friday "meat and carrots," Saturday "meat and sauerkraut," Sunday "beans and butter."[2]

Dinner proposed for young gentlemen at the new University of North Carolina in 1797 offers a glimpse of everyday fare: "A dish or cover of bacon and greens, or beef and turnips, together with a sufficient quantity of fresh meats, or fowls, or pudding and tarts, with a sufficiency of wheat and corn bread." The meals were to be augmented with "potatoes and all kinds of vegetable food usually served up in Carolina in sufficient quantities."[3]

Fascination with life on the frontier is apparent in English adventurer Francis Baily's notes on people, landscape, and lifeways. In 1797 Kentucky, at the simple home of a doctor, "At dinner time I observed a table prepared in the middle of the room, with some knives and forks and pewter plates placed on it, but without any tablecloth."[4]

> Our provisions consisted of some stewed pork and some beef, together with some wild sort of vegetable, which had been gathered out in the woods.... The inhabitants live a great deal upon deer and turkeys, which they shoot wild in the woods, and upon bacon, which they keep by them in case of need; and as to vegetables, they are seldom to be procured except in summer. The bread which is made here is chiefly of Indian meal; it is a coarse kind of fare, but after a little use becomes not at all unpleasant.[5]

Not all journal keepers were so tolerant. Travelers were dependent on the hospitality of homes along their way. Often times even a plantation kitchen offered only simple fare. Details of method, seasoning, and presentation may be drawn from historical receipts, setting aside modern thinking and perhaps substituting New World ingredients.

> The fare and accommodations a traveler meets with throughout this country, being very indifferent indeed, even at best, and generally miserable and wretched beyond description, excepting at warm or opulent planters houses, where there is always a profusion of everything, but in the coarsest and plainest style. [Traveling westward across North Carolina, 1784][6]

This profusion of food with its coarse and plain style disgusted one young French housewife recently settled in Virginia.

> You will want to know about the food they give us to eat. I cannot say that it is good, although most abundant, too abundant in fact, and

without any variety whatsoever.... People eat so much here! Indeed they seem to be doing nothing else, and it is all such heavy food that one wonders how they can digest it.[7]

On the other hand this Frenchwoman found some households setting forth grander and more sophisticated meals. When invited to dine at a neighboring plantation she was delighted with a "most sumptuous repast."

> You can not imagine all there was on the table: ducks, hams, roasted chickens, roast beef, roast pork, custards, jellies, sweetmeats of various kinds, twenty different sorts of tarts and cakes, Parmesan cheese, wine, porter, beer, punch, of course and two bottles of old French brandy for which the men could not find enough praise![8]

Many other travelers and newcomers left us descriptions of meals, some disappointing, some surprisingly tasty. Many complained of boring meals.

> Have had either Bacon or Chickens every meal since I came into the Country. If I still continue in this way shall be grown over with Bristles or Feathers. [1770s][9]

The lack of variety at mealtime continued to be the norm. Half a century later, a bride from England described her new life in the North Carolina backcountry with delightful detail:

> I will give you a regular bill of fare of the dinner which has little or no variety at any house I have visited. Ham and chickens, vegetables, tarts, custards and sweetmeats, the whole concludes with corn or wheat cakes and coffee the drinking of the latter appears a general fashion. [1827][10]

The French were particularly prone to turning up their noses at American food. Hélène de Maussion even criticized a dinner party at Mount Vernon:

> The dinner was good but plain. We had lamb and fowl. The fowl was tough but the lamb was good. Then beef and artichokes served together, which rather surprised me, and any number of different desserts, such as the terrible things they call puddings, tarts, pastries, fruit, ices, nuts and preserves.[11]

The Frenchwoman's dinner at Mount Vernon sounds far from plain. Perhaps the detested puddings soured her opinion of the meal. At least three meats and such an assortment of desserts seem quite nice. George Washington was said to be moderate in his own dining habits, while offering an elegant table to others.

At three he dines, commonly on a single dish, and drinks from half a
pint to a pint of Madeira wine.... But his table is always furnished
with elegance and exuberance; and whether he has company or not, he
remains at the table an hour in familiar conversation, then every one
present is called upon to give some absent friend as a toast.[12]

Like George Washington, William Byrd had a personal rule to eat only one
dish at dinner. And we are grateful that he daily noted the dish he chose. An
amazing variety of foods appeared on Byrd's table. The list reads like a table
of contents from a popular English cookery book of his day. The expected
mutton, pork, beef, veal, goose, and chicken were served roasted, broiled,
boiled, hashed, fricasseed, stewed, and in soup or pie. Calf's head, ox cheek,
cowheels, steer feet, poultry giblets, lamb stones, hog haslet (heart, liver, etc.),
tripe, tongue, or udder were among Byrd's choices for dinner.

American game mammals, fish, and fowls showed up in various preparations. The Byrd family and guests dined on venison, squirrel, turkey, pigeon,
duck, snipe, fish, and crab. On occasion Byrd and his guests shot at passenger
pigeons with bow and arrow for sport. He once "ate some beaver for dinner at
the Governor's."[13]

Byrd's one dish rule seems to have included an appropriate vegetable or
pudding to accompany the meat. Seasonal *sallets*, asparagus, cucumbers, artichokes, and green peas were particularly mentioned. In other seasons rice,
beans, peas pudding, turnips, and apples in many guises (stewed, roasted, or
as pudding, dumpling, or pie) were served.

The season's perishable fruits were enjoyed at breakfast, supper, and between meals, sometimes straight from the tree or vine several times a day.
Cherries, raspberries, and strawberries were particularly relished. William
Byrd's personal diary yielded glimpses into a wealthy planter's commonplace
dinners as well as the elegant dishes set before guests. English tastes persisted,
although hominy, pone, and hoecake were noted along with simple meals of
eggs or beans and bacon.[14]

The first American authored cookbook, Amelia Simmons' *Domestic Cookery*, contained few truly American receipts. Even potato and pumpkin receipts
followed English precedents; while corn breads and Indian meal puddings
illustrated New World adaptations. *The Virginia Housewife*, Mary Randolph,
simplified established recipes for the American table; and Lettice Bryan, *The
Kentucky Housewife*, not only identified older receipts still familiar in 1839, but
also provided significant details omitted by earlier authors.

While most cookery books put forth the ideal, some gave clues as to what
would have simmered in the everyday cook pot. *The Country Housewife's Family*

Companion shed light on everyday food of laborers as well as gentry in mid-eighteenth-century England. Von Rumohr compared European foods and methods. Travelers in the early mid-Atlantic and southern colonies allow us to peek into that pot hanging on a crane over the fire.

✒ Soups

I found the family just set down to some soup, or kind of broth (which was made by boiling Indian corn and bacon together, or in some such way). It was to me very good, as I was extremely hungry, though at any other time or place I might have rejected it with disgust.

> Francis Bailey, *Journal* (Near Knoxville, Tennessee, 1797), 263.

A good household soup can be made by pouring boiling, well flavored meat stock over slices of toasted bread. This is quite suitable even for breakfast and for feeding the sick. [In Germany and elsewhere in Europe, 1822.]

> Karl Von Rumohr, *Essence of Cookery*, 93.

Most writers considered soup stocks and gravies best if based on a combination of meats: beef, veal, mutton, and/or cured pork, perhaps fowl as well. Certainly, the reality of the family stew pot did not often match this ideal.

A young plantation mistress had the ingredients to produce a proper English broth in America. In 1742 Eliza Lucas wrote from the South Carolina lowcountry: "The Country abounds with wild fowl, Venison and fish. Beef, veal and mutton are here in much greater perfection than in the Islands [West Indies] tho' not equal to that in England; but their pork exceeds any I ever tasted any where. The Turkeys exceedingly fine."[15]

Wild fowl and game were enjoyed at all levels of society. New World vegetables, wild and cultivated, joined flavors with old familiar garden produce in the stew pot. Travelers venturing by boat down the Ohio River in 1796, found overnight accommodations at a farmhouse and a curious soup for supper: "[W]e went a little way into the woods, and killed some squirrels for our supper, and bringing them home, the old gentleman of the mansion . . . furnished us with some turnips, pumpkins, and other necessaries, and we soon had a dish of excellent soup."[16]

A German clergyman enjoyed dinner at the table of a Dutch justice of the peace and militia major. "He treated us to bear meat." The next day, at an inn in "wild and uncultivated country" in New York, "we were fed on raccoons . . . and pumpkins." Peter Kalm reported squirrel "reckoned a dainty," and raccoon "reputed to taste well." Raccoon and opossum seem to have been second only to squirrel and rabbit among small game. "[Opossums] and the raccoons are used for food, generally barbecued, or roasted, and their flesh is not unpleasant . . . wild turkies very large fat and fine, wild-geese, ducks, and squirrels innumerable, which make most excellent soup."[17]

On occasion gentleman William Byrd dined on squirrel and onions as well as hare and onions. Mary Randolph endorsed the same treatment for both meats. Hare or rabbit and squirrel were prepared like fowl, typically with onions and cured pork.[18]

Hare [or Squirrel] Soup

Cut up two hares, put them into a pot with a piece of bacon, two onions chopped, a bundle of thyme and parsley which must be taken out before the soup is thickened, add pepper, salt, pounded cloves, and mace, put in a sufficient quantity of water, stew it gently three hours, thicken with a large spoonful of butter, and one of brown flour with a glass of red wine; boil it a few minutes longer, and serve it up with the nicest parts of the hares. Squirrels make soup equally good, done the same way.

M. Randolph, *Virginia Housewife*, 35.

Brown flour was browned or toasted flour, not whole wheat. Other receipts simply called for butter rolled in flour to thicken the stew. You may choose either browned or plain flour, although the flavor will differ.[19]

✍ Stocks and Gravies

Most authors included basic recipes for stock to be used in soups and sauces. *Gravy* signified stock rather than the thick sauces we southerners think of as gravies. Typically gravy was a strong broth of several meats, as in the version below. Others obtained flavor from a single meat, from organ meats, from fish, or from vegetables alone. Bacon or butter added richness. Anchovy or lemon boosted the flavor.

To make Strong Broth to keep for Use

Take Part of a Leg of Beef, and the Scrag-end of a Neck of Mutton, break the Bones in Pieces, and put to it as much Water as will cover it, and a little Salt; and when it boils, skim it clean, and put in to it a whole Onion stuck with Cloves, a Bunch of Sweet Herbs, some Pepper, a Nutmeg quartered; let these boil till the Meat is boiled in Pieces, and the Strength boiled out of it; then put to it three or four Anchovies, and when they are dissolved, strain it out, and keep it for Use.

Glasse, *Art of Cookery* (1747), 63.

The clever onion stuck with cloves allows the cook to easily retrieve the whole cloves from the pot. The eighteenth-century cook used this trick in all sorts of dishes. An onion stuck with three or four cloves and a bundle of herbs may be placed inside a chicken before roasting or boiling to add just enough flavor.

Vegetables were included with meats to create stocks for Scots *stew soups* or *mouthful soups*, as for Meg Dods' mixed game soup.

[Stock for] Poacher's Soup

Take from two to four pounds of the trimmings or coarse parts of venison, shin of beef, or shanks or lean scrag of good mutton—all fresh. Break the bones, and boil this with a couple of carrots and turnips, four onions, a bunch of parsley, and a quarter-ounce of peppercorns, the larger proportion Jamaica pepper [allspice]. Strain this stock when it has boiled for three hours.

Dods, Cook and Housewife's Manual, 157

If the meat is in nicer bits the stock need not be strained. "This savoury and highly relishing new stew soup, may be made of any or every thing known by the name of game." After long simmering of the above rich stock, smaller game was added:

Poacher's Soup

A black-cock, or wood-cock, a pheasant, half a hare, or a rabbit, a brace of partridges or grouse, or one of each (whichever is obtained most easily), and season the pieces with mixed spices. These may be floured and browned in the frying-pan; but as this is a process dictated by the eye as much as the palate, it is not necessary in making this soup. Put the game to the strained stock, with a dozen of small onions, a couple of heads of celery sliced, half a dozen peeled potatoes, and, when it boils, a small white cabbage quartered, black pepper, allspice, and salt, to taste. Let the soup simmer till the game is tender, but not overdone; and lest it should, the vegetables may be put in half an hour before the meat—*Obs.* This soup may be coloured with wine and two spoonfuls of mushroom catsup, and enriched with forcemeat-balls.

Dods, Cook and Housewife's Manual, 157–58.

One can imagine a New World version beginning with odd pieces of venison and completed with some combination of turkey, quail, passenger pigeon, dove, squirrel, rabbit, and the list gets longer with raccoon, opossum, or whatever else the hunter happened upon. We might call this version hunter's soup rather than poacher's, as early Scots or Scots-Irish settlers were free to hunt in much of this wide open land.

Preference for such mixed meat and vegetable broths and soups was widespread in the Old World, and was brought to America by several cultural groups. Rather than simply boiling the ingredients as directed above, the meat or vegetables could have been browned first in butter or other fat. Alternately, meat was partially roasted before being added to the broth along with collected drippings.

Meatless receipts were recorded for Lent or when meats were scarce. Eighteenth-century onion soups generally were not based on meat broth as are today's "French" onion soups, nor was cheese added.

Onion Soup

Take Half a Pound of Butter, put it in a Stewpan on the Fire, and boil it till it has done making a Noise, then take ten Onions, pared and cut small, throw them in the Butter, and let them fry a while, then shake in a little Flour, keep it stirring all the while, and let them do a little longer; then pour in three Mutchkins [pints] of boiling Water, stir them round, cut small the upper Crust of the stalest Penny Loaf you have, and put in it, season it with Pepper and Salt, let it boil ten Minutes, take it off the Fire, beat the Yolks of two Eggs with Salt, a Spoonful of Vinegar, mix them, then stir it into the Soup; mix it well and dish it.

Cleland, *New and Easy Method*, 9–10.

This Scots receipt is nearly identical to an English version in which the cook is reminded to stir a little of the hot soup into the egg mixture before adding to the pot. Both authors proposed thickening the soup with flour, bread, and egg yolks. Other cooks left off the flour or proposed only egg or bread alone. I prefer the simplest thickener, bread, which produces a nice consistency and dodges potential pitfalls of flour lumps or curdled egg.[20]

Vinegar was the important secret ingredient for balancing the sweetness of onions. Lemon juice was a nice alternative, suggested in a mid-eighteenth-century English cookery manuscript. According to another English author "Some add to this a large Glass of White-wine, which I think makes it better tasted than 'tis without it." Either of these acid ingredients can balance the flavor.[21]

While most early cooks agreed that onion soup required only butter for richness—or generous amounts of sweet oil (olive oil) in the case of "Onion-Soup the Spanish Way"—*The Experienced English Housewife* included "an old cock" and cream instead. She added an attractive touch of color: "A few heads of asparagus or stewed spinach both make it eat well and look very pretty." Common eighteenth-century onion soup, made without the meat stock we expect today, is surprisingly good. In contrast, one thoroughly outrageous receipt "especially for the most Grand and Sumptuous Entertainments" called for beaten almonds, a sweetbread, and a duck or two in "Pottage of Onions Santhy."[22]

Peas pottage was another simple, but tasty, soup with a characteristic eighteenth-century twist. Receipts abounded in early sources. The following was typical in flavorings, but dressier than most with its garnish of meat balls.

Pees Pottage

Take 3 points of pees and 6 quarts of Water set them on y* fire together with a large Onion Season it high then let them boyl together then Straine them through a Cullender and set them on the fire again and when they boyl put in four handsfull of Spinage 2 Leekes a Sprig of mint and a Spoonfull of flower Temper'd with Water then put in your forst meat balls and a little after a pound of fresh butter keep it Sturing tell the butter is melted then Dish it to the Table and dont shred the Leeks nor the Spinage to Small

                                             Pre-1744 Virginia cookbook, 60.

Peas Pottage (Interpretation, one-third receipt)

Two cups of dried split peas to two quarts water with a small onion boiled
    until soft.
Rub through a colander if a smoother texture is desired.
Add coarsely chopped herbs: one large handful spinach, one small leek, a small
    sprig of mint.
1 teaspoonful flour, stirred with a little water until smooth
One-third pound butter; salt and pepper to taste.
Simmer until thickened; adding flour or water if needed to adjust consistency.

Mint with peas was a signature combination found throughout early sources. Mace, cloves, and ginger were occasionally mentioned as were parsley, thyme, and *sweet herbs* in general. The manuscript belonging to Martha Washington mentioned: "If you love it, put in a little elder vinegar." Vegetables deemed appropriate for peas soup included carrot, turnip, celery, sorrel, cabbage, and beet leaves. Pork, beef, veal, or mutton (sometimes herring or anchovy) might contribute a more robust base. Or "If you please, you may put boyled pigeons in the dish." With these options, the cook can certainly find a combination that turns humble peas soup into a genteel dish. Actually, the modest receipt above is perfectly delicious as is. Don't forget the mint.[23]

Forcemeat balls make a nice garnish but may be treated as optional, for they did not show up in every peas soup. Forcemeat balls should be at least partially cooked before adding.

✍ Boiled, Stewed, Hashed

Two rules to be observed in boiling were universal. Meat should be started in cold water, and as scum forms, it should be carefully skimmed. "Gradual heating softens, plumps, and whitens the meat, and, above all, facilitates the separation of the scum, on the removal of which the goodness, as well as beauty, of boiled meat so much depends."[24]

Early cookery authors gave several versions of a clever trick for preventing foods from scorching and sticking to the pot. When stewing fowls or a knuckle of veal Glasse directed "lay four clean Skewers at the Bottom" upon which to place the meat. Simmons agreed with using skewers or twigs or "put some bones across the bottom of the pot to keep from burning" the meat.[25]

Receipts for the dish we might call pot roast came under titles such as *a la mode, a la daube, the French Way*, or simply *to stew*. (See Beef a la Mode in Chapter 1.) These ranged from simple to extraordinary. It is evident the following beef a la daub receipt was shared among South Carolina gentry. We see an identical version passed from Eliza Lucas Pinckney (c. 1740) to her daughter Harriot Horry and eventually to Sarah Rutledge (c. 1847). This southern "dobe" is quite similar to Glasse's and Cleland's Beef a la Daub, although simplified; as the English and Scots daubes called for pan browning the beef before stewing.[26]

To Dobe a Rump of Beef

Bone it and lard it with Bacon, Season it with Sweet herbs, Challots, Pepper, and Salt, Put it into your Pot (with just water enough to cover it) with Carrotts, Turnips, Onions, and whole Pepper, cloves and Mace; let it stew over a slow fire for three hours till tender, then make a good Sauce with rich gravey, Morrells, Truffles, and Mushrooms over it.

Horry, *Colonial Plantation Cookbook*, 54.

This is a good example of a dish where mushroom ketchup or powder (Chapter 9) might provide a shortcut, substituted for the mushrooms and spices. *The Virginia Housewife*'s Beef a-la-Daube showed up half a century later in Hill's Civil War era cookbook, made more complicated rather than simplified. Then as now, pot roasts were dressed variously. Not only beef, but also mutton and turkey received this treatment. More complicated daubes called for wine or for a forcemeat stuffing. Instead of larding, bacon could be laid under and over the meat. Artichoke bottoms, celery, sweetbreads, or palates amplified beef a la daube. Other suggested embellishments included fried forcemeat balls and sippets (toasts), or "garnish the brims of the dish with parsley and with flowers."[27]

✍ The Basic Stewed Dish, Plain & Fancy

A plain stewed dish of beef, veal, or mutton was also dressed up with a fancy name. As a pot roast was *a la mode* or *a la daube*, so another rather basic stewed meat dish was elegantly titled *haricot*. This method can be easily traced through the two centuries explored here. From *The French Cook* of 1653 through the 1747 English *Art of Cookery*, the 1829 Scots *Cook and Housewife's Manual*, the 1824 *Virginia Housewife*, and William Blackford's 1852 manuscript volume. Whether you fancied it a haricot or just plain stew, you have probably prepared a version of this stewed meat dish. There are a special few touches that will turn your twenty-first-century stew into an eighteenth-century stewed dish. (Note: *Stew* was seldom encountered as a noun in early sources.)[28]

Mutton Harico [*or Beef or Veal*]

Take a neck of mutton, cut it into chops and fry them brown. Then put them into a stew pan with a parcel of sweet herbs, 2 or 3 cloves, a little mace, and pepper and salt to your taste. Cover them with boiling water and let them stew slowly for about an hour. Then cut some carrots and turnips into dice, slice some onions and cut up a head of celery; put them into a stew pan and keep it closely covered except when you are skimming off the fat. Let the whole stew gently for an hour longer and then send it to table in a deep dish, with gravy about it. You may make a similar haricot of veal steaks or of beef cut very thin.

Blackford, "Recipes in the Culinary Arts," 9.

Ingredients common to *haricots* through two centuries were the bundle of sweet herbs, mace, salt and pepper, turnips, carrots, and onions. If cloves were added they were sometimes stuck into an onion for ease of removal before serving. These touches transform the stewed meat into an historical dish.

A preference for mixed meat flavors showed up in William Byrd's *History of the Dividing Line*. Byrd's survey party comrades were thwarted in hopes of a venison and wild turkey stew by Native conviction that creatures of land and air must not be cooked together.

These two kinds of Meat [deer and turkey] boil'd together, with the addition of a little Rice or French Barley, made excellent Soupe, and, what happens rarely in Other food things, it never cloy'd, no more than an Engaging Wife wou'd do, by being a Constant Dish.[29]

We made good chear upon a very fat Buck, that luckily fell in our way. The Indian likewise Shot a Wild Turkey, but confest he wou'd not bring it us, lest we shou'd continue to provoke the Guardian of the Forrest, by cooking the Beasts of the Field and the Birds of the Air together in one vessel.[30]

✍ Olla Podrida, Olio Podrido, Hotchpotch, Hodge-podge

But, after all, if the Jumbleing of two Sorts of Flesh together be a Sin, how intolerable an Offence must it be to make a Spanish Ole [olla], that is a Hotchpotch [hodge-podge] of every kind of thing that is eatable? And the good People of England wou'd have a great deal to answer for, for beating up so many different Ingredients into a Pudding.
        William Byrd, *Histories of the Dividing Line*, 194.

William Byrd was obviously well acquainted with this family of traditional European dishes in 1728. The continental European names olla podrida or olio podrido seem to have been widely recognized along with the English names hodge-podge or hotchpotch, under an array of spellings.

The ancestral stewed dish composed of a bit of any available meat and vegetable may date back to the first cook pot. *Olla* was the name given to a traditional ceramic vessel of ancient lineage as well as to the mixture itself. Certain heavily tempered clay pots can withstand a flame; typical eighteenth-century earthenware cannot. In an European style pottery vessel the olla podrida was cooked in an oven or set in a pot of boiling water (i.e. jugged). A metal pot or Indian made clay pot was the commonly employed stew pot in eighteenth-century America.

The Spanish *olla podrida* translates as "rotten pot." *Podrida* generally indicates the ingredients are stewed until falling to pieces, rather than putrid. However, in a hardscrabble setting, where new bits might be added each day to yesterday's stew, there would be opportunity for *rotten* to take its less savory meaning.

Outrageously complex versions of olla podrida, olio, or hodge-podge are found among early sources. In 1685 Robert May began directions for his olio podrida with beef, sausages, and tongue, joined by "Gubbins as big as a Ducks Egg" of mutton, venison, pork, bacon to which he added a quantity of domestic and wild fowl ranging from a goose or turkey to forty-eight larks. The expected array of root vegetables and cabbage were to be added near the end of cooking. His suggested faggot of sweet herbs included spinach, sorrel, borrage, endive, marigolds, and for spice—cloves, mace, and saffron. White wine or lemon added tartness. For variety May proposed chestnuts, pistachios, pine nuts, almonds, and pomegranate, with all but chestnuts unlikely to enter into

Large Iron Pot. Scotland, Carron Iron Works, 1810–1815. Courtesy of the Museum of Early Southern Decorative Arts (MESDA) at Old Salem.

a New World olla. In other words, almost anything can go into an olla or olio. The cook can have fun with this in any time period.[31]

"Spanish Olio" as well as "An Hotch-Potch" were found among dishes for the most elegant English tables in *The Complete Practical Cook*, 1730. Hannah Glasse offered five sorts of hodge-podge, running the gamut from compound to simple, from simmered over the fire to jugged in a water bath. That practical Scot, Margaret Dods, defined an *Olio* as "composed of a due admixture of meat, fish, fowl, vegetables, and roots." She contrasted a proper olio to the haphazard pepper pot which was "a sort of clear-larder, Saturday's dinner-dish, composed of all sorts of shreds and patches." The divide between numerous versions of olio, hodge-podge, and the later pepper pot is ambiguous. Dods recorded a ditty to describe the basic stewpot meal, whether labeled olio, hodge-podge, or pepper pot.[32]

> Where every thing that every soldier got,
> Fowl, bacon, cabbage, mutton, and what not
> Was thrown into one Bank, and went to pot.

Everyday meals enjoyed by the well-travelled German author, von Rumohr, illustrated just how sophisticated a one-pot dinner might become. He described the preparation of his common *olla* in the voice of his servant:

[*Ollapodrida*]

I used to place in this pot each day: a small piece of bacon, two pounds of beef, one pound of veal, a young chicken and a young pigeon. . . . When the meat had been skimmed and cooked sufficiently, I added whatever roots, herbs and fine vegetables were available in the market and let these cook. I then set the vegetable soup in the middle of the table, surrounded by the four types of meat, accompanied by anchovies, fresh butter, radishes, cucumber salad and similar dishes. As the vegetable mixture varied . . . this simplified, perhaps even refined form of 'Ollapotrida' never became tedious.

Von Rumohr, *Essence of Cookery*, 91.

The names *hodge-podge* and *olla podrida* seem to have been interchangeable. Not only can we have fun inventing an olla or hodge-podge from almost endless possibilities among seasonal ingredients, we can also draw from interesting modes of presentation and garnishing. Such stewed dishes were often served with special flair. A 1671 source suggested "the Broth is rather to be drunk out of a Porringer, than to be eaten with a spoon." Other sources direct arranging the components in a common dish with the broth as sauce. We see that von Rumohr was served the meats in separate dishes arranged around the tureen of soup with interesting cold accompaniments. The meats, ringed by the vegetables, might be crowned with a whole bird or several small birds that simmered in the olla.[33]

Cabbage, carrot, turnip, and onion were typical for the winter pot; vegetables suggested for other seasons included green peas, celery, endive, broccoli, asparagus, even violet leaves, marigold flowers, spinach, or lettuce.[34]

"If you would make a very fine dish" of "Breast of Veal in Hodge-podge" you included a stuffed or forced head of lettuce in the stew, to be served in the center of the veal and sauce. A cabbage pudding might occupy the place of the stuffed lettuce. One can imagine the historical cook tossing other sorts of complementary puddings into the hodge-podge.[35]

The Virginia Housewife documented evolution of the olla into a thoroughly New World version. "To Make an Ollo—A Spanish Dish" began with directions for a typical traditional base (beef, mutton, chicken, and pork), but suggested an interesting new selection of summer fruits, vegetables, and seasonings, including tomatoes.

To Make an Olla—A Spanish Dish

Take 2 lbs. beef, 1 lb. mutton, a chicken or half a pullet, and a small piece of pork; put them into a pot with very little water, and set it on the fire at ten o'clock to stew gently; you must sprinkle over it an onion chopped small, some pepper and salt, before you pour in the water; at half after twelve, put into the pot two or three apples or pears peeled and cut in two, tomatas with the skin taken off, cimblins [summer squash] cut in pieces, a handful of mint chopped, lima beans, snaps, and any kind of vegetable you like, let them all stew together till three o'clock; some cellery tops cut small and added at half after two, will improve it much.

M. Randolph, *Virginia Housewife*, 96–97.

Mrs. Hill's 1872 *Southern Practical Cookery* gave the same American "Olio" with added corn and Irish potatoes, and included a similar receipt that she called "Hotch Potch." While Mary Randolph's Olla and Annabella Hill's Olio were thoroughly New World and thoroughly nineteenth-century in character, the 1859 *Southern Gardener and Receipt-Book* harkened back to European ancestry of a century before in "Hodge-Podge Soup." Beef, mutton, pigeons, rabbits, veal, and poultry were joined by onions, carrots, parsley, parsnips, and turnips, seasoned with shallots, garlic, allspice, thyme, and basil. Only the garlic and basil would have been unusual, but not unheard of, a century before.[36]

The more affluent the household, the more meats and fewer vegetables appeared on the table. Vegetables were commonly treated as sauces and flavoring for broths rather than a central component of the fashionable meal. Specific vegetables were paired with particular proteins: as turnip or cauliflower with mutton or venison; onions, celery, or cucumbers with chicken; peas or beans with pork; cabbage or greens with salted beef or cured pork; carrots with fresh beef; and spinach or sorrel with eggs. These combinations turned up repeatedly, but were far from rules. Individual cooks had other favorite flavor blends. Certainly, availability guided the combinations, as the unlikely squirrel, turnip, and pumpkin that cooked into an "excellent soup" for travelers on the Ohio River in 1796.[37]

✦ The Made Dish

What is technically called a made-dish presupposes either a more elaborate mode of cookery than plain frying, broiling, or roasting; or else some combination of those elementary processes, as, for example, half-roasting and finishing in the stew-pan.

Margaret Dods, *Cook and Housewife's Manual* (1829), 269.

Cast Iron Pan. Chatham County, North Carolina, c. 1778–1800. John Wilcox, maker. Collection of the Museum of Early Southern Decorative Arts, Old Salem Museums & Gardens.

In other words *made dishes* involved multiple steps or tricky sauces. The cook's skills with seasonings and presentation were displayed in these special dishes. "The very name made-dish . . . implies something savory and highly relishing." Many of the recipes in this collection—well sauced meats and vegetables, puddings and pies—qualify as *made* dishes when they require extra labor, multiple ingredients, and creative presentation.[38]

William Byrd II of Virginia, a man of regular schedule and rather compulsive habits, who resolved never to eat more than one dish at dinner, occasionally noted "I transgressed my rule at dinner by eating a second dish." He did not record which particular dishes tempted him to break his resolve on those occasions. Simple boiled, roasted, broiled, or fried meats were noted among his dinner choices, as well as quite an assortment of stewed, hashed, or fricasseed dishes. Such *made* dishes might have been elegantly sauced and handsomely presented or a clever and economical use of leftovers (or both).[39]

Byrd's diaries reveal that he regularly dined on mutton, often hashed or stewed. The following method, from the manuscript cookery book of another tidewater Virginia household of his time, is several degrees beyond simple boiled mutton, thus a *made dish*.

To harsh Mutton

Take a shoulder of Mutton half Roasted cut it as thin as you can and take a Glass of Clarrit a blade of Mace 2 Anchovies a few Cloves a Shorlott [shallot] and Salt a

Sprig or 2 of time and Savory some Lemon Peel let it Stew half an hour Covered and when it is Enough shake in some Capers but not tell you take it up.

Pre-1744 Virginia cookbook, 63.

Hashed mutton seems to have been most often served with turnips, but also with fresh vegetables in season, especially cucumbers. Byrd enjoyed his mutton with asparagus, green peas, or *sallet* as well as with turnips.[40]

The combination of wine, anchovy, shallot, lemon, and capers with herbs and spices was typical. Receipts for made dishes provide excellent examples of eighteenth-century seasonings. Notice the signature balance of flavoring agents among recipes in this section: sweet herbs (thyme, savory, parsley, sage); spices (mace, nutmeg, cloves); something for tartness (wine, lemon); and that special ingredient for depth of flavor (anchovy, shallot).

Half roasting meat before hashing or stewing seems labor intensive and perhaps of questionable purpose. However, this technique was common among period receipts. A seventeenth-century hash recipe directed cutting off little bits of mutton "as it doth roast." Two centuries later Sarah Rutledge recommended beef to yield the best broth as "Mutton gives it an unpleasant flavor, but this may be remedied by using it after having been roasted, or broiled." Alternately, the eighteenth-century cook browned the meat in a little fat, as we do today, before adding liquid for stewing. Both methods added flavor and eye appeal.[41]

The French Cook (1653) left us with such a variety of methods for cooking fowls and meats that we may feel free to use our judgment. La Varenne approved the English preference to partially roast before stewing, but also often suggested "pass in the pan" (brown in a little fat) and then "seeth until well sodden" (simmer until tender). In other cases he directed the meat be first seethed until almost done and finally broiled or put on a spit and roasted. Thus we have documented a freedom to switch cooking methods when we deem necessary. Brown first, then stew; or stew first, then brown.[42]

The option for half roasting followed by stewing provides a handy technique for the recreated historic cook's repertoire. The following Virginia method produces a sauce along with nicely browned and thoroughly done meat.

Wild fowl to stew

Half roast them then set them over a Chafing Dish of Coals with a pint of Clarret as much Gravey season'd with a Shallot & spice stew it till it is well mixt.

Jane Randolph 1743, Harbury,
Virginia's Cooking Dynasty, 384.

Of course the basic method for stewing any meat is to omit the initial brown-ing and begin with raw meat in cold liquid. The sauce and garnish become ever more important as the meat will not be as attractive as when browned.

To Stew Chickens

Take Chickens and quarter them into white Wine and Water but most Wine and when they are Stew'd Tender put in a good quantity of butter and a bundle of Sweet herbes with large Mace then take Rasping of a Manchett [fine white roll] to thicken it with a good quantity of Parsley you may put in a little Sage if you like it Salt pepper and Nutmeg then Season your Chickens with Marrow [or butter] laid on the tops of them[,] with the Yolks of Eggs well beaten and Juice of a Lemon in the Sawce and Garnish with Parsley and Lemon.

Pre-1744 Virginia cookbook, 63.

This is a rather typical receipt for stewing chicken. Remember to skim the pot as it begins to boil. An onion may be added to the above seasonings and butter used in place of the marrow. Two or three egg yolks plus a little flour rubbed into butter were combined to thicken similar dishes. Adding a little cream at the finish can transform this dish into a *Fricassey*.[43]

This combination of flavors is widely appreciated by many today as it was two hundred years ago. However, one wonders if the French would have ap-proved. A French plantation mistress in Virginia found fault with such dishes: "Fricassees of Chicken, such as we like in France, are absolutely different from those served here and sauces are unknown. Everything is covered with a thick and most unappetizing gravy." The cook's finesse with stew or fricassee can make the difference between a nice sauce or gloppy, unappetizing gravy. Ap-propriate choice of thickening agent and balance of seasonings are arts of the good cook.[44]

And while we are on the subject of fricassees, let's look at another ancestor of traditional southern smothered fowl, rabbit, or squirrel dishes. A slice or two of bacon may be added at the beginning. Note this gravy is thickened with butter and flour instead of egg yolk as in the stewed chicken above.

Fricaseed Rabbits

The best way of cooking rabbits is to fricasee them. Take a couple of fine ones, cut up and disjoint them. Put them into a stew pan. Season them with cay-enne pepper, salt, chopped parsley and powdered mace. Pour in a pint of warm water, or veal broth if you have it, and stew it over a slow fire until the rabbits are quite tender, adding when they are about half done some butter in small lumps, rolled in flour. Just before you take it from the fire enrich the gravy with a gill [½ cup] or more of cream seasoned with nutmeg. Stir the gravy well but take care not to let it boil after the cream is put in lest it curdle.

Put the pieces of rabbit on a hot dish and pour the gravy over them.

Blackford, "Recipes in the Culinary Arts," 13.

An unusual but especially delicious stewed chicken comes to us under the misleading title "Sweet Potatoes Stewed." A Dutch oven works well for this dish as does a covered pot over a gentle fire. Unpeeled potatoes are indicated; however if the sweet potatoes are peeled, they may sufficiently thicken the gravy. Generally, no additional thickening is required if only a small quantity of water is used. If broth is too thin, a little flour rubbed into a lump of butter may be added.

Sweet Potatoes Stewed

Wash and wipe them [sweet potatoes], and if they be large cut them in two lengths; put them at the bottom of a stew pan, lay over some slices of boiled ham, and on that, one or two chickens cut up with pepper, salt, and a bundle of herbs; pour in some water and stew them till done, then take out the herbs, serve the stew in a deep dish, thicken the gravy, and pour over it.

M. Randolph, *Virginia Housewife*, 133.

This stewed chicken forms its own delicious and out of the ordinary sauce. One wonders why Mary Randolph gave this fine chicken and ham dish such a misleading name. Strange as it may seem from the titles, you will notice kinship between Cheshire Pork Pie, Sea Pie, and Sweet Potatoes Stewed. The methods and ingredients are similar with sweet potato in place of Irish potato. Add a crust on top and Mary Randolph's stewed sweet potato, ham, and chicken becomes an exceptional pie.

✍ Forcemeats

Forcemeats show up in everything from pies to soups to stuffings. Any finely chopped or pounded mixture might be called *forcemeat*. Not every forcemeat contained meat. Generally meant for a stuffing, at times forcemeat was made into balls for garnish or even molded around boiled eggs to create "Forced Eggs."[45]

As one might expect, Mary Randolph's American forcemeat was based on eighteenth-century English cookery authors, especially Hannah Glasse who observed "Force-Meat Balls are a great Addition to all Made-Dishes." Note the options to fry or to boil forcemeat balls, depending on whether they are to be added to a dish with brown sauce or white.[46]

Slip-decorated Earthenware Dish. Attributed to North Carolina Moravian potter, Aust, 1780–90. Although the original Guilford County owners likely treasured and proudly displayed this dish, later generations apparently found it homely. The plate was ultimately delegated to storing salt pork, which caused deterioration of the slip decoration. Collection of the Museum of Early Southern Decorative Arts, Old Salem Museums & Gardens.

Forcemeat Balls

Take half a pound of veal, and half a pound of suet cut fine and beat in a marble mortar or wooden bowl; add a few sweet herbs shred fine, a little mace pounded fine, a small nutmeg grated, a little lemon peel, some pepper and salt, and the yelks of two eggs; mix them well together, and make them into balls and long pieces, then roll them in flour, and fry them brown. If they are for the use of white sauce, do not fry them, but put them in a sauce pan of hot water, and let them boil a few minutes.

M. Randolph, *Virginia Housewife*, 109.

A Note on Suet: *The Carolina Housewife* inserted a useful bit of advice in a Christmas Pie receipt. "Bacon, chopped or beat up with the forcemeat, is preferable to suet, as it is nicer when cold, and keeps better." This is a fine substitution when good suet is unavailable or in dishes where the flavor of bacon is appealing, as in forcemeat balls.

A mid-eighteenth-century Virginia lady left us her "Frost meat" with directions for chopping the meats finely rather than beating in a mortar. Her forcemeat is related to today's bulk sausage; although, the seasonings from three centuries ago were quite different.

To make Frost meat [Forcemeat]

Take Veal Lean beef or pork is best take a pound of pork & Shred it very Smal then take as much Sewett [suet] as mea[t] & Shred it but not so smal, then take a Little Sprig of time & Sweet Marjoram one nuttmeg half an ounce of pepper with some Cloves & mace well beat & a handful of salt, then Roul it up into Small Balls

Jane Randolph 1743, Harbury, *Virginia's Cooking Dynasty*, 312.

Forcemeat might include fish as well, especially oysters, or might contain no meat at all. Among three mid-century Scots formulas for forcemeat balls, one offered a meatless option based on bread crumbs and butter.[47]

Another Sort of Forc'd meat Balls

Crumb a Penny Loaf, and add to it eight Ounces of Butter, or Beef Sewet, minc'd very fine, Lemon-peel, Parsley, and a Bit of Onion shred fine; season it with Pepper, Salt, Nutmeg, wet it with two Eggs, roll it in your Hands to a Paste, then make it in small Balls the Bigness of a Nutmeg, fry them in Butter.[48]

Forcemeat (Period appropriate optional ingredients)

>   Meats (including fowl, fish, shellfish, and organ meats)
>   Suet, bacon, or butter
>   Bread, egg (raw or boiled)
>   Onion, green onion, shallot
>   Mushroom, anchovy
>   "Sweet herbs" (as spinach, parsley, thyme, marjoram, winter savory,
>   sage, etc.)
>   Currants, lemon peel
>   Pepper, salt, spice (as nutmeg, mace, cloves, etc.)
>   and more.

Almost anything was mixed into a forcemeat. The stuffing or dressing accompanying our Thanksgiving turkey is today's most beloved forcemeat. Bulk sausage is another.

✍ The Cabbage Pudding Family of Receipts

Popular eighteenth-century cookery books included fascinating variations of cabbage pudding or forced cabbage. English authors gave rather complicated receipts.

Hannah Glasse's "A forced Cabbage" was stuffed with veal, bacon, cabbage, boiled eggs, bread crumbs, and mushrooms; seasoned with pepper, salt, mace, lemon peel, parsley, thyme, and anchovies; and bound together with egg yolk. This mixture was typical in its seasonings and was simply bound up with string rather than in a cloth.[49]

"Forced Cabbage" has long been one of our favorite dishes drawn from eighteenth-century sources. Therefore, we were led to further investigate its history and its relatives. *The Complete Practical Cook* of 1730 included "Cabbage Pudding with Flesh" to be tied up in a buttered cloth and boiled.

[Stuffing for] Cabbage Pudding with Flesh

[Chop the cabbage, scooped from the middle of the head, then mix with] a Pound of Veal, have [half?] a Pound of Beef Suet, a quarter of a Pound of fat Bacon; put to it some Thyme and Parsly, and two or three green Onions; season with Pepper, Salt, Nutmeg, and Ginger: mince it very well, put to the scalded Cabbage, and chop that a little with it; work it [meats, seasonings, and the chopped cabbage] up with grated Bread and the Yolks of Eggs with a White or two.

C. Carter, *Complete Practical Cook*, 111.

A century later Mary Randolph recorded a similar but simplified stuffed cabbage recipe which may become as elegant or as simple a dish as desired. Two centuries beyond, we find the direct descendant as "Stuffed Cabbage or Gefuellter Krautkopf" in *The Joy of Cooking*. In the mid-twentieth century this dish was still current in central North Carolina as remembered by one open hearth cookery student. She recollected her father filling a cabbage with "something like meatloaf" before tying it in a cloth to boil, seemingly a direct descendant of Mary Randolph's method.[50]

Cabbage Pudding

Get a fine head of cabbage, not too large, pour boiling water on, and cover it till you can turn the leaves back, which you must do carefully; take some of those in the middle of the head off, chop them fine, and mix them with rich force-meat; put this in and replace the leaves to confine the stuffing; tie it in a cloth and boil it; serve it up whole with a little melted butter in the dish.

M. Randolph, *Virginia Housewife*, 134.

The most amusing cabbage pudding was certainly "An Hogoo." After the cabbage was stuffed with forcemeat the cook was directed to "shape it long ways like the body of a Duck and boyle a Ducks head and Stick it on a little Scure [skewer] then bind the body close in a Cloath and . . . boyl it well."[51]

In "To boil Fowls and Cabbage" Eliza Smith recommended serving cabbage pudding with poultry: "When the out-side is tender, lay it between two bon'd fowls, and on them all some melted butter and slices of fried bacon."

On the other hand, in her "Cabbage Pudding," Smith seemed to suggest smaller bundles: "wrap it up in green cabbage leaves, tie a cloth over it, boil it an hour." The forcemeat for this pudding called for two pounds chopped beef suet and an equal quantity lean veal mixed with the chopped cabbage, seasoned with mace, nutmeg, pepper, salt, and optionally grapes—combined with beaten eggs. This large quantity could never fit into a whole cabbage. Additionally, the boiling time seems too short to adequately cook raw meats. These details indicate the probability of this receipt yielding individual puddings, cabbage rolls or dolmades.[52]

A short boiling time is problematic for any raw meat based pudding. The rather similar receipt below, for "dolmoe," solved that problem by thoroughly boiling the forcemeat before folding into leaves:

Dolmoe Mrs Surtees

Take part of a Loyn or Neck of Mutton fat & Lean together chop it fine with some Parsley & time a little onion & Mace Nutmeg pepper & salt & some Rice mix all up together with an egg & roll them into Balls then tye them up in cloths & boil them two Hours then take them out & put in some Beet Leaves into hot Water to green them roll the Balls into them & lay ym in the dish with a White fricasey Sauce with a spoonful of Gravy put to it & juice of Lemon.

South Carolina household book.

The *Dolma* is a Mediterannean cousin to cabbage roll or cabbage pudding. Dolmades were typically wrapped in pickled vine (grape) leaves. Cabbage leaves, either fresh or brined, were usual elsewhere. In the American recipe above, beet leaves served the purpose. I was surprised to find this receipt in an early South Carolina source. Such meat and grain filled leaves were sometimes simply poached in water, stock, or sauce, rather than boiled in cloths.

A Note on Cooking Times: Today's knowledge of health risks from undercooked meats guides us to be wary of short cooking times. The cabbage pudding, and other large puddings that called for boiling only an hour, are more safely prepared with precooked meats in the filling, or a longer cooking time.

Suet based puddings and pies are exceptions. The raw suet is an integral ingredient, filling the role of butter or other fat. In fact those puddings will not succeed unless prepared with raw suet. Plum puddings and their kin call for four hours or more in the boiling water, adequate time for thoroughly cooking the suet and other meats.

Vegetarian dishes are found among *meagre* receipts for Lent. Cookbooks gave certain dishes both with and without *flesh*. Seafood dishes were counted meagre, and suitable for meatless days. "A Farce Meagre Cabbage" was stuffed with flounder, boiled eggs, breadcrumbs, parsley, butter, egg yolk, and the finely chopped inner cabbage—then tied up with a string and simmered in a highly seasoned sauce.[53]

The beef a la daube and olla, cabbage pudding and dolma, may have been thrown together from whatever happened to be on hand, or such dishes may have been prepared from carefully selected ingredients and presented with style. The cook's specialty was considered a *made dish*.

Definition of *made dish* seems to have been broad. For example, Hannah Glasse titled a sweet, spiced custard pie with ground almonds and shred artichoke bottoms "A pretty Made-Dish." It seems we may consider any dish that is time consuming, requires hard to find ingredients, or messes up numerous utensils a *made dish*.[54]

CHAPTER 7

Vegetables

Salads, Potherbs, Sauces, Meagre Dishes

A Country Gentleman and Farmer may have every thing at home, and set out a
Table fit for a Prince, without being beholden to the Markets

Richard Bradley, *Country Housewife*
(1736), I: 128.

By the end of winter our ancestors' health suffered from lack of fresh foods.
Even their preserved fruits and vegetables were likely depleted. Earlier generations were intensely tuned to each season's bounty—springtime greens, peas,
and asparagus; summer fruits, berries, beans, and corn; autumn apples, root
vegetables, and pumpkins. Seasonal, health restoring vegetables and fruits
were enjoyed raw and cooked. They were dried, pickled, or preserved to store
against seasons of scarcity.

✌ The Tribe of Sallets

The salad family tree is rooted on raw or boiled seasonal vegetables simply
dressed. These may branch into Grand Salads and into the even grander Salmagundi. Many of today's creative salads would have been right at home on an
eighteenth-century table, with some notable differences. An examination of
ancestral salads reveals ingredients, combinations, and presentations worth
reviving.

Defining *salad* or *sallet* in eighteenth-century context is difficult. Salads
included three dissimilar groups of ingredients: simple fresh salads dependent on seasonal availability, winter salads of boiled or preserved vegetables,
and salads of cold meats. John Evelyn's 1699 *Acetaria: A Discourse of Sallets*
treated common herbaceous plants, especially the leaves, stems, buds, flowers, and stalks along with a few roots and fruits. Evelyn touted a plant based
diet, at odds with both earlier and later authors. His ingredients were typical

of salads that persist to the present day. Nor would we find his dressings unusual.

Delicate greens, tender herbs, and flowers in season were enjoyed raw. John Evelyn declared that lettuces formed "the principal Foundation of the universal Tribe of Sallets," as they do still. Purslane, violet leaves, endive, spinach, sorrel, tender tops of nettles, cleavers, lemon balm, basil, borage, chervil, clary, fennel, cresses, or tarragon found their way into salads. Radishes, scallions, chives, and tender young pea pods joined the list of salad vegetables. Cucumbers and beets were popular additions, then as now.

In *Acetaria* John Evelyn ranked cucumbers "the most approved Sallet alone, or in Composition." Other authors shed insight into how they were customarily served, with vinegar and a complementary pungent component. Hot, spicy onions or nasturtiums were considered necessary to balance the cooling nature of the cucumber.

To eat raw Cucumers [sic] in a wholesome pleasant Manner

When you have pared and sliced cucumers, put a little water and some salt over them, and let them stand so about ten minutes; then drain that from them, and just wash them with a little vinegar, throwing that away likewise, before you put oil and vinegar upon them. This will make them eat much crisper and finer. . . . The addition of a few green nasturtian [sic] pods fresh gathered and eat with them, correct them, and make them much wholesomer as well as pleasanter, especially to such as do not chuse to eat onions with them.

Ellis, *Country Housewife's Family Companion*, 449–50.

Of course simple sliced raw cucumbers have remained a highly approved salad right up to today. Cucumbers were formerly served cooked as well as raw.

To boil Cucumbers

Take your largest Cucumbers, and wash them and put them into boiling water made quick with Salt, then when they are boiled enough, take them and peel them and break them into a Cullender, and when the Water is well drained from them, put them into a hot Dish, and pour over them some Butter and Vinegar a little Pepper and Salt, strew Salt on your Dish brims, lay some of the Rind of them about the dish cut in several Fancies, and so serve them to the Table.

Wolley, *Queen-like Closet*, 110.

Lightly cooked broccoli was dressed with oil and vinegar and garnished with nasturtium pods as were cucumbers. Hannah Wolley recorded another simple raw salad in the seventeenth century that remains familiar today.[1]

A good Sallad in Winter

Take a good hard Cabbage, and with a sharp Knife shave it so thin as you may not discern what it is, then serve it with Oil and Vinegar.

Wolley, Queen-like Closet, 172.

That observant Swede, Peter Kalm, traveling through the mid-Atlantic colonies enjoyed such a salad. "This dish has a very pleasing flavor and tastes better than one can imagine."

[Cabbage Salad]

My landlady . . . took the inner leaves of a head of cabbage . . . and cut them in long, thin strips, about $\frac{1}{12}$ to $\frac{1}{6}$ of an inch wide . . . she put them upon a platter, poured oil and vinegar upon them, added salt and some pepper while mixing the shredded cabbage, so that the oil etc. might be evenly distributed, as is the custom when making salads. Then it was ready. In place of oil, melted butter is frequently used.

Kalm, Travels, II: 609.

Moreau de St. Méry also noted the American salad "may be thinly sliced cabbage seasoned to each man's taste on his own plate." The cabbage was considered nicest if very finely shredded. Slaw seems never to have fallen from favor. *The Kentucky Housewife* and *Mrs. Hill's Southern Practical Cookery* included both cold and hot slaws. And, of course coleslaw is ubiquitous today, with interesting regional variations.[2]

Winter salads formed a diverse group of vegetable dishes assembled from cold season ingredients. Boiled beets were lauded as "a grateful Winter Sallet." Beets, parsnips, turnips, cauliflower, and artichoke bottoms were pickled as well as boiled to be enjoyed hot or cold as winter salads. Carrots, onions, leeks, and cabbage seem to have been more often boiled than eaten raw. These were dressed with oil and vinegar or with butter, with or without vinegar. Butter generally dressed salads to be served warm; oil was good on either hot or cold vegetables. Wolley gave interesting pre-eighteenth-century hot and cold winter salads:

To make good cold Sallads of several things

Take either Coleflowers, or Carrots, or Parsneps, or Turneps after they are well boiled, and serve them in with Oil, Vinegar and Pepper, also the Roots of red Beets boiled tender are very good in the same manner.

Wolley, Queen-like Closet, 136.

To make boiled Sallads

Boil some Carots very tender, and scrape them to pieces like the Pulp of an Apple, season them with Cinamon and Ginger and Sugar, put in Currans, a little Vinegar, and a piece of sweet Butter, stew these in a Dish, and when they begin to dry put in more Butter and a little Salt, so serve them to the Table, thus you may do Lettuce, or Spinage or Beets.

Wolley, *Queen-like Closet*, 156.

In mid-seventeenth century a boiled onion with vinegar, oil, and pepper was considered "a good simple sallat." John Evelyn agreed, "an honest laborious Country-man, with good Bread, Salt, and a little Parsley, will make a contented Meal with a roasted Onion." Meg Dods noted, "Stewed and roasted onions used to be a favourite supper-dish in Scotland and were reckoned medicinal:"[3]

[*Roasted Onion*]

Onions are roasted before the fire in their skins, peeled, and served with cold butter and salt. They are eaten either alone or with roasted potatoes, or with red or pickled herrings. In the latter case, we would recommend mustard as well as butter.

Dods, *Cook and Housewife's Manual*, 212.

Rundell echoed this basic method. She suggested pairing a roasted onion with either roasted potato or beet root.[4]

 The beet was widely considered "an excellent garnish, and easily converted into a very cheap and pleasant pickle." In von Rumohr's experience: "Due to their excessive sweetness, the common red beetroots are rarely served as a hot vegetable side dish. They are either pickled in vinegar or served in salads, mixed with bitter herbs and potatoes."[5]

 Beets keep their color best when boiled or baked whole. Cooked beets may be peeled and sliced for sauce or pickle. Beet was, and is, easily cut into shapes "according to your fancy." The deep red of beet root was exploited for coloring other foods, particularly turnips, onions, red cabbage, or cauliflower. At times the color was further enhanced with a little cochineal, a tropical insect that yields a red dye utilized for fabric and food coloring.[6]

Beet-root [*and Turnip*]

Wash the beet-roots, but take care not to break the skin or the fibers which hang about it, else the colour will fly. Boil them softly for an hour, or more if they are large, or bake them, and as soon as they are cold enough to be handled, peel them, and, cutting them into slices, put the slices into a jar, and have ready to pour over them cold vinegar, in which black and Jamaica pepper, ginger, cloves, and a little cayenne have been previously boiled. . . . The slices, when to be used, may be cut in the form of leaves, flowers, or nicked round the edges; a few small silver onions, and turnips scooped out to the size of marbles will take the rich red tinge of this pickle, form an ornamental variety with the beet-root, and cost nothing. Cochineal will improve the colour.

Dods, *Cook and Housewife's Manual*, 266.

Some authors recommended pouring hot vinegar on the beets, more commonly it was added cold. Seasonings differed. The vinegar was boiled with mace, ginger, and horseradish (Raffald); or black pepper, cayenne, Jamaica pepper [allspice], ginger, and cloves (Dods).

Both early eighteenth-century manuscript cookbooks compared in *Virginia's Cooking Dynasty* included "To pickle Beets Roots or turnips" with vinegar, salt, and spice. Receipts for pickling beets changed little through three centuries. *The French Cook* of 1653 simply directed pouring vinegar over cooked beets, as did Hannah Glasse a century later and *The Kentucky Housewife* in mid nineteenth century. You will notice no sugar in eighteenth-century pickles. In 1872 we find Mrs. Hill's *Southern Practical Cookery* including sugar in the pickle as remains standard today. An African American cook, known for her pickles and preserves, gave exceptionally syrupy "Sweet Cucumber Pickles" in *What Mrs. Fisher Knows About Old Southern Cooking* (1881).[7]

Another category of winter salads featured preserved fruits and nuts along with pickled vegetables. Seventeenth-century versions were tagged "grand salad."

We would recognize two of Markham's 1631 basic salads; seven more receipts reflected earlier traditions involving a variety of pickled ingredients, dried fruits, almonds, and liberal use of sugar. Wolley, in 1672, echoed this type of salad in her "grand Sallad" which is actually a meatless salmagundi. Pickled and candied ingredients, dried fruits, and nuts arranged separately on a large dish diverge from our concept of salad. John Evelyn recorded a similar dish, calling it "an universal Winter-Sallet . . . fitted for a City Feast."[8]

In reaction to exotic and complicated Grand Salads of the seventeenth century, Evelyn declared "Grand-Sallet . . . shou'd consist of the Green blanch'd and unpickled." His fresh version of Grand-Sallet called for a garnish of buds and flowers topped by a "stately" centerpiece of celery stalks. *The Accomplisht Cook* of 1685 included fifteen grand salad receipts. These involved exotic ingredients in unusual combinations. Rather curious at that early date was "Virginia Potato" among a long list of ingredients that included almonds, figs, and pickled oysters. Two interesting and simpler permutations follow:[9]

[Grand Sallet] Otherways

The youngest and smallest leaves of spinage, the smallest also of sorrel, well washed currans, and red beets round the centre being finely carved, oyl and vinegar, and the dish garnished with lemon and beets.

May, *Accomplisht Cook*, 135.

Other Grand Sallets

All sorts of good herbs, the little leaves of [red sage, sorrel, parsley, spinage, burnet, lettice, white endive, and charvel] . . . all finely pick't and washed, and swung in a strainer or clean napkin, and well drained from the water; then dish it in a clean scowred dish, and about the centre capers, currans, olives, lemons carved and slic't, boil'd beet-roots carved and slic't, and dished round also with good oyl and vinegar.

May, *Accomplisht Cook*, 136.

Attention was paid to choice and arrangement of salading material: "any thing well-flavored, and of a good color." Colorful salad ingredients need little further adornment. Several fashionable decorative touches of that day are still familiar. Early authors suggested garnishing with egg white rings. Fresh or pickled edible flowers or seeds and tender herb sprigs were strewn on top. And most intriguing, "The Roots of the Red Beet, pared into thin Slices and Circles, are by the French and Italians contriv'd into curious Figures to adorn their Sallets." The mysterious *curious figures* sound much more interesting than the sliced beets commonly residing on our salad bars.[10]

A vegetable or salad may have been served from a homemade wooden bowl, an American earthenware or pewter bowl, or from an imported ceramic or silver vessel. English creamware and Dutch delft were common on well dressed tables. For the most elegant dinners the cook's specialty may have been presented in a treasured Chinese bowl.

A definition for *salad* remains elusive. Raw, cooked, pickled, even candied foods were incorporated into salads. Many featured cold ingredients, although some winter salads were served warm. Vegetables were (and are) regarded as fundamental, but meats might be included or even become the base of a salad. Simple salads of cold meats, fowl, or fish were found among period sources throughout our period of concern. The following ancestral chicken salad was actually a sort of salmagundi.

To make a Sallad of cold meat

Take the brawn [meat] of a cold Capon, or a piece of cold Veal, and mince it very small, with some Limon pill, then put in some Oil, Vinegar, Capers, Caviare, and

Chinese Export Bowl. South Carolina lowcountry, c. 1785. Connected to General Thomas Pinckney, "El Dorado" plantation. Courtesy of the Museum of Early Southern Decorative Arts (MESDA) at Old Salem.

some Anchovies, and mix them very well, then lay it in a Dish in the form of a Star, and serve it in; Garnish your dish with Anchovies, Limon and Capers.

Wolley, *Queen-like Closet*, 115.

French Salad

Chop three anchovies, a shalot, and some parsley, small; put them into a bowl with two table spoonfuls of vinegar, one of oil, a little mustard, and salt. When well mixed, add by degrees some cold roast or boiled meat in very thin slices; put in a few at a time, not exceeding two or three inches long. Shake them in the seasoning, and then put more; cover the bowl close, and let the salad be prepared three hours before it is to be eaten. Garnish with parsley, and a few slices of the fat.

Rundell, *New System of Domestic Cookery*, 174.

Period sources also yielded directions for lobster on salad greens with oil and vinegar, as well as a salad of boiled or pickled salmon minced with apples and onions.[11]

Salmagundi

Salmagundi, Solomon-Gundy, Sallad-Magundy, Salmy-Gundy, Salomongundy . . . the names are as interesting as the receipts. The eighteenth-century

Salomongundy, as penned into the pre-1744 Virginia cookery book is similar to the majority of English versions, although simplified. Collection of the Museum of Early Southern Decorative Arts, Old Salem Museums & Gardens.

salmagundi was generally indistinguishable from a *grand salad;* excepting salmagundis more often featured meats.

As usually detailed in period sources, salmagundi is the ultimate salad. The composition and presentation are limited only by the cook's imagination and available ingredients.[12]

A Salomongundy

Take Chicken or Veal minced very fine then lay a layer of it and a layer of the Yolks of hard Eggs and a layer of the White and a layer of Anchovies with a layer of lemon then lay a layer of all Sorts of Pickles that you have and between Every one of these a layer of Sorrell Spinage and Sivies [chives?] Shred very fine as the others and when you have laid your dish all round that it is full only leave a place a Top to Set an Oraing or a Lemon in and Garnish with horse Radish Raspt [grated] Lemon Orange and barbaries and this is proper for a Second Corse side Dish Or a midle Dish for Super

You must take 2 dishes and lay the uppermost Dish the wrong side uppermost to build your Salomungundy on it being out of fashion to mix alltogether but every one mixs's it on their plates as they please some likes it with Oyl and Venigar and some with only the Juice of Lemon

Pre-1744 Virginia cookbook, 74.

Only toward the end of the receipt does one realize that this author's "layers" must be rings around the central dish or perhaps spokes radiating from the center, as in other versions of salmagundi. Mid-eighteenth-century authors clarify this presentation: the components were arranged in rings around a small bowl or saucer turned up side down in the middle of a large plate. Dods commented on "ornamental Salmagundi" as one of the "frippery dishes of former times." Hers was exceptionally ornamental, "surmounted by a triumphal arch of herring-bones."[13]

Alternately one may "either lay all the ingredients by themselves separate on saucers, or in heaps in a dish." Half whites of eggs provided yet another clever presentation; "each half egg has but one ingredient." Ingredients were minced or otherwise cut small.[14]

Though it may have been considered "out of fashion to mix altogether," several authors gave receipts for presenting a mixed salmagundi. Moxon's and Dod's methods seem thoroughly bizarre: The flesh was removed from the herring bones "without breaking the skin, and keep on the head, tails, fins, &c." The mixture was then to be packed back into the skins around the bones "in the shape of an Herring." What a peculiar presentation![15]

Survey of a dozen receipts, dating from 1734 to 1824, yielded an intriguing list of period appropriate components. Salmagundis characteristically included pickled fish, fowl or other meat, boiled eggs, vegetables or fruits, and "all Sorts of Pickles." You may select "just what you fancy" from the following list of possibilities.

Salmagundi (Composite interpretation)

Base Ingredients

    Anchovies or Pickled Herring (perhaps Pickled Oysters)

    Chicken (or Turkey, Pigeon, Duck)

    Veal, Beef, Pork, Ham, or Tongue

    Eggs, boiled (yolks and whites separate)

    Apple

    Onion, Shallot, Chives

    Cucumber

    Celery

    Spinach, Parsley, Sorrel, Lettuce, or Watercress (laid between other ingredients)

    Pickled Cucumber, Mushroom, Beet root, red/purple Cabbage and "any Pickle you like" such as Asparagus, Cauliflowers, Onions, Artichoke bottoms, Purslane, Barberries, Grapes, Plums, Peaches, or French Beans (pickled or blanched).

Centerpiece
> Whole Orange or Lemon
> Mango (pickled melon, rather than the tropical fruit)
> Butter, formed into a pyramid, pineapple, or other shape

Garnish
> Capers (or pickled nasturtium or radish pods)
> Flowers, especially nasturtiums; herbs
> Butter curls or lumps, stuck with parsley sprigs
> Horseradish, grated
> Lemon, Orange

One finds confusion between *salmagundi* and *salmi,* particularly as the nineteenth century progressed. As the names suggest, both dishes involved salted foods. Salmi was a ragout, a stewed mixture of meats, often including game birds, bacon, and anchovy. The salmi was typically served hot with toast. Certain meat pies could be considered salmis. In Mrs. Hill's 1872 *Southern Practical Cookery* Salmagundi was a complicated stew put into a pie with Irish potato dumplings and calves foot jelly. She noted: "They are good Christmas pies." Are we confused yet? Salmagundi began to sound more closely related to olla podrida or hodge-podge than to salad. As long as we remain in an eighteenth-century mindset salmagundi is less perplexing.[16]

🐚 Dressing the Salad

Dressing a salad was simple: Olive oil, vinegar, and salt were basic. For boiled vegetables served warm the dressing might contain butter rather than oil with the vinegar. A dressing could be made richer with mashed boiled egg yolk and more flavorful with pepper, mustard, herbs, minced onion or shallot. While seventeenth-century dressings were typically sweet, sugar was generally absent from eighteenth-century versions. Sweet salad dressings reappeared in the nineteenth century. *The Virginia Housewife* summed up common proportions and method. Simply omit her sugar when working in an eighteenth-century context.[17]

To Dress Salad

Take the yolks [of two boiled eggs] in a soup plate, pour on them a table spoonful of cold water, rub them with a wooden spoon until they are perfectly dissolved, then add two table spoonsful of oil; when well mixed, put in a teaspoonful of salt, one of powdered sugar [optional], and one of made mustard; when all these are united and quite smooth, stir in two table spoonsful of common, and two of tarragon vinegar; put it over the salad, and garnish the top with the whites of the eggs cut into rings, and lay around the edge of the bowl young scallions, they being the most delicate of the onion tribe.

M. Randolph, Virginia Housewife, 115–6.

Such a dressing seems not at all strange today. Other herb flavored vinegars, including elder flower, rose, or pepper, would be proper period choices.

Von Rumohr summed up pan-European salad tastes, and indeed the history of the salad. "People have their own favoured methods of making all kinds of salads from herbs and roots, either cooked, raw or pickled, combined with meat, fish or salted products. German people are quite familiar with mixtures such as the so-called Italian salad and herring and sardine salads." With so many potential components, salads surely varied according to season, geography, fashion, and personal tastes—just as today.[18]

✐ Salad or Sauce?

When were cooked vegetables considered salad and when sauce? The answer may simply have depended on the preference or custom of an individual. A vinegar and oil dressing seemed to indicate a salad. Vegetables cooked with meats or served in the same dish were considered sauce. Exceptions abound. Whether salad or sauce, eye appeal was emphasized for the stylish table.

Sorrel is a pleasant leafy green worth inviting back into our gardens and kitchens. Its tartness adds interest when combined with spinach or foods that may want more zest, sometimes filling the role of lemon or vinegar. Culinary use of sorrel was well known from earlier times in Europe and in America. "Sorrel leaves can enhance the flavor of stocks, they can flavor a variety of sauces and can be consumed as a vegetable, either alone, or mixed with other herbs." Sorrel sauce was served with chicken at the Byrd plantation table in Virginia. Sorrel receipts illustrate the overlapping of salad and sauce.[19]

To make a Sorrel Sallad

Take a quantity of French Sorrel picked clean and washed, boil it with water and a little Salt, and when it is enough, drain it and butter it, and put in a little Vinegar and Sugar into it, then garnish it with hard Eggs and Raisins.

Wolley, Queen-like Closet, 136.

To Stew Sorrel for Roasts of Veal, Lamb, Fricandeaux, &c.

Wash and simmer it in an unglazed earthen or stone jar, very slowly, and beat it up with a bit of butter, or a little salad-oil. Add cayenne, pepper, and salt. A mixture of spinage and sorrel is dressed as spinage, where sorrel alone might be thought too strong in acid.

Dods, Cook and Housewife's Manual, 215.

Sorrel-sauce

Stew two handfuls of blanched sorrel very slowly, with a good bit of butter oiled. Season it with pepper, salt, and cayenne; add a little strong gravy, and beat it well.

Dods, *Cook and Housewife's Manual*, 238.

[*Sorrel Sauce for Chickens*]

Take as much [chicken broth] as you shall want for Sauce, and add to it a little Parsley, Thyme, and Sorrel, boil'd green, and shred small, half a Pint of thick Cream, two Yolks of Eggs well beaten, some grated Nutmeg; shake all over the Fire 'till 'tis thick, throw in half a Pound of Butter, and shake it 'till that is melted.

Kettilby, *Above Three Hundred Receipts*, 9.

Thickening with egg yolk remained customary a century later. "A sauce can be made by boiling freshly chopped sorrel in meat stock . . . and then thickening it with a few egg yolks." Vegetable sauces were alternately thickened with flour worked into butter or with bread crumbs. Lemon, vinegar, and wine were used more commonly than sorrel for a tart note in sauces.[20]

The technique of "shaking" or swirling a sauce while heating is a good one. Other receipts direct stirring only in one direction. Try these methods to see which you prefer and which leads to a smoother sauce. A double boiler method is nearly foolproof to avoid curdling sauces or custards. See stewed sorrel and melted butter receipts for examples of a double boiler created from equipment at hand.

✍ Sauces

Butter Sauce

While melting butter would seem to need no direction, melted butter as a sauce was more complicated than one might expect. A little flour and either water or milk were brought just to a boil with the butter.[21]

To Melt Butter

Nothing is more simple than this process, and nothing so generally done badly. . . . weigh one quarter of a pound of good butter, rub into it two teaspoonsful of flour; when well mixed, put it in the sauce pan with one table spoonful of water, and a little salt; cover it, and set the sauce pan in a larger one of boiling water, shake it constantly till completely melted and beginning to boil.

M. Randolph, *Virginia Housewife*, 112–13.

Melted butter was served with a variety of dishes, particularly seafoods, boiled meats, and vegetables. It also formed a base for other sauces. Mary Randolph

Saucepan. York County, South Carolina, 18th Century. William Hill Ironworks. By Teresa Myers Armour, courtesy of the Schiele Museum.

recommended adding parsley or other herbs to melted butter. "When herbs are added to butter, you must put two spoonsful of water instead of one. Chervil, young fennel, burnet, tarragon, and cress, or pepper grass, may all be used." The French method incorporated a little nutmeg and vinegar in the melted butter sauce.[22]

While many sources directed the cook to keep at hand a browned roux of flour and butter for thickening gravies and sauces, Dods disagreed with the usual method. We may also profit from her shortcut of keeping a supply of browned flour for thickening brown sauces. We surely want to avoid sauces with the *empyrematic* flavor (burnt taste) against which she warned.

Brown Roux

Melt what quantity of butter you like, very slowly. Stir into this browned flour, till of a proper consistence. Small cooking will make this roux if the flour is browned previously; and this will prevent the danger of the empyreumatic flavour.

Dods, *Cook and Housewife's Manual,* 231.

[Browned Flour]

Where browning or brown thickening is required for any dish, browned flour may be employed with much advantage. It is easily prepared by laying a quantity of flour on a plate, and placing it in an oven, or before the fire, till it takes the shade desired; for it may be of any tint, from that of cinnamon to the deepness of coffee. Turn it occasionally, that it may colour equally, and keep for use.

Dods, *Cook and Housewife's Manual,* 231 (note).

✍ Bread Sauce

Bread sauce generally referred to bread boiled to a pulp, usually with onion. On the other hand any sauce based on bread might have been called bread sauce. These sauces may be simple or complex and invite the cook's creativity.

Bread or Pap Sauce

Take a pint of water, put in a good pint of crumb of bread, a blade of mace, and a little whole pepper; boil it for eight or ten minutes, and then pour the water off; take out the spice, and beat up the bread with a little butter.

S. Carter, *Frugal Colonial Housewife*, 55.

To make [Bread] Sauce for a Turkey

Cut the crusts off a penny loaf, cut the rest in thin slices, put it in cold water with a few peppercorns, a little salt and onion, boil it till the bread is quite soft. Then beat it well, put in a quarter of a pound of butter, two spoonfuls of thick cream and put it into a basin.

Raffald, *Experienced English Housekeeper*, 31.

It seems that each cook created bread sauces according to personal taste and the dish to be sauced. Substitute finely chopped celery for the onion to create another popular sauce. We curious cooks can have fun creating our own signature bread sauces. Options assembled from a range of cookery books may serve as a guide to keep our bread sauces within the compass of historical accuracy.[23]

Bread Sauce, The Curious Cook's Specialty (Composite Interprtation)

Grate or crumble bread.
Prepare onion: slice or mince; leave whole; or stick several cloves into
    whole onion.
(For celery sauce, substitute celery for the onion.)
Boil bread crumbs to a pulp in a little water with onion or shallot and
    seasonings.
(Optional liquid) milk, wine, broth, or perhaps drippings
Season with salt and pepper. Ground or whole peppercorns, black or white,
    may be used.
(Optional seasonings) nutmeg, mace, sage, vinegar, lemon or orange peel
    or juice
(Optional ingredients) currants, raisins, or cherries
Strain off excess water if deemed necessary.
Remove whole onion, whole peppercorns, or lemon peel if present.
Mash or beat soft-boiled bread crumbs and remaining onion.

Stir in butter and/or cream. Heat to the boiling point.
Serve on or under meat or in a sauce dish.

✍ Fruit Sauce

Fruits to accompany poultry, game, or pork are of ancient ancestry. While sauces of apples and cranberries remain thoroughly familiar, peach, strawberry, raspberry, and cherry sauces and compotes are worthy of reintroducing to our tables. A sauce might be as simple as fresh or dried fruit stewed with a little water. One half or one whole cup sugar to one cup water and a quart of fruit were general proportions, adjusted according to juiciness and sweetness of the fruit. Fruits were poached whole, sliced or diced then simmered, or stewed to a pulp. A lump of butter was added when desired. A dash of spice or grated lemon brightened flavor. Hannah Glasse suggested "Add a piece of lemon-peel" to the following apple sauce.[24]

To make Sauce for a Goose

Pare, core, and slice your apples. Put them in a saucepan with as much water as will keep them from burning. Set them over a very slow fire, keep them close covered till they are all of a pulp, then put in a lump of butter, and sugar to taste. Beat them well and send them to the table in a china basin.

Raffald, *Experienced English Housekeeper,* 29.

Peaches in sugar

Blanch six or eight in hot water that they may peel easily, then give them a boil in syrup, and serve. The French serve all sorts of fruit en compôte, which forms tasteful and economical dishes.

Dods, *Cook and Housewife's Manual,* 359.

Cherry Sauce

Select large cherries that are ripe; break them over a pan to catch the juice, and pick out all the seeds: put them into a pan with a little water, a small lump of butter rolled in flour, and half a pound of sugar to each quart of the cherries. Stew them gently till they are a thick smooth pulp, stirring them frequently. Mould it in teacups; and when they get cold, turn them out smoothly into a glass dish; grate loaf sugar and nutmeg over them, and eat them with poultry and game.

Bryan, *Kentucky Housewife,* 176–77.

The flour thickening in the cherry sauce is atypical for an early fruit sauce. Without the flour this sauce would be quite appropriate for an eighteenth-century meal. With or without the flour, success in molding this sauce has eluded me; however, cherries make an excellent sauce.

✒ Mushroom Sauce

Mushroom sauces were favored by some. Fresh mushrooms, mushroom pickle or mushroom ketchup were regularly called for in made dishes.[25]

To make Mushroom-Sauce for White Fowls of all Sorts

Take a Pint of Mushrooms, wash and pick them very clean, and put them into a Sauce-pan, with a little Salt, some Nutmeg, a Blade of Mace, a Pint of Cream, and a good piece of Butter roll'd in Flour; boil these all together, and keep stirring them; then pour the Sauce into your Dish, and garnish with Lemon.

Glasse, Art of Cookery (1747), 34; & S. Carter, Frugal Colonial Housewife, 53.

Sauce for boil'd Fish

Take Beef-Gravy, an Onion, a little White-wine, some Horse-radish sliced, Lemon-peel, an Anchovy, a Bunch of Sweet-herbs, boil them well together, and strain off the Liquor, then put a Spoonful of Mushroom Ketchup to it, and thicken it with Butter mix'd with Flower: or for Fast-days the Gravy may be omitted, and in the place of it put Mushroom-Gravy, or a larger quantity of Mushroom-Ketchup, or some of the Fish-Gravy

Bradley, Country Housewife, I: 35.

See Chapter Nine for mushroom ketchup and powder, handy seasoning shortcuts. Mushroom fricassees and ragouts ran the gamut from mushrooms in a cream sauce to mushrooms sautéed in butter with parsley, thyme, sweet marjoram, onion, pepper and salt. White or red wine was included in some variations. Flour or egg thickened these sauces.[26]

✒ Onion Sauce

Onion sauces were much admired and oft recommended. Scottish author Margaret Dods quoted an amusing verse regarding the onion: "In the early part of the last [eighteenth] century Swift sung:"[27]

> There is, in every Cook's opinion,
> No savory dish without an onion;
> But lest your kissing should be spoil'd
> The onion must be thoroughly boil'd

We agree that onion is indispensable to most savory dishes. An onion sauce can transform a simple boiled meat or vegetable from ordinary to interesting.

Rundell advised "serve it for boiled rabbits, partridges, scrag or knuckle of veal, or roast mutton." Most cookery books offered at least one version.[28]

Onion Sauce

Peel the onions, and boil them tender; squeeze the water from them, then chop them, and add to them butter that has been melted rich and smooth [see melted butter method above] but with a little good milk instead of water; boil it up once, and serve it. . . . A turnip boiled with the onions makes them milder.

Rundell, New System of Domestic Cookery, 114–15.

Dods recommended adding chopped sage to such a sauce if intended for goose. She touted brown onion sauce as "a highly-relishing sauce, suitable to many different dishes, and a general favorite with thorough-bred gourmands." Wow! We certainly could not pass up such a receipt.

Brown Onion-Sauce

Slice large mild Spanish onions, brown them in butter over a slow fire, add good brown gravy, pepper, salt, cayenne, and a bit of butter rolled in brown flour. Skim this, and put in a half-glass of Burgundy, claret, or port, the same quantity of mushroom-catsup; or, if more suitable to the dish . . . a dessert-spoonful of walnut-pickle or eschalot [shallot] vinegar . . . This standard sauce is susceptible of many variations. It may be flavored with any pungent vinegar . . . [or with shallot, mustard, celery, turnip, or cucumber].

Dods, Cook and Housewife's Manual, 235–36.

Notice that both receipts suggested boiling other vegetables with the onions if a milder sauce is wanted. Celery and cucumber sauces were also favorites throughout the period.

✿ Cucumber Sauce

To fry Cucumbers for Mutton Sauce.

You must brown some butter in a pan, and cut the cucumbers in thin slices; drain them from the water, then fling them into the pan, and when they are fry'd brown, put in a little pepper and salt, a bit of onion and gravy, and let them stew together, and squeeze in some juice of lemon; shake them well, and put them under your mutton.

Smith, Compleat Housewife, 66.

The anonymous 1700 manuscript from Virginia included a similar "Regalia of Coocumbers" directing the cook to wrap the cucumber slices in a cloth in order to beat and squeeze dry. In another "Sauce for Mutton or Lamb" the seasoning was a bit stronger with claret, cloves, mace, and nutmeg. A South Carolina housewife proposed a related sauce for fowls rather than mutton.[29]

Sauce for Boiled Fowls Lady Robinson

Take three onions 6 Cucumbers 6 Cabbage Lettuce very white & hard. Slice them together & Stew them in Butter till they are tender then bruise them with a spoon very fine & put to them a little pepper & Salt four Anchovies washd & pounded a pint of white Gravy & a qr of a pound of Butter workd in flower season it to your taste

South Carolina household book.

✍ Vegetables as Sauce

The following *sauce* from 1765 "To boil a Haunch or Neck of Venison" offers a primer on preparing vegetables. The options are simple: boil; vary shapes and textures, some in sprigs, others cubed, slivered, and mashed; season with salt and butter or cream. A side dish of melted butter was commonly offered with boiled vegetables.

For Sauce

Boil some Colliflowers in Milk and Water, and pull them into little Sprigs; boil some fine white Cabbage likewise, and some Turnips cut in square Pieces, and some Beet-Root cut in long narrow Slips. Have some Turnips likewise mashed with a little Cream and Butter. Let your Cabbage, when boiled, be beat in a Saucepan with a Bit of Butter, and a small Quantity of Salt; lay that next to the Colliflowers, then the Turnips, then the Cabbage, and proceed in that Manner till your Dish be full. As to the Beet-Root, dispose of it in such Places where your own Fancy directs you. Set some melted Butter in a Bason on one Side, in case it should be wanted.

Johnson, *Every Young Woman's Companion*, 80.

The directions for presentation are puzzling. Are the several vegetables to be arranged in rings or spokes or piles on the dish? Either pattern would be attractive, especially when garnished with beet slips. The boiled meat likely occupied the center of the platter. Each cook might interpret this sauce differently:

The image of a chunk of boiled meat surrounded by pale lumps of similarly flavored vegetables seems uninteresting, reminiscent of meals on my first visit to England, in 1952. In a "polite Dish" of venison dressed with the above sauce, the variety in shape and texture and the garnish of colorful beet slivers enhanced rather dull cool weather ingredients. This sauce was ostentatious in the labor required to prepare each vegetable separately. Cooking vegetables and meats together was not only simpler but often yielded a richer gravy, as in an olla or hodge-podge.

Not every cultural group favored these particular vegetables as sauce for meats. One French lady in Virginia puzzled that her neighbors "seem to be particularly fond of turnips and other vegetables which we would scorn to eat in France."[30]

A list of ancestral plant foods contains the expected and the unexpected. Families of common vegetables included cabbages, carrots, turnips and turnip greens, parsnips, potatoes, onions, peas, green beans, shelled beans, beets and beet greens, celery, cucumber, lettuce, cauliflower, broccoli, asparagus, and artichokes. Radishes, roots of parsley and celery, turnip rooted cabbage or kohlrabi, and Brussels sprouts were more highly esteemed two centuries ago than now. Not until the end of the eighteenth century did field peas, lima beans, summer and winter squashes, tomatoes, and fresh green corn show up in cookbooks. However, personal accounts document these new plant foods in common use prior to appearing in publications.

When cooking in an eighteenth-century mindset one cannot err in boiling a vegetable. Seasoning with salt and pepper and butter was also basic. Boiled or stewed vegetables might be dressed up with cream sauce, brown gravy, oil and vinegar, or butter and vinegar.

Most sources agreed that vegetables should not be overcooked, but retain crispness. A copper or brass pot was recommended for preserving the beauty of colorful vegetables. On the other hand, vegetables were at times meant to disappear into a gravy or sauce. This topic of *sauce* does become tangled, does it not? A sauce can be a savory or sweet dressing or gravy; or a sauce can be a garnish or side item such as an attractive arrangement of vegetables to accompany meat.

Each season offered its medley of options. Asparagus, tender fresh peas, and greens were celebrated in springtime. Spinach served in mounds was commonly suggested as sauce and garnish. Surprising to us today, salad greens (not only spinach but endive and even lettuces) were frequently boiled as well as enjoyed raw.

❧ Potherbs

Spinach was a favorite green. Other common potherbs included cabbages, lettuces, sorrel, mustards and cresses, endive, and the young green tops of beets, turnips, and kohlrabi.

Wild plants were gathered as well. *Acetaria* of 1699 declared "every Hedge affords a Sallet." The pre-1744 Virginia manuscript included a *tansy* containing common violet leaves (a nice spinach-like wild green) as well as green wheat and strawberry leaves, which are more questionable additions. In the widely varying receipts for *tansies* the herb tansy was only mentioned as a minor ingredient, if at all. Early cooks apparently understood that tansy is not only a bitter herb, but toxic as well.[31]

✿ Wild Greens

Peter Kalm found wild greens being gathered in spring. The curled dock and lambsquarters were prepared as spinach or sorrel. "But they generally boil the leaves in the water in which they had cooked meat. Then they eat it alone or with the meat. It is served on a platter and eaten with a knife." Just as we enjoy greens with vinegar today, "vinegar is placed in a special container on the table" to pour on the greens. "I must confess that this dish tastes very good." Kalm noted that very young pokeweed was also gathered, and he had eaten it "without any bad effects."

Settlers were aware of cautions in gathering wild vegetables. A British Lieutenant followed the lead of settlers in the Virginia interior collecting pokeweed or *poke-sallet* in 1779.[32]

> Vegetables not being over abundant in these back woods at any time, and there being a great deficiency of them in the spring of year, we adopt the custom of the inhabitants who gather the leaves of the poke-plant, just as they shoot above ground and are tender and soft; it is no bad substitute for spinnage, and greatly resembles it in flavor, yet great care must be taken in gathering of it, that it is neither too old, nor the stalk grown, for . . . the consequence of eating it is inevitable death, as it purges the body to excess. Notwithstanding this plant has this pernicious quality, the children eat the berries of it in the Autumn, without any ill consequence [?] attending it.
>
> Anburey, *Travels*, 2 :218.

Note: Poke berries should not be eaten. Poke shoots and young leaves must never be eaten raw, but should be boiled, with the first cooking water discarded, before incorporating into recipes. The early spring shoots have traditionally been served as cooked greens or prepared as asparagus. Although pokeweed is not the lethal plant Anburey supposed, the "purging to excess" could make a body feel as if he or she might die.

A folk practice descended from eighteenth-century *tansies* is still found among traditional southerners who enjoy a "mess" of poke salad (or sallet) as a spring tonic. The pokeweed is always first boiled and drained before a second boiling with pork and onions, sautéing with salt pork, or scrambling with eggs. Other cooked greens, such as turnip, mustard, or collard, continue to be referred to as *salad* in some communities.[33]

❧ Asparagus

William Byrd's diaries documented his enjoyment of asparagus during April and May—with mutton, with fish, with pigeon, with squirrel. Most eighteenth- and nineteenth-century sources agreed on a very precise method for boiling asparagus. The stems are to be scraped, cut into equal lengths, and tied in bunches. Stand the bunches in a pan so that the tips are above the boiling water level, in order that the stem may cook until tender while the delicate tips are only lightly steamed. Brilliant.[34]

From English sources we learn lightly boiled asparagus was customarily served on buttered toast accompanied by melted butter. In the Italian fashion asparagus was dressed with olive oil, lemon juice, salt, pepper, and mustard. The Germans favored a white sauce of butter, flour, and egg yolk. The following dish is a more elegant option.[35]

Asparagus Forced in French Role

Take three French Roles, take out all the Crumb, by first cutting a Piece of the Top-crust off; but be careful that the Crust fits again the same Place. Fry the Roles brown in fresh Butter, then take a Pint of Cream, the Yolks of six Eggs beat fine, a little Salt and Nutmeg, stir them well together over a slow Fire, till it begins to be thick. Have ready a hundred of small Grass [asparagus, sparrow grass] boiled, then save Tops enough to stick the Roles with: the rest cut small and put into the Cream, fill the Loaves with them. Before you fry the Roles, make Holes thick in the Top-crust to stick the Grass in; then lay on the Piece of Crust and stick the Grass in, that it may look as if it was growing. It makes a pretty Side-dish at a second Course.

Glasse, *Art of Cookery* (1747), 99.

These stuffed rolls indeed furnished an attractive side dish. Today they make a splendid main dish for lunch or supper. The savory asparagus custard filling is delicious and the asparagus tips growing out of the top make a clever presentation.

True to form, *The Complete Practical Cook* of 1730 went a step further. He proposed a roll filled with "a Fricassy or Ragoust with the Tops of Asparagus" as centerpiece in a bowl of rich asparagus soup.[36]

❧ Cabbage, Broccoli, Cauliflower

The popularity and seeds of these vegetables traveled to America with European settlers. Plain green and red cabbages were common favorites. The crinkled leaf savoy cabbage and Brussels sprouts were considered a bit more elegant as were broccoli, cauliflower, and turnip rooted cabbage (kohlrabi), all prepared similarly.

Boiled broccoli was enjoyed as sauce, salad, or garnish. It was suggested that broccoli or the budding stalks of turnips be tied in bunches for boiling as was done with asparagus. In fact any vegetables that might prove difficult to fish from the pot could be handily tied into bundles or contained in a cloth or net. Glasse suggested filling rolls with broccoli and buttered (scrambled) eggs in similar fashion to "Asparagus Forced in French Role."[37]

Green (white) or red cabbage was sliced or chopped to be simmered in a minimum quantity of stock, adding a bit more stock, water, or butter if the cabbage became too dry. A little vinegar and caraway were approved additions. Cabbage contributed flavor and body to soups and was considered an appropriate ingredient "in the famous *olla podrida,* the delicious blend of vegetables and meats which is a favourite dish in Spain." Stuffed or forced cabbages came in many guises; homely or dressy (see Chapter 6).[38]

Slip-decorated Earthenware Dish. Central North Carolina, Moravian potter, 1771–1821. The basic "dirt dish" became elegant enough for a sophisticated table with slip decoration such as this tan, green, and cream fylfot-shaped flower on dark brown base. Collection of Old Salem Museums & Gardens, Winston-Salem, North Carolina.

Cauliflower was also commonly cooked in the least possible amount of meat broth or butter and water, as were most vegetables. Boiling cauliflower florets in a cloth was considered convenient. Boiled just until tender, cauliflower was dressed with oil and lemon juice or with a white cream sauce.[39]

The Scottish *Cook and Housewife's Manual* recommended soaking vegetables in salt water before cooking to "bring out every insect that may lurk in the leaves." This advice is still useful when we are fortunate to have organic produce fresh from the garden or farmers market, especially broccoli, cabbage, and other vegetables with lots of crevices.

To Stew Red Cabbage

Wash, pick, and shred what will fill a large pint-basin. Melt some butter in a sauce-pan, and put in the cabbage with only the water that hangs about it, pepper, cayenne, salt, and an onion sliced. Stew this, keeping the sauce-pan close covered; and when just ready, add a glass of vinegar, which may just boil up. French cooks add a bay-leaf and two cloves stuck in an onion, which must be picked out before serving.

Dods, *Cook and Housewife's Manual*, 214.

Vinegar is the magic ingredient with red cabbage for the acid turns the unattractive blue-grey cabbage a beautiful magenta. Sausages or boiled meats were served on a bed of red cabbage. Germans added caraway.

✍ Beans

An Englishman traveling through the southern wilderness in 1797 dined at a house near Nashville, Tennessee upon "a large piece of boiled bacon, and a great dish full of French beans, together with some bread made of Indian meal." William Byrd also dined on beans and bacon in his more elegant plantation setting.[40]

French beans were green string beans. Byrd's may have been either green beans in their pods or shelled mature beans of several varieties. Standard cookery books gave particular methods for preparing fresh summertime green beans for the pot. Most American authors agreed with English and German methods below, which are not what we think of as southern green beans. Not until the nineteenth century do we find green beans commonly cooked with pork, although they were often served with cured pork.[41]

To dress French Beans

First string them, then cut them in two, and afterwards across: But if you would do them nice, cut the Bean into four, and then across, which is eight Pieces;

lay them into Water and Salt, and when you Pan boils put in some Salt and the Beans; When they are tender they are enough; they will soon be done. Take Care they don't lose their fine Green. Lay them in a plate, and have Butter in a Cup.

Glasse, Art of Cookery (1747), 11.

French Beans, finely sliced in the German fashion

May be cooked through by steaming in stock and finished with butter, flour and chopped parsley. They may also be steamed in butter, garnished with a little vinegar, tarragon, basil and other pungent herbs. Finally, they may be served in a sweeter medium, with fresh cream and a little butter and flour.

Von Rumohr, Essence of Cookery, 155.

Shelled beans and peas were of Old and New World varieties. Fresh or dried shelled beans were boiled until tender and typically served with *bacon* (salt cured pork, either bacon or ham). The beans were drained and served in a dish with bacon in the middle. Most sources recommended boiling the meat separately from the beans.

Fresh green peas, simply prepared with a touch of mint, were much celebrated in season. Dried peas sufficed the rest of the year. See peas puddings and pottages in Chapters 3 and 6.

Corn

Fresh corn was much celebrated and customarily enjoyed boiled or roasted. A party of Moravians traveling through northeastern North Carolina in 1753 noted a pleasant meal, "a little old mother prepared the noon meal, we had a kettle full of corn on the cob, salt, and afterwards water-melons."[42]

Virginia plantation tutor Fithian, out horseback riding with one of his students, "gathered and brought home some good Roasting-Ears of Corn" (mid-August 1774). In the Carolina backcountry, land agent John Brown was also delighted over fresh green corn. On July 15, 1795 "we had Rosten Ears or Coarn for supper." The following description, from an Italian traveler, just makes ones mouth water for roasted corn:[43]

[Roasting Ears]

When the corn is not completely ripe, but the grains are already formed on the ear, the latter are picked, brought close to the fire and roasted all around. Thus roasted, these ears are taken, still warm from the fire, covered with fresh butter, and eaten, extracting the kernels with the teeth until they are all gone. The sweet milky juice . . . adds to a pleasant and very welcome flavor. This item of food is found alike on the tables of poor farmers and the wealthiest gentlemen and is generally highly appreciated.

Castiglioni, Viaggio,318.

Corn and potatoes were appreciated, but did not make up for a lack of bread. In the North Carolina backcountry "for a lack of bread some families have been using potatoes, or sweet potatoes, or new corn, grated and baked into bread." Similarly in western Virginia, "How delicious was the taste of the young potatoes when we got them! What a jubilee when we were permitted to pull the young corn for roasting ears! Still more so when it had acquired sufficient hardness to be made into Johnny cakes by the aid of a tin grater."[44]

✍ Potato

The potato grew to be more and more appreciated during the eighteenth century. Of course it had been a staple in the Americas from ancient times. In 1736 England the potato was discussed as a "very useful root, being either boil'd, or roasted in hot Embers; and after it is boiled, to be broiled" Other sources agreed that boiled potatoes might be served with butter, broiled on a gridiron, or fried in butter or drippings. Goose drippings gave a "very high relish" to potatoes fried by the French method. In Germany potatoes were served "with butter and meat stock, with cream, with herbs and with powerful sauces made of chopped herrings (or preferably sardines), shallots, and fine herbs" and also mashed. Mashed potatoes were seasoned with salt and thinned with butter and milk, cream, or broth. A little cinnamon was suggested along with salt. Or try the following herbed potatoes. You may be tempted to simply mash and chop potatoes and greens as we were. Whether sieved smooth as directed or left a bit lumpy these are interesting green mashed potatoes.[45]

Potato purée . . . with a mixture of fine herbs

One half of the quantity used should be spinach, and the other half sorrel, chervil, parsley, purslane and tarragon. These herbs should be heated in a little concentrated stock so that they retain their fine green color. Then chop them, taking care not to loose their juice. Take a quantity of dry potato purée which is twice that of the herbs with their juice and pass both potatoes and herbs through a coarse sieve, or through a metal colander. Return the sieved mixture to the fire with a little butter, add salt and allow it to just heat through.

Von Rumohr, Essence of Cookery, 139.

By 1829 in Scotland potatoes were lauded as "that root of superlative excellence and unbounded utility, which takes its honoured place on every dining table . . . and goes far to equalize the dining enjoyments of every grade of society."[46]

Often we find it difficult to know whether a writer referred to the white Irish potato or the sweet potato (sometimes called yam). They were considered interchangeable by some.

Journals furnish clues regarding common preparation methods. According to Kalm, "They [sweet potatoes] are prepared in the same manner as common potatoes and are either mixed and served with them or eaten separately." From Castiglioni we learn sweet potatoes were "eaten roasted or boiled, puddings are made from them, and cakes that appear as if they were made of sweet almonds and which are served instead of bread in the morning with tea."[47]

The Virginia Housewife closed her receipt for sweet potato pudding with the note, "Irish potato pudding is made in the same manner, but is not so good." *The Carolina Housewife* gave multiple receipts for both potato puddings. With the quantities of butter, sugar, egg, brandy, nutmeg, and lemon peel called for, either Irish or sweet potato pudding would be tasty. These ancestors of southern sweet potato casseroles and pies were baked in a buttered dish or in a paste. Many were extremely rich, as are many of our handed down versions.

When visiting a lowcountry South Carolina plantation you might have been served Harriot Horry's "Yam Pudding," made by her mother's receipt with a pound of butter to each pound of sweet potato. Such lavish use of butter was a greasy fingerprint of upper class cookery. Many pies or puddings were excessively rich. Potato, pumpkin, and carrot were essentially interchangeable in pie and pudding receipts. Contrast pumpkin and carrot puddings below with this potato custard to understand the range of possibilities. Jane Randolph's had no butter at all, but more egg.[48]

Potatoe Custeard very good

To a quart of Potatoe Pulp, put a quart of good top of Milk, Six Eggs 2 spoonfuls Rose Water, half a Nutmeg, sweeten it to your Taste, then bake it in good Paste.

Jane Randolph 1743, Harbury, *Virginia's Cooking Dynasty*, 418.

Jane Randolph's Potato Custard (Interpretation, one-half receipt)

    2 cups cooked mashed potato
    3 eggs
    2 cups milk
    1 tablespoon rose water, ¼ teaspoon nutmeg
    ½ cup sugar
Mix and pour into pastry lined dish
This quantity fills an average baking dish or two thin pies.

You may prefer to bake Jane Randolph's potato custard in a greased dish rather than in a paste, as custards do tend to make an under crust soggy. This is the sort of pudding for which a twist of pastry just around the rim is attractive and practical. I find a rim of Ellis' "good crust" perfect.

Sweet potatoes became a favorite root at all levels of society. Italian traveler Castiglioni reported sweet potatoes "so common that not infrequently they are given as food even to the slaves." On the other end of the economic scale, South Carolina plantation mistress Eliza Lucas Pinckney wrote to headmaster of her children's school in England that she would have sent some "potatoes of this country" along with the children's favorite, rice, "but they have not yet come in."[49]

A French traveler found "Sweet potatoes in Norfolk are delicious and extremely cheap." Swedish traveler, naturalist Peter Kalm praised the sweet potato's "sweet and very agreeable taste, which I cannot find in the other potatoes, in artichokes, or in any other root, and they almost melt in the mouth." The North Carolina Moravians evidently also enjoyed these "good roots which taste much like mashed chestnuts."[50]

Carrots (and other Old World root vegetables)

Root vegetables were most simply cooked in a small quantity of water or meat stock and dressed with a little butter and parsley. They also added flavor to all sorts of broths and sauces.

Carrots were combined with other root vegetables or with peas, cabbage, or asparagus. "In some parts of Germany, a good robust piece of bacon [ham] steamed with carrots and well soaked [boiled] potatoes is a regional dish." Beef with carrots was customary in England. Carrots "the Flemish way" produced a rather fussy, but attractive garnish, sauce, or side dish: "Prepare (after boiling) in nice forms, as stars, wheels, &c., and stew them in melted butter, with minced parsley, young onions, salt and pepper."[51]

Early in this project we noticed carrot puddings everywhere, as were sweet egg pies (see Chapter 1), in early and later manuscripts and in nearly every publication consulted. This appeared to have been a favorite dish and the receipts sounded so good that we figured one should definitely be included in this collection. Setting carrot pudding aside to work on more puzzling and challenging topics, we finally got around to testing. So confident in this dish, another curious cook and I cockily prepared it for dinner, using a pre-1744 Virginia method.[52]

What did we learn? Carrot pudding must have been another of those creations for displaying one's affluence, a rich dish indeed. An outrageous quantity of butter bubbled around the edges, puddled on top, and ran over the edges. The aroma and flavor were lovely (and buttery), but just a taste was quite enough for most people.

Carrot puddings fit into a category with mainstream sweet egg pies and potato and pumpkin puddings and pies. Although a period perfect dish from the eighteenth century, we are not likely to want the typical version on a twenty-first-century buffet. The search for a carrot pudding containing more carrot with significantly less butter did not uncover such an exception.

We did discover carrot pudding receipts with a greater quantity of bread and liquid that yield a nice result when either baked or boiled. Flavoring options are interesting. Among five early southern manuscript sources two were flavored with nutmeg, three with orange flower water, one with rose water, four with sack (Madeira or sherry is nice), and one with candied lemon and citron peel. We can have fun developing our own favorite combinations from these possibilities. The lovely flavor of the manuscript receipt we first tried derived from nutmeg, sack, and orange flower water.[53]

We tested the following pudding with one-half teaspoon nutmeg and two teaspoonfuls orange flower water. That proved delicate and delicious. Leftover pudding reheated nicely, and with fresh fruit made an outstanding breakfast.

A Second Carrot Pudding

Take two Penny-loaves [one pound or more of bread], pare off the Crust, soak them in a Quart of boiling Milk, let it stand till it is cold, then grate in two or three large Carrots, then put in eight Eggs well beat, and three quarters of a Pound of fresh Butter melted, grate in a little Nutmeg, and sweeten to your Taste. Cover your Dish with Puff-paste, and pour in the Ingredients, and bake it an Hour.

Glasse, *Art of Cookery* (1747), 107.

The butter may be reduced to one half pound and still be in line with period receipts. Paring the bread crust is only necessary if the crust is heavy or tough. Other authors noted these puddings may be either boiled in a cloth or baked. Both cooking methods work well with this receipt.

Carrot Pudding (Interpretation and combination, one-half receipt)
> ½ pound crumbled bread (about two large buns or rolls) soaked in
>> 2 cups hot milk
> 1 ½ cups grated carrot
> 4 eggs, well beaten
> 4 to 6 ounces melted butter
> ½ cup sugar
> ¼ teaspoon nutmeg

Add other seasonings to your taste. (Madeira or sherry, orange flower water, rose water, candied lemon peel)

Bake in paste or buttered dish; or boil in a buttered cloth.

A young French woman, Hélène de Maussion, who generally distained American food, found favor with certain pastries. "I have a cook who is a marvel for her pastry and her "pies," as they call them here.—like our French pâtés with the difference that they are stuffed with fruit instead of meat, are really wonderful and melt in one's mouth." One wonders just which pies she enjoyed. Carrot pudding and sweet egg pie seem to fit her comparison with pâtés.[54]

By the end of the eighteenth century, puddings of potato and pumpkin joined the carrot. Most were awfully buttery with up to a whole pound of butter proportional to each pound of vegetable. We were pleased to find the above leaner exception.

The root tribe of vegetables is quite large containing celery root, parsley root, skirrit, and salsify along with turnip, carrot, parsnip, and beet. Any of these roots were employed to add body and character to stewed and made dishes. Interesting combinations may be simply boiled and seasoned or tossed in a cream sauce. By the end of the century the New World Jerusalem artichoke root was also generally known and well liked for its flavor similar to the unrelated artichoke.

✐ Artichokes

Artichokes vied with potatoes on some tables. "For three months of the year, the artichoke occupies approximately the same position in the diet of southern Europeans as the potato has occupied for a generation in the diet of the Northerners. The heart of the artichoke is rich in starch and even the outer leaves are fleshy and nutritious before the flower begins to develop."[55]

Artichokes were popularly enjoyed fresh or pickled. Artichoke bottoms were preserved by drying. Quartered young artichokes, fresh, brined, or pickled, were broiled or boiled and served with butter or olive oil, lemon juice, or a cream sauce. The boiled "leaves" (actually a budding flower head) were enjoyed dipped in butter as we do today. Artichoke bottoms or young tender artichokes were called for in a variety of pies and made dishes.

Europeans brought to America a liking for the artichoke. William Byrd's short temper flared at his cook "for neglecting to boil some artichokes for dinner." This incident lets us know the taste for artichokes was lively; however, we are left with a question as to the sort of artichoke Byrd expected with his boiled pork. At that early date, we imagine the green bud.[56]

But then the Jerusalem artichoke, from the root of a species of sunflower, came into the picture. This New World plant had been introduced into Europe, but was slow to gain general esteem there. Although quite different in form and from opposite ends of their respective plants, there is a similarity in taste. Just as it can be difficult to decipher which *potato* is meant, so also *artichoke* became confusing by the end of the eighteenth century.

By early nineteenth century artichokes of both types showed up in cookbooks on both sides of the Atlantic. *The Carolina Housewife* gave methods for artichoke bottoms and also Jerusalem artichokes in cream sauces. *The Kentucky Housewife* gave directions for boiling both sorts as well as mashing, baking, and saucing the Jerusalem. Back in Scotland Dods did the same.[57]

Jerusalem Artichokes

May either be boiled plain, taken up the moment they are done, and served with melted butter poured over them, or cooked with a rich white or brown-sauce. They are very good roasted; they are served in a napkin, and melted butter is eat with them. They are also mashed, and made in pie.

Dods, *Cook and Housewife's Manual*, 208.

Pickling was particularly common. Jerusalem artichoke pickles and relishes are still to be found in southern pantries. However, today's evolved versions tend to be sweet and piquant, not the super tart and spicy ones of the eighteenth-century table. Where these sunflowers were planted years ago their late summer blooms still mark the spots where we may return to harvest tubers in their wintertime prime. Jerusalem artichokes are sometimes found in supermarkets labeled as *sunchokes*.

✒ Pumpkin

Pumpkin showed up on the table much more often than cookbooks indicated. Peter Kalm observed pumpkins "much used by the Dutch, the English, the Swedes, and others here in America" and even the French to some extent. Similarly, the North Carolina Moravians extended otherwise scanty foodstuffs with pumpkin throughout fall and winter.[58] Most simply, pumpkin was cut, the seeds removed, and the halves roasted before the fire or baked in an oven. "When they are roasted butter is spread over the inside while it is still hot so that the butter is drawn into the pumpkins after which they are especially good eating." Fresh or dried pumpkin was boiled in water and mashed to be made into a porridge or soup with milk.

Potage of pumpkin with butter

Take your pumpkin, cut it into peeces, and seeth it with water and salt. After it is sod, strain it, and put it into a pot with an onion sticked with cloves, fresh butter and pepper.

La Varenne, *French Cook*, 127.

In additional receipts for pumpkin potage *The French Cook* suggested adding milk. Von Rumohr preferred meat stock to earlier milk based soups.[59]

[Regarding Pumpkin Pottages and Purées]

A purée made of the flesh of overgrown pumpkins, mixed with milk and season-ing, was served even on Papal tables. This purée is most insipid and rather sweet when made with milk but is much better if strong stock is used and the mixture is then served buttered, with fine herbs and spices . . . [also] pepper and lemon juice.

Von Rumohr, *Essence of Cookery*, 139, 143.

That early nineteenth-century German foodie further observed that pump-kins "can also be stuffed and then steamed in concentrated meat stock." *The Virginia Housewife* and *The Kentucky Housewife* suggested baking pumpkin or winter squash filled with forcemeat. The trick in either steaming or baking the forced pumpkin lies in achieving thoroughly cooked stuffing before the pumpkin collapses. You may play it safe with precooked meats or with bread, vegetable, or fruit stuffings.[60]

Pumpkin mixed with corn meal was boiled or fried as dumpling or pancake. And pumpkin was elevated from subsistence fare to the fashionable table in pudding, pie, or tart. It might have been made savory or sweet. Sliced apple or applesauce was commonly combined with pumpkin.[61]

To make a Pompion-Pie

Having your Paste ready in your Pan, put in your Pompion pared and cut in thin slices, then fill up your Pie with sharp Apples, and a little Pepper, and a little Salt, then close it , and bake it, then butter it and serve it in hot to the Table.

Wolley, *Queen-like Closet*, 123.

Pumkin Pye

We pare and cut the pumpkins in slices, then lay the slices in a glazed ea[r]then pot with salt between each layer of them, all night, for extracting their watry juice: Then chop them with the like quantity or less of apples, and with sugar put them into a crust and bake. The pumpkins save apples, and by some are liked better than apples alone.

Ellis, *Country Housewife's Family Companion*, 316.

Pumpkin Pudding

Stew a fine sweet pumpkin till soft and dry, rub it through a sieve, mix with [one pint pumpkin] pulp six eggs quite light, a quarter of a pound of butter, half a pint of new milk, some pounded ginger and nutmeg, a wine glass [¼ cup] of brandy, and sugar to your taste [¾ cup]. . . . put a paste round the edges and in the bottom of a shallow dish or plate, pour in the mixture, cut some thin bits of paste, twist them and lay them across the top and bake it nicely.

M. Randolph, Virginia Housewife, 154.

Today's widely used pie receipt from the label of a popular brand of canned pumpkin is a direct descendant of Mary Randolph's Pumpkin Pudding, differing in seasoning balance and fewer eggs. Even if you begin with canned pumpkin, try Randolph's proportions. The extra lightness and haunting flavors of the ancestral version is a pleasant variation. One teaspoonful ginger and one-quarter teaspoonful nutmeg is a subtle combination. You may add more if your taste buds call for strong spice.

Eliza Leslie suggested an extra half cup cream or milk in place of the butter, for a total of one and one-half cup milk in Randolph's receipt. Glasse's first American edition, Leslie's *Seventy-Five Receipts*, and Simmons' *American Cookery* offer options for interpreting and varying pumpkin puddings or pies. Wine alone or combined with rose water might be substituted for the brandy. This would be a great place to use rose brandy. The hint of rose is delightful with pumpkin.[62]

Squash

Winter squashes were treated as pumpkins. "Squashes are a kind of pumpkin which the Europeans got from the Indians . . . they are eaten boiled, either with meat or by themselves . . . they are put on the edge of the dish round the meat."[63]

Winter Squash alias Cashaw

This is much finer than the summer squash. Pare it, take out the seeds, cut it in pieces, and stew it slowly till quite done, in a very little water. Afterwards, drain squeeze and press it well, and mash it with a very little pepper and salt.

Blackford, "Recipes in the Culinary Arts," 17.

Summer squashes of various shapes were boiled and mashed with cream, butter, salt, and pepper. The scalloped patty pan squash or cymling and the yellow crookneck are appropriate varieties.

Okra, Tomato, Peppers

An Italian traveler through the southern backcountry (1774–77) noted the early combination of okra with tomatoes. Okra "Cut into pieces, it is boiled with the flesh of veal, very tasty soups being made of it with the addition of a little tomato, or *pomo d'oro*, and Indian pepper (*Capsicum annuum*)." It is unclear how commonly these vegetables were eaten by European settlers at that early date. Okra, tomatoes, and peppers began showing up in published receipts in the early nineteenth century.[64]

❧ "Veritable Household Medicines"

Vegetables were not consumed in quantities considered healthful by today's standards. Fresh fruits and vegetables were only available seasonally; but, beyond that fact, vegetables were not considered nutritious since most are low in calories. However, combinations of particular vegetables with specific meats, legumes, or grains were thought beneficial. "Some act as purgatives while some refresh and cleanse the body fluids; in short, if consumed in sensible quantities, vegetables are veritable household medicines. Every good housewife should be aware of their different effects." But that is another study and another book.[65]

CHAPTER 8

For Special Occasions

The Balls, the Fish-Feasts, the Dancing-Schools, the Christnings, the Cock fights, the Horse-Races.

Philip Fithian, *Journal and Letters* (1773–74), 168.

Tutor Philip Fithian was astonished at the festive lifestyle he found among Virginia's plantation gentry, "The Balls, the Fish-Feasts, the Dancing-Schools, the Christnings, the Cock fights, the Horse-Races." Festive gatherings most certainly called for the cook's best creations. Beverages, rather than food, may have been of primary importance to the cock fights and horse races.[1]

Barbecues, Fish Feasts, and Turtle Feasts were stylish events. A Collation of Sweetmeats was likely to be offered at a ball. An outrageous parade of carefully arranged dishes graced the formal dinner table. Scaled down versions were enjoyed by common folk.

Fish Feasts

Although fish feasts were mentioned over and over in Fithian's journal, he offered details of neither food nor entertainment. We can be pretty certain that yesterday's Fish Feast was not the buffet of brown, greasy seafood we find at today's southern fish fry. Although we have found neither menu nor details of the dishes served on any particular occasion, we can trace popularity of seafood recipes from early English cookery books and manuscripts through American cookbooks up to the present. From these we can create a feast of authentic seafood dishes from two centuries past if not a replicated Fish Feast. The selected receipts offer diverse styles, flavors, and presentations. Choose several for a feast or enjoy them separately for lesser occasions.

A fish feast probably included shellfish and crustaceans along with fish. The oyster was a favorite, showing up in all sorts of unlikely dishes. Crab, crawfish, and lobster were stewed, creamed, or gravied. Shrimp figured less often in period recipes. Among eighteenth-century sources you will find familiar dishes with unfamiliar names, receipts with familiar names but surprising results, and delectable new ideas for serving favorite sea foods.

✍ Fish

Freshwater and sea fish (bream, carp, catfish, eel, shad, salmon, flounder, herring, cod, and more) were prepared in expected ways: boiled, broiled, baked, fried, and in made dishes. Seafood receipts tended to be delicate, prudently allowing the flavor of the fish or shellfish to shine.

Basic boiled fish bore such names as (English) Water-Sokey, Dutch Water Souchy or Soochy, and (French) Water Suchet. According to Richard Bradley "'Tis an odd way to the English, but is much admired by many Gentlemen who have traveled." This is such a perfectly simple method one wonders that it merited recording at all. Scotswoman Dods wrote, "Eels, gudgeons, whitings, flounders, &c. were all employed for this dish" while *The French Cook* and *The Experienced English Housekeeper* thought this a proper method for perch and trout. Most sources recommended serving water sokey with bread and butter.[2]

To dress Perch [or trout or other fish] in Water Sokey

Scale, gut and wash your perch, put salt in your water. When it boils put in the fish with an onion cut in slices, you must separate it into round rings, a handful of parsley picked and washed clean, put in as much milk as will turn the water white. When your fish is enough, put them in a soup dish and pour a little of the water over them with the parsley and onions. Then serve it up with butter and parsley in a boat. Onions may be omitted if you please. You may boil trout the same way.

Raffald, *Experienced English Housekeeper*, 19.

Milk in this dish was unusual; plain water was usual; some receipts recommended fish stock. There should be just enough liquid to cover the fish. Von Rumohr cautioned that the fish should not be placed in the liquid until at a full boil. Parsley, salt, and several whole peppercorns flavored water souchy, sometimes slivered parsley root along with the leaves.

Onion was a nice addition, although von Rumohr thought the simpler, the better. "In some parts of Germany all fish are boiled with onions, vinegar and pepper. Although this is not in itself a bad method, it does tend to mask the differences in flavor between individual fish." He considered simmering trout in wine good, although masking "the subtle finesse of its flavor."[3]

French techniques with fish were also delicate but more flavorful. French cookery was much imitated throughout western Europe and in the New World's more sophisticated kitchens. A delicious and historically accurate sauce or stewing liquid may be produced with chives or onion, white wine or a little vinegar, butter, parsley, capers, salt, and pepper. Less common were mushrooms, asparagus, lemon or orange peel. Although French sauces for fish were generally thin, some were thickened with breadcrumbs or egg yolks.[4]

If crackers are layered with the fish and onions in a greater quantity of liquid, another simple and basic dish results, fish stew or chowder. Early chowders were typically fresh fish, salt pork, onion, and crackers, gently seasoned with salt, pepper, and butter. Cream or milk, potatoes, and sometimes tomatoes showed up in chowder pots of the nineteenth century.[5]

Both saltwater and freshwater fish entered into stews. By 1833 we have a chowder receipt that presages fish stews still traditional in parts of the South:

Chowder

Four pounds of fish are enough to make a chowder for four or five people; half a dozen slices of salt pork in the bottom of the pot; hang it high, so that the pork may not burn; take it out when done very brown; put in a layer of fish, cut in lengthwise slices, then a layer formed of crackers, small or sliced onions, and potatoes sliced as thin as a four-pence, mixed with pieces of pork you have fried; then a layer of fish again, and so on. Six crackers are enough. Strew a little salt and pepper over each layer; over the whole pour a bowl-full of flour and water, enough to come up even with the surface of what you have in the pot . . . [cover closely] Do not open it, except when nearly done, to taste if it be well seasoned.

Child, *American Frugal Housewife*, 59.

Flour mixed into the water may be considered optional, for crackers and potatoes will thicken the stew. Butter rolled in flour, added near the end of cooking, if needed, is a better practice adopted from earlier receipts.

Fish Pies took many forms. Some began with cooked, minced fish in a rich and heavy filling. In simplest form, the raw fish is placed in a paste lined dish with butter and seasoning, covered with paste, and baked. Various fishes, including eel, might be used for this pie.

Rich Fish-Pie, a maigre dish

Clean and nicely trim either soles, trout, salmon, turbot, whichever is intended for the pie, and cut them into handsome fillets. Season the fillets inside with pepper, cayenne, mace, and salt. They may either be turned round or laid flat in the pie-dish, packing them neatly. . . . Put bits of butter below and above the fish. . . . Season nearly a pint of stock made of the heads and trimmings; thicken and strain this over the fish, and cover the dish with a good puff-paste. It will require less cooking than a meat-pie of the same size.

Dods, *Cook and Housewife's Manual*, 191.

Note that the amount of stock needed will be less for our customary pie size; other fish pies omitted the liquid and relied on butter for sauce. The above receipt gave the attractive option of rolling the fish fillets. Dods proposed elaborations for the pie: "If to be very rich, the pie-dish may be lined with fish-forcemeat . . . [or] strew in, if to be very rich, chopped shrimps or prawns, or the soft part of oysters, or lobster-meat." Two Virginia manuscripts illustrated such elaborated fish pies:

A Salmon [or other fish] Pye

Take a convenient piece of fresh Salmon, 2 quarts of Shrimps or prawns, & ye like quantity of Oysters, Half a quarter of an Ounce of whole Mace, ye like of Beatton Pepper, & 4 Anchovies, Spread your Pye Bottom with a good piece of Butter, then lay in your Sallmon, first Laid 3 or 4 hours in white Wine, then Strane your Seasoning upon it, lay good Store of Butter on ye Topp then Cover it & Bake it.

English cookery receipt book, c. 1730–1760, 29.

The above receipt was lavish with shrimp and oysters. Anchovy seems redundant in fish dishes, doesn't it? Strong fish flavor must have been well liked. You may be relieved to learn that not all seafood dishes included anchovy; thus, we may consider it optional. The receipt below is complex, but if forcemeat is omitted it reverts to simple fish pie.[6]

Sallmon [or other fish] Pye

Take Puff past lay it in the bottom of your Dish or pan then take Midle peice of Sallmon season it with salt pepper Cloves Mace and Nutmeg so lay your Salmon in and lay a layer of butter and a layer of Salmon tell it is layed all out Cut your Salmon in 3 pieces and make forst meat balls with a large Eal chopt fine with the Yolks of hard Eggs with 2 or 3 Anchovies Marrow and Sweet herbes a little graited bread a few Oysters if you have them then lay them round your Sallmon and on the Top season them with Salt and pepper and what other Spice you like . . . but I like Salt and pepper only and Season'd high

Pre-1744 Virginia cookbook, 56.

Fish pies are easily made in the eighteenth-century manner and draw rave reviews in this century as well. Use the catch of the day common to your coastal region; I have had great success with wahoo and mahi-mahi pies. Mace or nutmeg seems to have been a must for fish pies, but you may wish to go light with those spices at first to educate your taste buds.

Fish Pie (Interpretation)

Layer filleted fish with onion and dot with butter.
Season with salt, pepper, a dash of mace, gentle herbs (tarragon, chervil, parsley).

Add a splash of white wine.

Cover with pastry.

An eight inch, quart sized fish pie bakes in about forty-five minutes.

Options:

Artichoke bottoms, capers, hardboiled egg yolks, mushrooms, asparagus,
    and/or bread crumbs are period appropriate additions.

A bundle of sweet herbs, bay leaf, or horseradish may elevate the seasoning.[7]

Eel entered into all sorts of fish receipts and starred in some. Early southerners found eels in local waters, as explorer John Lawson noted, "Eels are
no where in the World better, or more plentiful, than in Carolina." A French
traveler was delighted at the availability and reasonable price of eels near Norfolk, but perceived, "Americans are not interested either in catching or eating
them." For pie, an eel was cleaned, skinned, and cut into pieces "half as long as
your finger," seasoned, then placed into paste, usually without butter as eel is a
very oily fish. Oysters or even currants might enhance an eel pie.[8]

Broiling was a favored method for preparing fish, as it is again today. See
Chapter 5 for tasty variations on broiled and planked fish.

✐ Crab

Ancestors of today's beloved deviled crab and crab cakes are intriguing. This
family of dishes bore such names as Buttered Crabs or Stewed Crabs. Butter,
white wine, nutmeg or mace, and pepper were signature seasonings in this
ancestral dish. Bread crumbs were included less often than in today's recipes.
Glasse included two recipes "to butter Crabs or Lobsters," one without crumbs
and another with "as many crumbs of bread as will make it thick enough."
One receipt called for anchovy, the other did not. This affords us a choice. The
pre-1744 Virginia manuscript receipt below was quite similar in seasonings to
Glasse's method.[9]

To Butter Crabes

Take Crabs boyl them in Salt and Water and when they are hot have redey dis-
solvd in a little Water and white Wine a Anchovie a little Nutmeg and whole
pepper then take out all the Meat out of the bodies and Claws take care you do
not break the shell of the body for that must hold the meat then put it into your
Sawspan and rowl up a Good peice of butter in flower with a little Lemon shred
in shake it up well together to a good thickness with the Meat and put it in to
the bodies of the Crabs and stick in it Tosted Sippetts then Sarve it up hott Take
Care you don't Curdle it nor let your butter Oyl. A side Dish.

Pre-1744 Virginia cookbook, 73.

It is interesting that this early receipt called for flour to thicken the sauce, while later authors reverted to older techniques involving bread crumbs or egg yolk as thickening agents. Cleland recommended egg yolk along with bread crumbs. Hannah Wolley included bread crumbs in an older, but similar, method for buttering lobsters, crabs, or crayfish. "You may do Shrimps or Prawns thus, only you must not put them into the shells, again, but garnish your Dish with them." Eighteenth-century sauces were generally not as thick as we favor today. Richard Bradley's buttered crabs had no thickening. He recommended buttered crabs in their shell as garnish for fish. "Or this Mixture may be serv'd on a Plate, upon Sippets, with Slices of Lemon or Orange."[10]

Similar crab dishes served with *sippets* (small toasts) seem to have been the mode for at least a century. Harriot Pinckney Horry of the South Carolina lowcountry echoed Glasse's method "To dress a Crab" and was in turn echoed by Sarah Rutledge in *The Carolina Housewife:*[11]

To Stew Crabs

Choose three or four Crabs, pick the Meat clean out of the body and claws, take care no spungy part be left among it or any of the Shell, put this clean meat into a stew pan, with a little white wine, some pepper and salt, and a little grated Nutmeg, heat all this, well together, and then put in some Crums of Bread, the yolks of two Eggs beat up and one Spoonfull of Vinegar. Stir all well together, make some toasted Sippets, lay them in a plate and pour in the crabs. Send it up hott.

Horry, *Colonial Plantation Cookbook, 59.*

This early lowcountry stewed crab is nice, although a bit bland. Von Rumohr listed shallot and "fine herbs" in a crab pie filling. Dods included mustard. A gentle touch of such flavors might enliven the stewed or dressed crab receipts while staying within compass of early tastes. The toasted sippets may be buttered to add richness. Some receipts directed frying bread slices or cubes in butter instead of toasting.[12]

By 1881 we have Crab Croquettes that we would recognize as fried crab cakes. Cooked crab was mixed with cracker crumbs, celery, onion, and "seasoned high to be nice" with salt, pepper, and red pepper. This method, from *What Mrs. Fisher Knows About Old Southern Cooking*, probably originated in a South Carolina plantation kitchen and was carried in this African American cook's memory to California. Our southern love of croquettes had developed by that date as Fisher included seven receipts utilizing various meats, chicken, fish, oysters, and even liver, in addition to crab. Meat, oyster, and fish croquettes called for mashed potato rather than cracker.[13]

Rotating Trivet. Kentucky, 1775–1800. This trivet improves heat control by allowing a cooking vessel to be rotated nearer and away from livelier coals. Collection of the Museum of Early Southern Decorative Arts, Old Salem Museums & Gardens.

℘ Oysters

"Americans have almost a passion for oysters, which they eat at all hours" according to a late eighteenth-century French traveler in America. Oysters were eaten raw or cooked in every imaginable way.[14]

From the number of receipts for oyster loaves, we judge these must have been popular through generations. Nearly every author suggested serving stewed oysters in hollowed rolls. Charles Carter's *The Complete Practical Cook* offered his usual impractical and complicated method which included sweetbreads and morelles with the oysters. He also recommended serving an oyster loaf in the middle of a dish of rich oyster and lobster soup. Carter's flamboyant court dishes would seem to muddle the simple deliciousness of the more approachable receipts of popular authors such as M. Randolph, E. Smith, Moxon, or Glasse. Oyster loaves were suggested accompaniment on the serving dish with a stewed turkey "the nice Way."[15]

To Make Oyster Loaves

Take little round loaves, cut off the top, scrape out all the crumbs, then put the oysters into a stew pan with the crumbs that came out of the loaves, a little water, and a good lump of butter; stew them together ten or fifteen minutes [Raffald directed only five or six minutes], then put in a spoonful of good cream, fill your loaves, lay the bit of crust carefully on again, set them in the oven to crisp. Three are enough for a side dish.

M. Randolph, *Virginia Housewife*, 78.

Mary Randolph simplified the wording from Elizabeth Raffald's earlier cookery book, changing only the cooking time. Jane Randolph's 1743 manuscript simply directed: "fil the hole with the stew'd Oisters" as did Elizabeth Moxon. The pre-1744 Virginia manuscript suggested a more highly seasoned liquor for stewing the oysters, much like Hannah Glasse's delicious sauce:[16]

To make Oyster-Loaves

Take half a Pint of Oysters, stew them in their own Liquor . . . [add] a Glass of White Wine, a little beaten Mace, a little grated Nutmeg, a quarter of a Pound of Butter rolled in Flour, shake them well together, then put them into the Rolls.

Glasse, *Art of Cookery* (1747), 99.

Lemon juice and peel were added along with the wine in a Scots version and egg yolks were recommended instead of flour. Parsley is a pleasing addition. You may choose from these seasonings and thickening agents to develop your personal eighteenth-century style oyster speciality.[17]

✑ Shrimp

Shrimp pie showed up in a variety of sources, usually quite simple. As with fish pies, the dish was filled with shrimp, butter, and seasoning. Some cooks added a little liquid. This pie should be cooked only long enough to lightly brown the crust, as shrimp toughens when overcooked.

A Savoury Shrimp or Prawn Pie, maigre

Have as many well-cleaned shrimps or prawns as will nearly fill the pie-dish. Season with pounded mace, cloves, a little cayenne and Chili [red pepper] vinegar. Put some butter in the dish, and cover with a light puff-paste. Less than three quarters of an hour will bake these pies.

> Dods, *Cook and Housewife's Manual*, 192.

Earlier receipts agreed with mace and cloves, but added a glass of white wine and a couple anchovies. Fancier pies combined lobster with shrimp; seasoned with salt, pepper, mace, and nutmeg; moistened with a little gravy, oyster liquor, white wine, or lemon juice.[18]

An 1847 South Carolina receipt morphed the shrimp pie into what we might call shrimp casserole. This evolution continued with later authors. Shrimp was combined with bread, butter, pepper, salt, mace, nutmeg, (white wine optional) and then baked in a dish or shells. Crab or oysters were also proposed for filling scallop shells. These might be baked or broiled on a gridiron and browned. "Take a red hott Iron fire Shoevell and hold over them to Brown and Crisp the Crumbs."[19]

✑ Turtle Feasts

Did turtle, "the King of Fish," show up at fish feasts? One imagines an overlap between fish and turtle feasts. Perhaps a dish of local terrapin or tortoise fit into the fish feast. A giant sea turtle offered a whole feast in itself.[20]

Festive turtle dinners were widely popular. The Reverend Woodmason railed against South Carolina lowcountry frivolity: "Luxury and Extravagance —Balls—Concerts—Assemblies—Private Dances—Cards—Dice—Turtle Feasts—Above all—A Playhouse." He was especially critical of the self-made gentry who "enjoy'd their Claret Madera and Turtle, and the Cries of the Poor was Deem'd Insolence and Impudence."[21]

We learn a little more about these dinners from another mid-eighteenth-century traveler, further north. Near New York "amusements are much the same as in Pennsylvania . . . where it is common to have turtle-feasts: these happen once or twice in a week. Thirty or forty gentlemen and ladies meet and dine together, drink tea in the afternoon, fish and amuse themselves till evening, and then return home."[22]

Turtle was relished in England as well. South Carolina plantation mistress Eliza Lucas Pinckney shipped turtles to English friends and relatives with marginal success. Time and again the creatures perished on the voyage. After one unsuccessful attempt she wrote "we very unlucky not to get one Turtle safe out of 6 fine ones all in good order . . . before they went on board." Mrs. Pinckney left one culinary clue. She sent a bottle of *Cayan* [cayenne] to accompany a turtle, indicating a fondness for piquant seasoning. She may have developed a taste for turtle and peppers as a girl in the Carribean. One visitor to Antiqua noted that both fish and turtle were "generally dressed with rich sauces; the red pepper is much used, and a little pod laid by every plate, as also a lime."[23]

English recipes were quite involved. A single sea turtle could yield soup, several different stewed dishes, and a pie. Raffald gave directions for such a spread involving six different dishes. Glasse recommended serving turtle soup in the middle of the table flanked by a dish of fins, a fricassee of the entrails, and two other preparations served in the *callapee* and *callapash* (shells) of the turtle. The shell supplied a handy and attractive serving vessel as in the baked turtle receipt below; or the shell could be lined, edged, or covered with pastry for a turtle pie. Although most of the turtle organs were consumed, the cook was warned to take care "not to break the gall, but to cut it off from the liver and throw it away."[24]

Scottish traveler Janet Schaw raved over turtle, "young, tender, fresh from the water," which she enjoyed almost daily in Antigua in 1775 and found much better than the old ones she had tasted back home. "They laugh at us [Scots, English] for the racket we make to have it divided into different dishes. They never make but two, the soup and the shell." American recipes were closer to the original West Indian methods, with only a soup and one *made dish* baked in either the turtle shell or a ceramic dish.[25]

Did turtle feasts generally feature sea turtles or were the smaller terrapins also employed for festive occasions? While visiting a North Carolina coastal plantation, Schaw enjoyed a dinner featuring turtle. "We had a Tarrapin dressed there for turtle. They have really an excellent cook and she made it as good at least as any I ever eat in Britain." The receipts below provide some clues as to how that terrapin may have been dressed.[26]

To dress a small river turtle

The Soup

You must cut the head off over night next morning cut off the fins and legs then open it by separating the under from the upper shell then take out all the intestines eggs and so forth rip them clean them and throw them in to warm salt and water—then cut off all the meat as clean out of both shells as you can get them and lay the best peices aside then take the guts the heart the liver the fins after they are scalded and scraped and any of the small pieces of the meat that will not and the under shell scalded and scraped do [ditto] for the dish—and put them in your pot with 6 onions a bunch of pasely [*sic*] choped very fine a faggot of thyme and summer savory tyed up—Some fine pepper cloves and alspice and salt sprinkled over season it with the spice high or low as you like it—put about half a pound of buter into the pot and flour it all well then set it over the fire and Let it stew in the butter till it is brown mind to stir it as it is doing or it will stick then put about a pint or a half pint as you like it of white wine—and a pint of water and let it stew gently have a tea kettle of water boiling by the fire and fill it up as it boils by puting about a pint at a time till you have about the quantity that you think will do for dinner if it is not thick enough to your mind beat the yolks of two eggs in a little flour and stir in put the fins heart and liver and all the scraps of meat in your turrene and serve it up add a few of the force meat balls that may be made for the baked part

Stockton receipt book, 68.

To make the baked dish

Take onions parsely thyme peppers alspice and cloves all choped and pounded very fine with a plate full of grated bread mix them together and rub every piece with it and lay it in a deep dish leaving enough of the same seasoning to rub in the back shell of the turtle then put in a pound of good sweet butter a pint of wine in your dish and about a quart of water Set it in your oven to bake if your turtle is large make force meat balls of the turtle meat if not part of a leg of veal will do fry them in a pan and when your Dish has been in a hot oven about an hour and a half it will be done put the shell in at the same time with a little piece of butter and a gill [½ cup] of water and when you serve it up put the meat and as much of the gravy as it will hold in the shell garnish with hard eggs and lemon if you have it and serve it up the rest of the gravy that may be in the dish serve in a sauce boat

Stockton receipt book, 70.

The above receipts produced a feast fit for a plantation table. However, turtle prepared more simply was also esteemed. One Englishman traveling in the Virginia interior and over the mountains wrote, "One of our company shot a turtle which made us an excellent supper" and on another occasion, "Stopped to cook our breakfast on a small gravelly Island where we found plenty of Turtle eggs, with which we made pancakes equal in goodness to those made with hen's eggs." William Byrd's party had a similar experience while surveying the boundary between Virginia and North Carolina. "We catcht a large Tarapin in the River, which is one kind of Turtle. The flesh of it is wholesome. . . . It lays a great Number of Eggs . . . very Sweet and invigorating, so that some Wives recommend them earnestly to their Husbands."[27]

The female turtle seems to have been the most desirable. African American cook, Abby Fisher, specifically called for a female terrapin and the land turtle receipt below includes the turtle eggs. Hard boiled chicken eggs were also commonly added to turtle dishes. Fisher's 1881 receipt continued traditions from a century earlier. She seasoned her terrapin and green turtle stews with salt, pepper, allspice, and sherry.[28]

Turtle was enjoyed by all classes in the New World, for a simple meal as well as for a feast. The following turtle dish might have been accomplished in a modest household or when traveling as well as in a finer kitchen.

To dress land Turtles

They must be starved for three or four days before they are killed then cut their heads off and let them bleed well—wash them in cold watter and put them into a pot of boiling water with a handfull of salt. let them boil until you can pull off the shells with ease then open them, and take out the nice meat with the eggs and the part of the liver that is separated from the gaul, put it into an dish with pepper butter and salt, and stew it on the coals for a few minutes

Stockton receipt book, 98.

Apparently not everyone fancied turtle on their dinner tables. Bear, deer, raccoon, rabbit, and numerous bird species were listed as good to eat in a mid-eighteenth-century survey of inland Carolina plants and animals; however, regarding the tortoise, the Moravian surveyor only commented "The Indians eat them."[29]

✍ Barbecues

A whole young pig slowly cooking over gentle coals all day was reason enough for a gathering. This method differed from roasting (cooking with radiant heat, beside a fire) and from broiling (quick cooking over hot coals). The method and the very name *barbecue* came from the West Indies.

In 1737 Georgia a gentleman "hearing of some preparations made for a small collation. . . . I went out of curiosity to see what passed. There I found a table spread with a cloth &c. . . . A young shoat just ready barbecued over a fire in the wood was set on the table." A traveler in 1759 Virginia reported "now and then a party of pleasure into the woods to partake of a barbecue." Four decades later in Virginia circuit preacher Frances Asbury found "The gentry had made a dinner at a small distance from the town—a kind of green corn feast, with a roasted animal, cooked and eaten out of doors, under a booth" in early September. And in Norfolk, as finale to a May first celebration, "everyone repairs to the common behind the town, where there is a barbecue—animals roasted whole on crisscrossed pieces of wood over a great fire, in the open air."

(This traveler's description of the method is puzzling. Crisscrossed wood, if fresh and green, may work; but the required slow, gentle cooking could not be accomplished "over a great fire.") Plantation tutor Phillip Fithian also found such parties of pleasure organized among the gentry: "I was invited . . . to a Barbecue: this differs but little from the Fish Feasts, instead of Fish the Dinner is roasted Pig, with the proper apendages, but the Diversion & exercise are the very same at both."[30]

What were "the proper appendages"? That most helpful author *The Kentucky Housewife* noted barbecued shoat should be accompanied with "melted butter and wine, bread sauce, raw sallad, slaugh [slaw], or cucumbers, and stewed fruit."

At least one young lady in South Carolina preferred certain of the *appendages* to the barbecued pig itself. She was hoping for more than salad and stewed fruit when she wrote, "Let me tell you our greater inducement for going [to a dance party] was to stuff ourselves with niceties, for some person informed us there was to be . . . minced pyes and nick nacks; but to my great disappointment the first object I discovered was a smoking shoat." A 1784 letter from Virginia to London described such a party with hints of the Diversion:

> I am continually at Balls & Barbecues (the latter I don't suppose you know what I mean) I will try to describe it to you, it's a shoat & sometimes a Lamb or Mutton & indeed sometimes a Beef splitt into & stuck on spits & they have a large Hole dugg in the ground where they have a number of Coals made of the Bark of Trees, put in this Hole & then they lay the Meat over that within about six inches of the Coals, & then they Keep basting it with Butter & Salt & Water & turning it every now and then, until it is done, we then dine under a large shady tree or an harbor made of green bushes, under which we have benches & seats to sit on when we dine sumptuously.[31]

English gentleman, Richard Bradley gave detailed directions for preparing such a "smoking shoat." He suggested a different geometry for the barbecue apparatus, a large gridiron instead of spits, "take a large Grid-iron, with two or three Ribs in it, and set it upon a stand of iron, about three Foot and a half high" and recommended "This should be done in a Yard, or Garden, with a Covering like a Tent over it." Bradley reminded the reader that in order to preserve the gravy the skin of the pig should not be cut.

An Hog barbecued, or broil'd whole

Stretch out the Ribs, and open the Belly, as wide as may be; then strew into it what Pepper and Salt you please. . . . lay your Hog, open'd as above, with the Belly-side downwards, and with a good clear Fire of Charcoal under it. Broil that side till it is enough, flouring the Back at the same time often. . . .When the Belly-part of the Hog is enough, and turn'd upwards, and well fix'd to be steady upon the Grid-Iron, or Barbacue, pour into the Belly of the Hog, three or four Quarts of Water, and half as much White-Wine, and as much Salt as you will, with some Sage cut small; adding the Peels of six or eight Lemons, and an Ounce of fresh Cloves whole.

Then let it broil till it is enough, which will be, from the beginning to the end, about seven or eight Hours.

Bradley, *Country Housewife*, II: 165–66.

Bradley's method is quite clear and practical. And, best of all, we have found his wine, sage, lemon, cloves, and pepper basting sauce extraordinarily good. You may add the American touch, cayenne.

The Virginia Housewife gave a receipt for barbecued shoat and a similar method to roast a pig. She defined *shote* [shoat] as "the name given in the southern states to a fat young hog." Mary Randolph's seasonings were similar to the Stockton receipt below, although her method was less clear. She suggested stuffing the pig with a forcemeat of the pig's liver, bread crumbs, onion, parsley, butter, egg, salt and pepper. During roasting Randolph directed "rub it frequently with a lump of lard wrapped in a piece of clean Linen," a useful technique worth trying. After roasting, wine and drippings were mixed with the stuffing for sauce. Butter took the place of lard for the following method.[32]

To barbecue a pig

Season your pig well with black pepper and cian [cayenne] lay it on your grid-iron and with a brush made of old linnen baste it with salt and water till it is about half done then baste with butter till the skin is crisp then serve it up with a strong gravy you must make your gravy with a bit of beef and the pigs heart boiled in a skillet with a blade of mace a few pepper corns and a sprig of sage then take out the heart and chop it very fine and put it with a lump of butter rolled in flour a glass of wine and stired one way into strong gravy.

Stockton receipt book, 14.

✌ The Wedding

In the back settlements as in the plantation society of coastal regions, a combination of meats was central to a feast. A vivid word picture of a frontier wedding dinner illustrates the dinner was expansive, although the setting was rustic:

The ceremony of the marriage preceded the dinner, which was a substantial backwoods feast of beef, pork, fowls, and sometimes venison and bear meat roasted and boiled, with plenty of potatoes, cabbage, and other vegetables. During the dinner the greatest hilarity always prevailed; although the table might be a large slab of timber, hewed out with a broad axe, supported by four sticks set in auger holes; and the furniture, some old pewter dishes and plates; the rest, wooden bowls and trenchers; a few pewter spoons, much battered about the edges, were to be seen at some tables. The rest were made of horns. If knives were scarce, the deficiency was made up by the scalping knives which were carried in sheaths suspended to the belt of the hunting shirt.[33]

An abundance of meats, as described above, might well have been showcased in a hodge-podge, also called olla podrida or simply olla. An interesting array of ingredients also marked salmagundi as a special occasion dish. Olla podrida or hodge-podge (Chapter 6) and salmagundi (Chapter 7) were—and are—well suited for large gatherings. Either could be simple or quite elaborate. Both made the most of available ingredients and varied with season and cook's whim. Creative presentation transformed the stew pot or an assortment of cold foods (even leftovers) into special occasion dishes.

Either of these could become your new party favorite in both eighteenth-century context and at a twenty-first-century entertainment. Planning and preparation can be as much fun as the serving and enjoying.

These imaginative presentations of meats and vegetables served stylish society or "a substantial backwoods feast." Either hodge-podge (olla) or salmagundi would be an outstanding central dish to celebrate a wedding, christening, or other proud family occasion.

🥧 Plum Cake for Weddings, Baptisms, Christmas,
  and other festive occasions

Among English in Pennsylvania a stream of friends customarily visited couples during the first few weeks of married life. After enjoying wine and tea with the newlyweds, guests were presented a piece of wedding cake to take with them. "If the cake was not provided, the bride was either considered stingy or ignorant. . . . The wedding-cake was made of eggs, flour, butter and sugar mixed and thoroughly beaten with some sweetmeats added." A similar custom, involving the same kind of cake, followed baptisms.[34]

Alternately called wedding cake or bride cake, this special occasion cake was actually a rich plum cake. Today we would call it fruit cake. Of course the cake size depended on the number of guests expected. A mid-eighteenth-century English version was based on four pounds each of butter, sugar, and flour. In mid-nineteenth century *The Carolina Housewife's* "Plum Cake for Weddings" began with twenty pounds of butter combined with proportionate amounts of other ingredients. Aside from size, the methods are nearly identical. An early nineteenth-century Salem, North Carolina manuscript listed ingredients in more conservative and manageable quantities. Published sources provided us with details and variations for a composite interpretation.[35]

Bride Cake or Wedding Cake (Composite interpretation)
> 1 lb butter
> ½ lb (1 cup) sugar (or as much as 1 lb if candied fruits are not included)
> 8 eggs
> 3 ½ cups flour
> ¼ oz spice (mace, nutmeg, or cloves)
> 1 gill (½ cup) brandy
> 1 lb currants
> ¼ lb almonds (slivered; or up to 1 lb ground almond)
> ½ lb citron (or combine citron, candied orange and lemon peels)

Combine ingredients in the order given, beating thoroughly after each addition.
Candied fruits may be stirred in or layered with the batter.
Bake in medium oven until done; time will vary according to pan size(s).

A 1769 English cookbook suggested a daunting mixing method that will make you hugely grateful for an electric mixer if you are preparing this cake in a twenty-first-century kitchen:

To make a Bride Cake

First work the butter with your hand to a cream, then beat in your sugar a quarter of an hour. Beat the whites of your eggs to a very strong froth, mix them with your sugar and butter, beat your yolks half an hour at least and mix them with your cake. Then put in your flour, mace and nutmeg, keep beating it well . . . put in your brandy, and beat your currants and almonds lightly in . . . lay your sweetmeats in three lays with cake betwixt every lay.

Raffald, *Experienced English Housekeeper*, 134.

This large cake wants a bake oven. Cake size as well as long cooking time makes Dutch oven baking difficult. Raffald warned that baking in a pot will only burn the outside while undercooking the center. The determined cook might divide the above batter and succeed with small cakes at the hearth. Although, today one wants a wedding cake as large and impressive as possible, was that the norm two centuries ago? The above receipt bakes nicely in three average sized redware baking dishes. Cakes were also baked in hoops. Stacking smaller cakes creates an impressive presentation. One imagines at least twenty cakes resulted from *The Carolina Housewife* receipt with its hundred pounds of ingredients. That would certainly be cake enough to serve guests visiting the new bride and groom for many days.

Celebratory plum cakes have survived the centuries with few variations, differing mainly in quantity of almonds. An 1839 Kentucky "Wedding Fruit Cake" contained the greater quantity of almonds, the nuts being ground rather than slivered. This almond rich version persists in *Larousse Gastronomique*. Almonds were not included in *The Carolina Housewife*'s 1847 "Plum Cake for Weddings." This almond-less cake has been passed down in Charleston, South Carolina families for weddings and other special occasions. The 1924 *Boston Cooking-School Cook Book* also omitted almonds in "Wedding Cake I."[36]

Mary Eaton's 1822 cookery dictionary described wedding cake as a typical pound cake with fruit and almonds, while her bride cake was a simple yeasty plum cake. *The Kentucky Housewife* gave a fruit and almond wedding cake receipt, but also a dissimilar "Bride's Cake," a delicate white cake with white icing quite different from all the others. We would recognize that bride's cake as today's ordinary wedding cake. "It should be considerably elevated upon the table, and stick firmly in the centre of it, a handsome assemblage of real or artificial leaves and white flowers."[37]

✍ Icings

Of course, since the cake was the centerpiece of the celebration, it was dressed with icing. Two sorts of icing were suggested for a wedding cake or other special plum cake; both are of meringue, one containing almond flour. Either appropriately frosts this rich cake. The two icings were sometimes used together.

To ice or frost a bride's-cake, or a very large plum-cake

To a half-pound of fine sifted sugar put the whites of two eggs, beaten with a little orange-flower-water, or simple water, and strain. With this whisk the sugar for a long time, till it is quite smooth. This may be tinged with the juice of strawberries or currants, or with prepared cochineal.

Dods, Cook and Housewife's Manual, 443.

These proportions were typical for simple sugar icings. The c. 1700 Virginia manuscript required three egg whites per half pound of sugar, scented with rose water. Harriot Horry's "Ice for Plumb Cake" called for four egg whites. Horry also suggested alternate flavorings: rose water and lemon or lime juice instead of orange flower water. Since egg whites differ in volume, we may judge quantity by size of our available eggs.[38]

Icing (Interpretation based on Dods, Horry, and c. 1700 Virginia ms.)

Beat 2, 3, or 4 egg whites very well, until stiff.

Add 1 cup extra fine white sugar, 1 teaspoonful at a time.

Flavor with a teaspoonful of rose water or orange flower water.

Spread on cake, and as Harriot Horry advised "put them in an oven not hot
    but warm enough to dry them."

This icing is typical of the period, although rather different from our idea of
cake frosting. It is actually meringue with close kinship to kisses and their
ancestral cakes, biscuits, or puffs. See details in the discussion of kisses as
Christmas treats. This icing forms a shell over the cake that is very pretty but
shatters when the cake is cut.

A second group of receipts is typified by the following eighteenth-century
English almond icing. *The Kentucky Housewife* and Mrs. Beeton echoed this
receipt a century later, but with four egg whites rather than three to a pound of
sugar.[39]

To make Almond icing for the Bride Cake

Beat the whites of three eggs to a strong froth; beat a pound of Jordan almonds
very fine with rosewater. Mix your almonds with the eggs lightly together [with]
a pound of common loaf sugar beat fine, and put in by degrees. When your cake
is enough, take it out and lay your icing on and put it in to brown.

Raffald, *Experienced English Housekeeper*, 135.

Half the above receipt (2 egg whites, 1 cup extra fine sugar, ½ pound almond
flour and a little rose or orange flower water) makes a good batch of almond
icing. You may notice this is identical to the macaroon receipt. It is not spreadable, but can be rolled into a layer to cover the cake. The cake with almond
topping may be put back into the oven for a few minutes. More commonly, the
icing was not browned, but simply set by the fire or in a warm oven to dry or
harden.

On occasion the two icings were used in tandem. "On very rich cakes, such
as wedding, christening cakes, &c., a layer of almond icing is usually spread
over the top, and over that the white icing as described. All iced cakes should
be kept in a very dry place."[40]

Other special foods accompanied the cake for a wedding celebration. "Norfolk weddings are extremely gay. A dear female friend of the bride prepares
pastries of all kinds for the occasion."[41]

One suspects a rich plum cake made up part of the "nice cakes and dain-
ties" baked by neighbors for a Virginia christening. "We had a real reception

after the christening. All our friends came in to congratulate us. You should have seen the table when the dining-room doors were opened. It was covered with game, fruits, preserves and cakes. And of course there was plenty of wine and beer and punch. Punch is so popular here that no festivity can go on without its being brought to the guests on their arrival and handed to them continually afterward."[42]

A pre-1744 "Extraordinary plum cake" illustrated a second family of plum cakes, with yeast and therefore fewer eggs. Jane Randolph collected the same cake receipt; both appear to have been taken from a common English cookery book. Our sweet fruity holiday breads descend from these yeasty plum cakes.[43]

๑ Celebrating the Agricultural Round

Planting and harvest were the busiest, and most critical, times of the year. More than just the obvious spring planting and autumn harvesting, the need for extra help popped up throughout spring, summer, and fall. Midsummer brought the labor intensive grain harvests. In those seasons family, friends, and neighbors often pitched in to help one another. A prosperous farmer might hire or rent extra hands.

Beyond the field work many other tasks called for a work party—threshing, hog killing, and the jolly corn huskings—some more *work* and some more *party*. Folks gathered to share the work but also to enjoy each other's company at the end of a full day. Thanksgiving days happened throughout the year.

Housewives were charged with feeding hungry workers. Surely somebody remembered to bring restorative beverages as well. When time and resources allowed, special foods were prepared to celebrate completion of seasonal tasks.

๑ Seed Cake

Seed cake was traditionally connected with sowing and harvesting. William Ellis described seed cakes made simply of flour, yeast, rich milk, sugar and caraway seeds "baked in a round, deep, earthen or tin pan, on a hearth, or at the oven's mouth." Other receipts included egg. Seed cake was taken to harvest workers in the field to be dipped into ale or offered for supper with cheese.

The "good housewifely" farmer's wife was admonished to keep on hand "this cake or wig, or plumb-cake, especially in harvest time" or to serve to visitors along with a cup of ale. Two centuries earlier, one of Thomas Tusser's *Points of Huswifery* urged the preparation of seed cake to celebrate wheat sowing:[44]

Seed-Cake

> Wife, some time this week, if the weather hold clear,
> An end of wheat sowing we make for this year:
> Remember thou therefore, though I do it not,
> The seed-cake, the pasties, the furmenty pot.[45]

Among yeasty seed cake receipts from over a dozen sources, published and handwritten, English and American, few were alike. Some included butter, some required eggs, some called for both. And even when the lists of ingredients matched, the quantities varied greatly. Some seed cakes called for an astonishing amount of caraway. The common half ounce, or one tablespoonful, for one pound of flour was, and is, about right for most tastes.[46]

In trials with various seed cakes, we found Scots and English proportions identical except for spices. You may wish to try it first with only caraway and then decide which optional ingredients to add for your special seed cake. You may prefer it simple as we do.

A Common Seed Cake

Mix a half-pound of beat white sugar with two pounds of flour in a large bowl or pan. Make a hole in the centre, and pour into it a half-pint of lukewarm milk, and two spoonfuls of yeast. Mix a little of the surrounding flour with this, and throwing a cloth over the vessel, set it in a warm place for an hour or two. Add to this half a pound of melted butter, an ounce of caraway-seeds, a little allspice, ginger, and nutmeg, and milk sufficient to make the whole of a proper stiffness. Butter a hoop, and pour in the mixure. Let it stand a half-hour at the mouth of the oven to rise, and then bake it.   Dods, *Cook and Housewife's Manual*, 445.

Seed Cake (interpretation based on Dods, Raffald, and others, one-half receipt)

Mix ½ cup sugar with 3 cups flour (stir in spices, if desired)
Mix ½ cup lukewarm milk with 1 package dry yeast dissolved in 1 tablespoon warm water.
Pour milk-yeast mixture into hole in middle of flour-sugar mix.
Stir a little of the surrounding dry ingredients into wet ingredients.
Set in warm place for an hour or two.
Add ¼ pound melted butter in an additional ½ cup lukewarm milk.
Stir in 1 tablespoon caraway seeds.
(Optional: Add spices, flavorings, or sweetmeats.)
Stir all together. Put into buttered hoop, baking pan, or 2 eight-inch earthenware dishes.
Set in warm place to rise. Bake 45–60 minutes or until deeply browned.

In an alternate mixing method the baker was directed to add all liquid ingredients at one time (lukewarm milk, butter, and yeast); allow to rise; gently work in caraway; allow to rise again. A third mixing method suggested rubbing the butter into the flour before adding the warm liquids. It seems each cook had a preferred mixing order as well as a personal favorite receipt for yeast raised cake.

Secrets to success with this cake seem to be to cook thoroughly; the crust may become deeply browned before the center is done. Allow to cool before slicing. The aroma from this cake is so luscious that one must fight the temptation to cut into it straight from the oven.

Options: Whether the seed cake was of the yeast type or pound cake, diverse enhancements were proposed in addition to the caraway. Finer seed cakes were made with exotic and expensive ingredients such as rose or orange flower water, sack or brandy, cloves, mace, nutmeg, allspice, ginger, saffron, fresh or candied orange or lemon peel, currants, or raisins. Such variety opens the door to experimenting with delicious combinations.

Although yeast-variety seed cake receipts differed widely, the pound cake with caraway was standard. Few varied from the expected equal weights of butter, sugar, and flour with about a dozen eggs per pound of flour.

To Make a Light Seed Cake

Take a Pound of Flour well Dried, a Pound of Sugar well Sifted, a Pound of Butter, the yelk [*sic*] of Twelve Eggs & the whites of Six and a ½ oz Carraway Seeds Mixt well together & Bake it.

Goelet household book, 3.

About one tablespoonful caraway is good in this cake. You may enjoy experimenting with additional period appropriate flavors or sweetmeats. Your seed cake can acquire a personality of its own. And, it really is enjoyable served with cheese and dunked in ale as the harvesters did.

✿ Wigs

Actually a small seed cake, wigs were particularly enjoyed at spring planting time. Wigs were ubiquitous in period cookery books. The basic wig was a bun made with flour, butter, yeast, milk, and caraway. Richer versions included sugar, egg, and perhaps spice. The pre-1744 Virginia manuscript volume included two typical receipts. This is a good basic one.[47]

To make Wiges [Wigs]

Take a quarter of a peck of Flower a pound of Suger some Carraway seeds half a pound of Butter melted in the Milk so much as will make it a very light past

4 spoonsfull of Yeast when it is Mixed set it to the fire to Rise and then lay it out in Wigs let them stand in ye Oven 3 quarters of an hour.

Pre-1744 Virginia cookbook, 57.

Wigs (Interpretation and comparison, half receipt)
>   4 cups flour
>   1 cup sugar (or less)
>   ¼ pound butter melted in 1 cup warm milk
>   1 teaspoonful dry yeast in 2 tablespoons warm water
>   (Add a little more milk, if needed.)
>   2 tablespoons caraway
>   (Optional: 1 egg, nutmeg or mace, salt)

Let rise, form buns, let rise again. (See Seed Cake for mixing methods.)
Bake in medium oven for 30 minutes or until done.

Scotswoman Dods' bun receipts provide insight into this family of breads. Her version with caraway was essentially wigs but more forthrightly named Seed-Buns. She presented a Common Buns receipt and expanded it into Cross-buns with additional sugar and spices and a cross pressed or cut into the top. Plum-buns were cross-buns with currants, candied orange peel and almonds. One finds the ancestry of today's springtime hot cross buns in these receipts as well as sweet Christmas breads.[48]

✍ Pot Pie or Sea Pie

A meat pie was traditional for rural work parties, as was seed cake. "The standard dish for every log rolling, house raising and harvest was a pot pie, or what in other countries is called a sea pie." The *sea pie* was not of seafood as the name might indicate, but of preserved pork or beef and other ingredients that might be available on an ocean voyage. Cheshire pork pie is an example. Chicken, pigeons, or other fowl were sometimes included with the cured meat.[49]

The ham and potato pie below is a prime example. Glasse's pork and apple pie is only a bit fussier, with nutmeg and white wine. These two Cheshire pie receipts illustrate wide flavor differences to be achieved from a few basic ingredients.

Cheshire-Pye with Pork

Take some salt Loin of Pork, or Leg of Pork, and cut it into Pieces, like Dice, or as you would for an Harsh. If it be boiled or roasted, it is no matter; then take an equal quantity of Potatoes and pare them, and cut them into dice, or in slices. Make your Pye-Crust, and lay some Butter, in pieces, at the bottom, with some

Pepper and Salt; then put in your Meat and Potatoes, with such seasoning as you like, but Pepper and Salt commonly, and on the Top some pieces of Butter. Then close your Pye, and bake it in a gentle Oven, putting in about a Pint of Water [much less water needed for an ordinary sized pie], just before it is going into the Oven; for if you put in your Water over Night, it will spoil your Pye.

Bradley, Country Housewife, II: 171–72.

Our ancestors understood that pork should be thoroughly cooked. Salt cured meats were often boiled to draw out excess salt. Fresh meats might be lightly browned, then simmered in a little liquid. This step partially cooks the meat and produces a nice gravy for the pie.

When the pie is assembled from raw meat the cook must be attentive to assuring the meat cooks thoroughly. In the following receipt Glasse seemed to indicate the pork entered the pie uncooked; another of her Cheshire pies called for boiled pork. Either way will make a nice pie.

A Cheshire Pork-Pye

Take a Loin of Pork, skin it, cut it into Stakes, season it with Salt, Nutmeg, and Pepper; make a good Crust, lay a Layer of Pork, and then a large layer of Pippins pared and cored, a little Sugar, enough to sweeten the Pye, then another Layer of Pork; put in half a Pint of white Wine, lay some Butter on the Top, and close your Pye.

Glasse, Art of Cookery (1747), 72.

A quarter cup wine is about right for an ordinary baking dish. Consider the juiciness of your apples in judging quantity of wine. A century later a nearly identical recipe showed up in Virginia as simply "Pork Pie," with water in place of wine.[50]

Assemble meat pies in a pie dish or directly in the Dutch oven. Virginia housewife Mary Randolph outlined the latter method in her Sea Pie: Layer slices of boiled salt pork or beef, sliced potatoes and onions, and a fowl cut in pieces. Season with salt, pepper, (perhaps cloves), thyme, parsley, and butter between layers. Add water, wine, and mushroom catsup. Cover with pastry. The Dutch oven is then set to simmer until the meat and vegetables are nearly done, at which time shovel coals onto the lid and finish browning the crust.[51]

During a hearth cookery class one student was intrigued when I introduced the topic of these special occasion meat pies. As I spoke about *sea pie,* she heard *cipaille,* a meat pie traditional in the Gaspésie area of Canada, where she formerly lived. Thoroughly fascinating! A web search revealed French Canadian layered meat pies made of all sorts of game or of domesticated meats.

Pork layered with chicken is purported to be the oldest type of cipaille, which reflects mid-eighteenth-century sea pies or Cheshire pork pies. Is *cipaille* a corruption of *sea pie*? That recipe did not appear in early French sources examined. Perhaps this is an example of an English receipt adopted by French settlers—an unusual New World cultural exchange as European exchanges of foods and customs were usually in the reverse direction.

✒ Melon Frolic

Just as family and friends gathered for fish feasts, turtle feasts, and barbecues, so were other foods celebrated. Often a single food was featured, as fish, turtle, young pig—or spring greens, corn, or watermelons. "In the month of August there is a celebrated Melon Frolic which brings together all the neighboring people to eat watermelons and dance."[52]

✒ Spring Tonic

Early spring greens were health restoring after winter's scarcity. An array of dishes combining eggs and spring greens were celebrated. These took the form of pudding or pie, pancake, or omelet. Choose from receipts for spinach puddings, tansies, wild greens, omelets, and asparagus forced rolls for your spring tonic.

✒ Hedgehog

One of the most playful names for an eighteenth-century dish came from that charismatic Old World creature, the hedgehog. *The Art of Cookery Made Plain and Easy* included three receipts for Hedge-Hog, first in the chapter "For Lent, or a Fast Dinner" and again among showy conceits in "Of Cheesecakes, Creams, Jellies, Whip-Syllabubs, &c." Although hedgehogs, the animals, are not found in the America, the pre-1744 Virginia manuscript lets us know the idea for this charming dish immigrated to the New World. The receipt resurfaced in an 1832 American cookbook.[53]

A hedg hogg

Take a pound of Jorden Allmonds blanch and beat them in a Morter with a Spoonfull or 2 of Sack or Orainge flower Water to keep them from Oylin make it into a stif Paste [or begin with prepared almond flour] then beat in 6 Yolks and 3 whites of Eggs sweeten it with double Refin'd Suger to your Tast [½ cup is good] with half a point of Cream and a quarter of a pound of Sweet butter Melted set it over your Stove keeping it Sturring tell it is as stif as you may make it up in the Shape of a Hedghog stick it full of Allmonds blanched Slit thin like the brisells of a Hedghog then set it in your Dish then boyl [one half pint] Cream and thicken it with the Yolks of 2 Eggs but not to thick and sweeten it with loaf Suger to your Tast and pore it round it set it to be cold Sarve it to the Table . . . A side Dish

Pre-1744 Virginia cookbook, 75.

Half the receipt makes a lovely little life sized hedgehog. English and Scots receipts suggested the perfect finishing touches: "plump two currants for the eyes" and add "a bit of candied Orange for Tongue." A hedgehog is indeed simple enough for a side dish and ostentatious enough for a party table, "in the middle for supper, or in a grand desert [*sic*]."[54]

A variety of round puddings were enhanced by studding with slivered almonds, a popular touch through several centuries. A 1672 receipt suggested sticking almonds in a bread pudding "and it will look like a Hedgehog." And Eliza Leslie's 1828 plum pudding was to be stuck all over with slips of almond or citron or both.[55]

✍ Christmas

To create "A Scotch Christmas Bun, from Mrs. Fraser's Cookery" the basic bun dough enclosed a layer of currants, raisins, almonds, candied orange peel, citron, and spices. With this receipt Dods noted, "Every country-town, village, and rural neighbourhood in England, Scotland, and Ireland, has its favourite holiday-cake, or currant loaf." This tradition carries over today in our Christmas breads.[56]

✍ Kisses

On Christmas Eve 1804 in the North Carolina Backcountry we discovered Margaret Steele "preparing kisses maricles &c. for Christmas." Kisses remain a traditional southern sweet; however, *maricles* are a mystery. Might Steele's maricles have been macaroons or perhaps marvels, fried dough cakes?[57]

Kiss was a fashionable new (early nineteenth century) name for an older sweetmeat, a super sweet meringue. The pre-1744 Virginia manuscript called such little lemon confections "Lemon Biskett;" Cleland, 1759, called hers "Lemon Puffs;" Raffald, 1769, named a related receipt "Cream Cakes." Eliza Leslie's 1828 receipt for Kisses was a bridge from older, denser versions to the many that followed. The following receipts illustrate the genealogy of these historical sugar plums.[58]

Lemon Puffs

Beat and sift a Pound of Loaf Sugar, mix it with the Juice of two Lemons, and the Rind grated fine, whisk the Whites of three Eggs to a Snow; then beat all together very well, sift Sugar on Papers, and drop it on by Spoonfuls, don't let them be too near one another, put them in a very slow Oven. You may make Orange Puffs the same Way.

Cleland, *New and Easy Method*, 151.

The Blackford manuscript of a century later (1852) included a lighter version with a greater proportion of egg white. We agree with other early authors who advise using only lemon peel rather than the juice or essence.

Kisses

Powder a pound of the best loaf sugar. Beat to a strong froth the whites of 6 eggs and when it is stiff enough to stand alone, beat into it the powdered sugar (a teaspoonful at a time), adding the juice of two lemons or 10 drops of essence of lemon. After beating well drop it on sheets of white paper, making it into regular shapes with the spoon. Place them in a moderate oven (if it is too cool they will not rise, but flatten and run together) and bake them until colored of a very pale brown. Then take them off the papers carefully, place two flat sides together, so as to unite them in an oval ball and lay them on their sides to cool.

Blackford, "Recipes in the Culinary Arts," 3.

A friend who continues the tradition of making kisses for Christmas each year follows the same proportion as Blackford, six egg whites to two cups of sugar. This queen of the meringue offers important advice: Have egg whites at room temperature. Use extra-fine sugar if available or make standard granulated sugar finer in a blender. Beat and beat and beat the egg whites. Add sugar very gradually, by the teaspoonful, beating thoroughly after each addition. After slow baking, dry the kisses in a cool oven several hours or overnight.

18th-century Lemon Puffs or 19th-century Kisses (Composite interpretation)

Beat 3–6 egg whites very well, until stiff.
Have ready two cups fine white sugar (not confectioners sugar).
Add sugar, one teaspoonful at a time, beating thoroughly between each addition.
Add grated peel of 2 or more lemons.
Drop in little lumps or cones on paper-covered tin.
Bake at low temperature (250 degrees in modern oven) until barely colored.
While warm, place two meringues together, forming an oval.

Raffald suggested "You may lay raspberry jam or any other sort of sweetmeat betwixt them before you close the bottoms together to dry." A bit of candied orange or lemon peel is especially nice. An eighteenth-century collation of sweets might have included these delicious sweets, although they were more likely called lemon puffs or lemon biscuits in those days, rather than kisses.[59]

Early versions called for as few as two egg whites, and most called for only the rind of the lemon. *The Carolina Housewife* 1847 called for a dozen egg whites to a pound of sugar. She also recommended flavoring with rose rather than lemon.

My trusty *Joy of Cooking* brings the kiss tradition right up to the present. Recipes are directly descended from eighteenth- and nineteenth-century meringue cakes with either four or six egg whites per two cups sugar. Traditional flavoring from lemon rind is suggested, but also thoroughly twentieth-century flavors such as vanilla, nuts, bits of candied cherry, or cocoa.

The 1839 *Kentucky Housewife* included "Kisses and Secrets" with a delightful twist, an amusing tradition that will be fun to emulate when we are not working in a strictly eighteenth-century mindset. "[W]rap round each a slip of paper containing a single verse or pun, and envelope them separately in small pieces of fine white paper that is neatly fringed, giving each end a twist." While this custom may not date back into the eighteenth century, it is a charming branch of the family tree of these small meringue confections.[60]

✍ Ginger Cakes for Christmas

Gingerbread was enjoyed year round, but especially at Christmas time. Ginger cakes or ginger breads came in a variety of guises through several centuries. (See recipes in Chapter 4.) Spicy cookies were a specialty of the Moravians, being sold in village shops and taken along to sell during Court Days. At Christmas services in North Carolina Moravian settlements, gifts of foods were distributed to children along with "a pretty Christmas verse" and perhaps a candle.[61]

> On Christmas Day the English children from the mill [children of families seeking refuge from Indians] came to see our Christmas decoration [in Bethabara].... We told them why we rejoiced like children and gave to each a piece of cake. In Bethania... a Lovefeast for the 24 children there, at the close of the service each received a pretty Christmas verse and a ginger cake, the first they had ever seen.[62]

As we have seen in the chapter on baking, ginger cakes may have been simple drop cakes or rolled out and cut. But what about molded or stamped ginger cakes? Although very few receipts suggested stamping with a design, carved wooden cake molds survive from the period. Old Salem curates two interesting cake molds among early Moravian artifacts. In our experiences with period doughs we find a number of ginger cakes and other little cakes lend themselves to stamping. Perhaps this was so common a technique as to need no mention.

Cake Mold. Salem, North Carolina, c. 1800–1815. John Blum, carver. Collection of the Museum of Early Southern Decorative Arts, Old Salem Museums & Gardens.

During the years 1760–1773 special Christmas foods recorded in Moravian diaries included pieces of cake, ginger cakes, honey cakes, or apples. The cake might have been plum cake, seed cake, or plain. Either eggs or yeast may have been employed for lightness.

✐ Christmas Pie

Tidewater plantation tutor Fithian noted on December 29th 1773, "We had a large Pye cut to Day to signify the Conclusion of the Holidays." That Christmas pie may have contained two or more boned fowl stuffed one inside the other. Or perhaps it was a mincemeat pie.

Glasse's "Yorkshire Christmas-Pye" contained a boneless turkey, goose, chicken, partridge, and pigeon, one inside the other. A hare, woodcocks, and other game were to be arranged around the layered birds within the pie. Glasse noted the standing paste (coffin) for this pie would require a bushel of flour. Twenty-four pounds of flour and six pounds of butter were called for in Raffald's goose pie receipt, to contain a goose, stuffed with a turkey and rabbit, flanked with ducks and woodcocks. Receipts from this family of flamboyant holiday dishes were alternately titled goose, turkey, or duck pie.[63]

To create your own Christmas pie, consider which fowls are available. Flavor contrast and eye appeal may also influence your choice. For example, the dark flesh of duck lends a nice contrast to turkey or chicken, the fatty goose may improve the drier turkey. You may even find such a bird within a bird already prepared at your supermarket. We have found the cleverly named *turducken* among frozen meats. Two receipts are given here to compare details and period character of this holiday specialty.

This pretentious dish did not become simpler, as did other receipts when transplanted to America. *The Carolina Housewife* followed earlier tradition for a complicated Christmas pie with her own touches.

A Christmas Pie

Make the walls of a thick standing crust, to any size you like, and ornamented as fancy directs. Lay at the bottom of the pie a beef steak. Bone a turkey, goose, fowl, duck, partridge, and place one over the other, so that, when cut, the white and brown meat may appear alternately. Put a large tongue by its side, and fill the vacancies with forcemeat balls and hard eggs; then add savory jelly [jellied broth or gravy]. . . . Bacon, chopped or beat up with the forcemeat, is preferable to suet, as it is nicer when cold, and keeps better.

Rutledge, *Carolina Housewife*, 85.

The raised or standing crust generally functioned more as container than to be savored. We were happy to find that Rundell suggested the option to bake this sort of pie in a dish. In her pie of duck stuffed with chicken and tongue, she directed: "Bake in a slow oven, either in a raised crust, or pie dish, with a thick crust, ornamented." Cleland also gave this option in her goose pie receipt: "You may either raise it or put it in a Dish."[64]

Another Scots version, directed layering only two birds and stewing them partway done before assembling the pie. Even so, the estimated baking time was three hours. Larger pies must bake longer. This was obviously not Dutch oven baking.

A Christmas goose-pie

Bone and season highly a goose and a large fowl. Stuff the latter with forcemeat made of minced tongue or ham, veal, parsley, suet, pepper, and salt, with two eggs [or other forcemeat]. Stew them for twenty minutes in a little good broth in a close stew-pan. Put the fowl within the goose, and place that in a raised pie-crust, filling up the vacancies with forcemeat or slices of parboiled tongue or pigeons, partridges, &c. Put plenty of butter over the meat. This pie will take three hours to bake. It will eat well cold, and keep a long while.

Dods, *Cook and Housewife's Manual*, 388.

It seems next to impossible to thoroughly cook the birds without overcooking the pastry. Raffald directed covering sides and top with three layers of paper to protect the crust during the long baking. She challenged the cook to decorate the pie with pastry vine leaves, flowers, or shapes of the birds.

A quite different Christmas pie was of mincemeat. The Virginia pie of Fithian's journal may have been more like Bradley's "minc'd Pyes, or Christmas Pyes" the filling of which "you may keep it till Candlemas [February 2], if you make it at Christmas." Although the Christmas pie of fowl was also said to keep well, we would consider it unsafe to consume either of these pies after it sat around through the holidays. The pre-1744 Virginia cookery manuscript contained a mince pie similar to those of Bradley, E. Smith, and other English sources. Many receipts combined boiled and minced beef heart, tongue, or sirloin with the suet and fruits.[65]

The c. 1700 Virginia cookbook outlined an even more basic mincemeat, much like Hannah Glasse's "To make Mince-Pies the best Way."[66]

To make Mince Pyes. Mrs. Street

Take one pound of Suet, One pound Currants, One pound of apples being right golden runnets, one pound of sugar, one ounce of Cloves Mace & Nutmegs each beaten together the juice of two Lemons & one Sevil Orange with the rinds finedly greated, a gill of sack, Candyed Orang and Lemon Peel & Citron.

Unidentified cookbook, c. 1700, Harbury, *Virginia's Cooking Dynasty*, 158.

Curious cooks who tested this receipt prefer less clove, but otherwise give this mince pie high praise. Mincemeat has survived the centuries little changed, as has plum pudding.

✍ Plum Pudding

Virginia and South Carolina plantation mistresses copied nearly identical plum puddings into their personal cookery books. Harriot Horry added more flour (six tablespoonfuls) than Jane Randolph plus a half teaspoonful nutmeg. She also offered the choice of currants or raisins.

A rich plumb Pudding

Take 1 lb Suit shred fine 1 lb Rai[sins] Ston'd 4 spoonfulls of Flower & 4 Do. [spoonfulls] of Sugar 5 Eggs but 3 whites beats the Eggs with a little Sack & salt boil 4 hours at Least.

Jane Randolph 1743, Harbury, *Virginia's Cooking Dynasty*, 382.

"There are a thousand other ways of making a plum-pudding." Some contained both currants and raisins along with candied lemon peel, orange peel, citron, and almonds. Plum puddings were spiced according to the cook's fancy with some combination of ginger, cinnamon, cloves, nutmeg, and mace. Flour, bread crumbs, or biscuit served as thickening; wine, brandy, or rum added flavor. "The wine or spirits may be spared, and the pudding flavoured with distilled waters, as rose-water, peach-water, orange-flower-water." Slices of cold pudding may be nicely rewarmed in a Dutch oven.[67]

Two other sorts of plum puddings are included in Chapter 3 under the simple titles "a Pudding" and "Very fine Hogs Puddings." The latter produced individual plum puddings boiled in sausage casings.

✍ Christmas Pottage

Plum pottage offered a different and thoroughly appealing way of preparing the traditional combination of beef and dried fruits for Christmas or other occasion. Two dishes, a boiled leg of beef and fruit soup, were simply prepared in one pot. Bread was suggested to thicken the soup. Some added a little sugar, others salt and pepper, with the spices.[68]

Plum-Pottage, or Christmas-Pottage

Take a Leg of Beef, and boil it till it is tender in a sufficient quantity of Water, add two Quarts of red Wine, and two Quarts of old strong Beer; put to these some Cloves, Mace, and Nutmegs, enough to season it, and boil some Apples, pared and freed from the Cores into it, and boil them tender, and break them; and to every Quart of Liquor, put half a Pound of Currans pick'd clean, and rubb'd with a coarse Cloth, without washing. Then add a Pound of Raisins of the Sun, to a Gallon of Liquor, and half a Pound of Prunes. Take out the Beef, and the Broth or Pottage will be fit for use.

Bradley, *Country Housewife*, II: 147–48.

From early Virginia we glean touches that mark "Plum Porrage" as a special dish. A few prunes tied in a cloth may be dropped into the soup just long enough to "Plump them to Garnish your Dish and lay them in as many shapes round your dish as you fancy and Grait a brown Crust round the brimes of your dish."[69]

✍ Twelfth Night Cake

On January 7, 1740 William Byrd noted that he "drew twelfth cake, gave the people cake and cider." We wish he had given a few more details. What sort of cake was served? Were there guests or only family and servants? A visitor to Alexandria some years later left us more particulars regarding a twelfth night festivity.

[Alexandria Va, Jan. 6, 1775] It seems this is one of their annual Balls supported in the following manner: A large rich cake is provided and cut into small pieces and handed round to the company, who at the same time draws a ticket out of a Hat with something merry wrote on it. He that draws the King has the Honor of treating the company with a Ball the next year.... The Lady that draws the Queen has the trouble of making the Cake. Here was about 37 ladies dressed and powdered to the life, some of them very handsome and as much vanity as is necessary. All of them fond of dancing, but I do not think they perform it with the greatest elegance. Betwixt the Country dances they have what I call everlasting jigs. A couple gets up and begins to dance a jig (to some Negro tune) others comes and cuts them out, and these dances always last as long as the Fiddler can play. This is sociable, but I think it looks more like a Bacchanalian dance than one in a polite assembly. Old Women, young wives with young children in the lap, widows, maids and girls come promiscuously to these assemblies which generally continue till morning. A cold supper, Punch, Wines, Coffee and Chocolate, but no Tea. This is a forbidden herb. The Men chiefly Scotch and Irish. I went home about two o'clock, but part of the company stayed, got drunk and had a fight.[70]

There is no hint as to the sort of "large rich cake" served at this lively ball. It may have fit into the family with either pound cakes or sweet yeast breads. See Wedding or Bride cakes and Seed Cakes for examples of each type. Twelfth Night Cake or King's Cake passed down through the intervening two centuries is of the yeast bread-cake type. French versions contain fresh lemon or orange peel, and a Scots Yule Cake receipt calls for raisins, and candied peel. A New Orleans King Cake is plain.[71]

✍ The Funeral

When William Byrd attended a funeral in 1712 Tidewater Virginia he was served "wine and biscuits according to custom." Elizabeth Steel purchased thirty dozen "Bisquet" and thirty-two pounds beef for her husband William Steel's funeral in 1773 North Carolina backcountry.[72]

What sort of biscuits were those customarily served at funerals? See possibilities in Chapter 4. The "tavern" or "wine" biscuit seems likely.

Buns were customary at important occasions in Moravian settlements. The 1767 North Carolina Moravian records reveal "After the funeral, buns and a little wine were served the attendants in the Tavern and Gemein Haus,— there were more than a hundred who had come" We suspect those early buns may have had the same delicate flavor of mace as lovefeast buns still baked by descendants of those early settlers.[73]

CHAPTER 9

Miscellanies
and Musings

This chapter might alternately be titled Tangents. Here are odds and ends of topics which have long intrigued us curious cooks. Newly discovered manuscript references have led in new directions. Some of these miscellanies were common knowledge to our ancestors. Other whimsical or flamboyant foods were not particularly basic, nor were they necessarily common; however, all are documented from our times and places of interest.

✒ Traveling Foods

Travelers encountered a broad range of hospitality and provisions. Taverns or ordinaries offered food of varying quality for humans and horses. In the back-settlements travelers were dependent on hospitality at homes along their way. A tantalizing soup simmering in the family cook pot would have been a pleasant discovery at the close of a day's journey. The fortunate traveler supped on cold boiled meat left from dinner. Corn cakes, eggs, and ham or bacon were quickly and easily prepared.

> [South Carolina Upcountry, 1767] laid my Self down for the Night frozen with the Cold—without the least Refreshment—No Eggs, Butter, Flour, Milk, or anything, but fat rusty Bacon, and fair Water, with Indian Corn Bread, Viands I had never before seen or tasted.[1]

> [Hillsboro to Salisbury, North Carolina, 1769] found little to eat, and that little very poor and very nasty.
> [Near Cross Creek, North Carolina 1769] went to bed supperless because the House looked too nasty for Christians to eat in.[2]

> [Ferry house, lower South Carolina or northern Georgia, 1775] My Friends would have smiled to see my repast and the figure I cut in eating it. Fried pork & milk was a dish to which necessity gave a high relish.[3]

> [Virginia, 1779] Having several times mentioned an ordinary, it may not be amiss to acquaint you, that out of the principal towns, all taverns and

public houses are, in Virginia, called ordinaries, and 'faith not improperly in general; they consist of a little house placed in a solitary situation, in the middle of the woods ... the entertainment you meet with is very poor indeed, seldom able to procure any other fare than eggs and bacon, with Indian hoe cake, and at many of them not even that; the only liquors are peach brandy and whiskey. For this miserable fare they are not remiss in making pretty exorbitant charges.

[Richmond, 1779] before the war, the hospitality of the country was such, that travelers always stopt at a plantation when they wanted to refresh themselves and their horses, where they always met with the most courteous treatment, and were supplied with every thing gratuitously[4]

[Valley of Virginia, 1780s] stopped at a lonely house, belonging to an Irishman by the name of Macdonald, where I found eggs, ham, chicken, and whiskey, and where I had an excellent dinner.[5]

[Norfolk, 1796] For board and lodging whilst I was there, they charged one dollar per day, for which they provide you with breakfast and dinner only: if you eat supper, (which here is very seldom done,) you are charged separately for it. Their breakfasts consist of beefsteaks, sausages, stewed veal, fried ham, eggs, coffee and tea, and a dish, or rather a cake, peculiar to the southern states, made out of the meal of Indian corn, and called hoe-cake, of which the inhabitants are very fond. Its taste I do not dislike when buttered and eaten with eggs, though to many it is disagreeable: it is simply a mixture of Indian meal and water, and baked on an iron plate over the fire.[6]

[Western Maryland and Pennsylvania, 1796] Our charges on this part of the road were half a dollar each for breakfast and dinner and supper, without any distinction of fare. If our table were spread with all the profusion of American luxury, such as ham, cold beef, fried chicken, &c. &c. (which are not uncommon for breakfast in this part of the world), or whether we sat down to a dish of tea and hoe-cake, our charge was all the same.[7]

[Western North Carolina 1811] No coffee—other materials for breakfast very good.[8]

[Western Tennessee, 1811] Miserable lodging—this night slept on slab boards & under a dirty Coverlet—nothing but Corn for my horse & Bacon & eggs for supper—Cost 25 cents.[9]

These descriptions lead one to understand the need to pack provisions for a trip. For a gentrified meal on the road boiled or roasted meats and eggs, cheese, boiled or pickled vegetables, fruits, breads, pies, and cakes were among period foods that might travel successfully. Meat and bread were often eaten together but were not referred to as sandwiches.

A loaf filled with cold ingredients seems the ancestor of today's giant party submarine sandwich; with warm ingredients it becomes our trendy bread bowl. Mention of "traveling loaves" has not been found anywhere other than in one 1730 English cookbook, although the idea is too intriguing to leave out of this collection, however atypical.

Travelling Loaves

Take Chickens or Pullets, Pheasants or Partridges or Rabbets, and a Neck of Mutton or Lamb, and roast it off cold, and cut your Fowl in Joints, and your Mutton into Cutlets; take large French Loaves of three Pence apiece, or other Bread; cut a hole in the Top, and scoop out most Part of the Crumb; you may put Fowl into one Loaf, Mutton or Lamb into another, a Salad-Mogundy into another, and slic'd Ham and Tongue into another, putting a little Salt in a Paper with your fresh Meat: And as you travel you may eat any where on the Road in your Coach, carrying some Bottles of Drink likewise; so, in haste, you may eat on the Road without staying by the Way.

C. Carter, *Complete Practical Cook*, 81.

This receipt fuels the imagination. Whether enjoyed on a comfortable rock by a stream, under an arbor in the garden, in a horse drawn coach traveling to Charleston, or tailgating today, sharing a traveling loaf with friends seems a delightful prospect.

✿ Basic Provisions

Certain foodstuffs were considered basic to have on hand in the well stocked larder or for emergency rations when traveling. Shipboard provisions for the first colonies of debtors on the passage to Georgia shed light on basic English diet of the 1730s.

Passengers shall have in every week four beef days, two pork days and one fish day... [also bread, beer and water] with a sufficient quantity of... flour, peas, butter, suet and plums.[10]

The Trustees were so careful of the poor people's health that they put on board turnips, carrots, potatoes and onions which were given out with the salt meat and contributed greatly to prevent the scurvy.[11]

While root vegetables were not the answer to preventing scurvy, they certainly provided nutrition and variety to shipboard meals. Flour and suet or plums (raisins or currants) were to be given out with the beef, peas with the pork, and butter with the fish. One of the settlers on the first voyage verified these combinations, the ordinary meal being beef with suet pudding and when the supply of suet ran short "plums in the room of it." Vinegar and treacle were added to the weekly ration. There were live chickens, hogs, and sheep on board, some for the new colony, some eaten during the trip by the ship's officers and gentry. On Christmas, after prayers and a sermon, all passengers and crew enjoyed mutton, beef broth, and pudding.[12]

Unsatisfactory meals were among the many trials experienced by an Anglican clergyman traveling and preaching in the 1767 South Carolina Upcountry.

> In all these Excursions, I am obliged to carry my own Necessaries with me—As Bisket—Cheese—A Pint of Rum—Some Sugar—Chocolate—Tea, or Coffee—With Cups Knife Spoon Plate Towels and Linen. So that I go alway[s] heavy loaded like a Trooper. If I did not, I should starve.[13]

Supplies thought essential for gentleman travelers give us insight into tastes. Benjamin Franklin saw to the outfitting of twenty British officers with "necessaries and refreshments" appropriate for their march through the wilderness in 1755. Each officer received a parcel containing the following:

> 6 lbs. loaf sugar. 6 lbs. good Muscovado do. [ditto]
> 1 lb. good green tea. 1 lb. good bohea do.
> 6 lbs. good ground coffee. 6 lbs. chocolate
> ½ cwt. best white biscuit
> ½ lb. pepper
> 1 quart best white wine vinegar
> 1 Gloucester cheese
> 1 kegg containing 20 lbs. good butter
> 2 doz. old Madeira wine. 2 gallons Jamaica spirits
> 1 bottle flour of mustard
> 2 well-cured hams. ½ dozen dry'd tongues.
> 6 lbs. rice. 6 lbs. raisins.[14]

Just imagine the very nice meals that might have been prepared by enhancing everyday meats, vegetables, and game animals, with these "necessaries." This list helps us envision a well provisioned household cupboard as well.

✒ Eggs

Eggs were prepared by all the expected methods with a few interesting twists. They were poached, buttered (scrambled), boiled, or fried. Eggs were commonly served to travelers or as a simple meal at home. Regarding fried eggs with "bacon-ham" or sausage Dods noted "But for this homely dish many an honest traveler would go without his dinner." Poached eggs were suggested for floating in soup or serving with poultry or green vegetables. Boiled eggs showed up in expected and unexpected places as seen in sweet egg pie and onion pie. Hard boiled yolks were put into meat pies, often accompanying forcemeat balls, as in giblet and chicken pies. Today's scrambled eggs were then known as *buttered eggs*. A dish of eggs scrambled with asparagus or pokeweed was a welcomed springtime tonic. We might reasonably serve these green buttered eggs on toast or stuffed in a roll as suggested for broccoli in eggs or asparagus in custard sauce.[15]

Those who like eggs softly cooked may enjoy broiled eggs, a clever alternative to poached egg on toast. This tidy method may be used for a single diner, or to prepare a side dish for the table. A large slab of bread would be needed for the six or eight eggs called for in the receipt, a smaller toast would do for a single egg or two.

To Broil Eggs

Cut a Toast round a Quartern Loaf, toast it brown, lay it on your Dish, butter it, and very carefully break six or eight Eggs on the Toast, and take a red-hot Shovel and hold over them. When they are done, squeeze a Seville Orange over them, and grate a little Nutmeg over it, and serve it up for a Side-plate.

Glasse, *Art of Cookery* (1747), 102.

Omelets were varied then as now. From a pre-1744 "Amlett of Eggs," Cleland (1759), and Raffald (1769) to Mary Randolph (1824) and Rutledge (1847) we find a continuing preference for parsley in a simple omelet. Chives or onion, "any kind of sweet herb," clary, and even mint were suggested as well as minced ham, tongue, beef, or anchovy. Asparagus, orange sections, or sprigs of parsley were mentioned as garnishes. Cleland's omelet is characteristic of the period.[16]

To make an Amulet

Get what Quantity of Eggs you think will fill the Dish; season them with Pepper and Salt; ten Eggs will fill a small Dish; shread Parsley and Chives, and beat them and the Eggs with a Gill of Cream very well; then fry them in a Pan of good clarified Butter or Beef-driping on both Sides. You may put in Gravy instead of Cream: You may put cut Slices of Oranges over it in the Dish.

Cleland, *New and Easy Method*, 129.

For a smaller omelet, the proportions are five teaspoonfuls cream to two eggs. The omelet may be turned over as the above receipt recommends or you may hold a hot salamander or fireplace shovel above the pan "to take off the raw look of the eggs."[17]

A spoonful pudding is yet another quick and simple egg dish. One can imagine it as a small supper dish or a meal for child or invalid. Perhaps several individual puddings could embellish a well sauced made dish.

A Spoonful Pudding

Take a Spoonful of Flour, a Spoonful of Cream or Milk, an Egg, a little Nutmeg, Ginger, and Salt, mix all together, and boil it in a little wooden Dish half an hour. You may add a few Currans.

Glasse, *Art of Cookery* (1747), 112.

A small earthenware bowl serves this purpose as well as a wooden dish. The pudding and dish should be tied up tightly in a wet and floured cloth, which is amazingly successful at keeping boiling water away from the contents. The individual sized spoonful pudding is interesting as an experiment or as a manageable little pudding for historical demonstration.

✿ Cheese

All classes of Americans consumed cheese. A wide variety was produced at home, "some tasted pretty well; but most varieties were poor. . . . Some of it could rival the English variety." Cheese was enjoyed with bread, biscuit, or cake and with apples or other fruits for breakfast, supper, and between meals refreshment. On occasion imported cheese was served with the final course of a formal dinner. When cooking with an historical mindset we must remember that cheese was seldom suggested in early English or Scots cookery.[18]

European cookery employed cheese more broadly. "Rasped Parmesan is largely used by Italian and French cooks to flavor ragouts and soups, and many dishes of vegetables. It is seldom employed in our insular [Scottish] cookery."[19]

The Experienced English Housekeeper of 1769 recorded an ancestral macaroni and cheese calling for parmesan. Macaroni and cheese was not a cheap every-day comfort food, but a showy addition to a sophisticated dinner table.[20]

To dress Macaroni with Parmesan Cheese

Boil four ounces of macaroni till it be quite tender and lay it on a sieve to drain. Then put it in a tossing pan with about a gill of good cream, a lump of butter rolled in flour, boil it five minutes. Pour it on a plate, lay all over it parmesan cheese toasted. Send it to the table on a water plate, for it soon goes cold.

Raffald, *Experienced English Housekeeper*, 144.

This dish traveled to America and became more common as the nineteenth-century unfolded. In a simplified Virginia method butter and parmesan cheese were stirred into the macaroni and then baked.[21]

Cheese showed up more commonly in occasional receipts for toasted cheese on bread or a sort of fondue. That popular mid-eighteenth-century author, Hannah Glasse, gave methods for Scotch-Rabbit, Welch-Rabbit, and English-Rabbit—all variations on cheese toast, with or without mustard, some crisp others soaked with red wine. A French cheese toast from the same period was titled *ramequin* rather than *rabbit* or *rarebit*.[22]

To make an English-Rabbit

Toast a Slice of Bread brown on both Sides, then lay it in a Plate before the Fire, pour a Glass of Red Wine over it, and let it soak the Wine up; then cut some Cheese very thin, and lay it very thick over the Bread; put it in a Tin Oven before the Fire, [or hold a hot salamander or fire shovel above the cheese] and it will be toasted and brown presently. Serve it away hot.

Glasse, Art of Cookery (1747), 97.

Ramequin of Cheese

Take some Cheese, melt it with some butter, an onion whole or stamped, salt and pepper in abundance, spread all upon bread, pass the fire-shovell over it red hot, and serve it warm.

La Varenne, French Cook, 91.

Although little used in cookery, cheese was without a doubt part of the eighteenth-century diet and was considered essential to have on hand whenever possible. An itinerant Anglican minister carried cheese in his emergency rations when traveling through the Carolina Backcountry. Benjamin Franklin considered cheese one of the necessities to provide to British officers on a wilderness campaign. A Charlotte innkeeper provided a student traveler with biscuit and cheese to "serve as a repast at Noon." Cheese was an ideal traveling food.[23]

✌ Beverages

Lists of basic provisions give us an idea of beverages. Gentlemen travelers desired a range of liquid refreshments: rum, chocolate, tea, and coffee for traveling in the Carolina back settlements; both green and black tea, coffee, chocolate, wine and rum on a military campaign west from Philadelphia.

> [Pennsylvania, 1747] Tea, coffee, chocolate ... are at present even the country people's daily breakfast.[24]

[Delaware Valley, 1759] Milk and water is the common drink of the people....Tea, coffee, and chocolate are so general as to be found in the most remote cabins, if not for daily use, yet for visitors, mixed with the Muscovado, or raw sugar.[25]

🐌 Cider, Beer, Wine, and Spirits

[Delaware Valley, 1759] Still liquor, brandy made of peaches or apples ... is not regarded as good as rum. Whisky is brandy made of grain. It is used far up in the interior of the country, where rum is very dear on account of the transportation.[26]

Small beer from molasses ... Mead is made of honey and water boiled together, which ferments of itself in the cask.... Table beer made of persimmons.... When these have been well frosted, they are pounded along with their seeds, mixed with wheat-bran, made into large loaves, and baked in the oven. Then, whenever desired, pieces of this are taken and moistened, and with these the drink is brewed.[27]

Apples are ground up in a wooden mill, which is worked by a horse. Then they are placed under a press until the juice is run off, which is then put in a barrel, where it ferments, and after some time becomes clear.[28]

[Virginia, 1773–74] In the Evening the Colonel began with a small Still to distill some Brandy from a Liquor made of Persimmonds.[29]

[Bethabara, North Carolina, 1794] An attempt was made to stop the sale of strong drink in the tavern, and to serve only cold water with meals ... but there would be no objection to serving molasses beer with meals; and travelers on their way to Charleston or New Bern may be offered coffee or milk at breakfast and supper.[30]

[At an ordinary near Halifax, North Carolina, 1782] A bowl of Grog was called for. The fellow came out to us with the half of it in a small pewter basin, and as he was sensible it was too strong, he was prepared with a little gourd full of water. 'Pray sir, why did you not make it in a bowl?'— 'I have none.' 'A mugg?' 'none either' ... Three or four of the inhabitants of the lower class ... were drinking hot Eggnog out of a little gourd.[31]

The various sorts of wines and flavored brandies along with such spirituous mixtures as punches, shrubs, cordials, eggnogs, and grogs require a book of their own. Let us just take a brief look at punches as examples of fashionable refreshment in common use.

Delft Punch Bowl. Holland, 1680–1700. Collection of the Museum of Early
Southern Decorative Arts, Old Salem Museums & Gardens.

[William Byrd, with friends in Williamsburg] After dinner we went to
Colonel Carter's room where we had a bowl of punch of French brandy
and oranges. We talked very lewdly and were almost drunk.
[The following morning] Colonel Carter and several others came to my
lodgings to laugh at me for my disorder last night.
[Two days later Byrd apparently behaved more decorously.] We were
merry till the evening and then we drank a bowl of punch made of
French brandy and oranges which I drank for my cold and ate roast
apples with it.[32]

[Northeastern North Carolina, 1753] A little old mother prepared the
noon meal … punch for us to drink.[33]

[Delaware Valley, 1759] Punch is made of fresh spring-water, sugar,
lemon-juice, and Jamaica spirits [rum]. Instead of lemons, a West India
fruit called limes, or its juice, which is imported in flasks, is used. Punch
is always drunk cold; but sometimes a slice of bread is toasted and placed
in it warm to moderate the cold in winter-time, or it is heated with a red-
hot iron.[34]

George Washington is reported to have had three dishes of tea with his breakfast. His final refreshment of the day, an hour before the setting sun was "one small glass of punch, a draught of beer, and two dishes of tea."[35]

✐ Tea

[Traveling in 1750] Tea ... is differently esteemed by different people, and I think we would be as well, and our purses better, if we were without both tea and coffee. However, I must be impartial, and mention in praise of tea that if it be useful it must certainly be so in summer on such journeys as mine through a vast wilderness, where one cannot carry wine or other liquors and where the water is generally unfit for use, being full of insects. In such cases it is very refreshing when boiled and made into tea, and I cannot sufficiently describe the fine taste it has under such circumstances. It relieves a weary traveler more than can be imagined, as I myself have experienced, and as have also a great many others who have travelled through the primeval forests of America. On such journeys tea is found to be almost as necessary as food.[36]

[Delaware Valley, 1759] Tea is a drink very generally used. No one is so high as to dispise it, nor any one so low as not to think himself worthy of it. It is not drunk oftener than twice a day. It is always drunk by the common people with raw sugar in it. Brandy in tea is called lese.[37]

[Eastern North Carolina, 1785–87] Tea is drunk at breakfast and in the afternoon, although the milk and butter that they take with it are very scarce.[38]

Various wild and cultivated herbs were substituted for tea. Some were considered medicinal. Others filled the need when imported Asian tea was in short supply or as a political statement preceding and during the American Revolution. Yaupon (a small-leafed shrub of the holly family) yielded a popular tea.

[Virginia, 1728] Carolina-Tea calld Japon [yaupon] ... This is an Evergreen, the Leaves whereof have some resembalance [*sic*] to Tea, but differ very widely both in Tast and Flavour.[39]

[Traveling along the eastern seaboard, 1783–1784] Careful housekeepers have the leaves [yaupon], which may be gathered at any season of the year, culled out in a cleanly way, and dried in an iron kettle over a slow fire; they pound them a little in a mortar, so as to keep them the better in glass bottles, but before putting them up they let them evaporate a while in the air.... It is claimed here that at one time this Japan-tea began to be much liked in England ... but importing was forbidden, lest the sale

Teatime Finished. By Teresa Myers Armour, courtesy of the Schiele Museum.

of the Chinese tea should be diminished. All the good qualities of this tea, praised as they are, cannot however prevent the sickliness of the inhabitants.[40]

The ceremony attached to sharing tea or coffee in stylish company seemed to have puzzled newcomers, whether from France or a Backcountry settlement. Was this a common experience or a widespread legend?

[Traveling in 1793–98] Evening tea is a boring and monotonous ceremony. The mistress of the house serves it and passes it around, and as long as a person has not turned his cup upside down and placed his spoon upon it, just so often will he be brought another cup. You hear a thousand true and false accounts of Frenchmen who, in their ignorance of this peculiar custom, have been so inundated by tea that they have suffered intensely.[41]

One backcountry settler described the same befuddlement upon going to town as a young man and encountering coffee for the first time, finding it "nauseous beyond anything I ever had tasted in my life."

[Backcountry Virginia or Pennsylvania, c. 1760s] I well recollect the first time I ever saw a tea cup and saucer and tasted coffee.... I continued to drink, as the rest of the company did, with the tears streaming from my eyes, but when it was to end I was at a loss to know, as the little cups were filled immediately after being emptied. This circumstance distressed me very much, as I durst say I had enough. Looking attentively at the grown persons, I saw one man turn his little cup bottom upwards and put his little spoon across it. I observed that after this his cup was not filled again. I followed his example, and to my great satisfaction the result as to my cup was the same.[42]

That fellow (Joseph Doddridge) later declared "A genuine backwoodsman would have thought himself disgraced by showing a fondness of those slops [tea and coffee]."

♨ Coffee

Although some backwoodsmen had an aversion to this popular beverage, coffee seems to have been ordinary with such diverse groups as gentry, tradesmen, farmers, students, travelers, and soldiers, as was tea. In his later years (c.1739–41) Virginian William Byrd had only tea or coffee for breakfast most days when at home. (As a younger man he started his day with milk.)

[Delaware Valley, 1759] Coffee ... is sold in large quantities, and used for breakfast.[43]

[Virginia, 1773–74] We have omitted Supper, & in its place substituted Coffee which we commonly take about seven in the evening[44]

♨ Chocolate

Chocolate also seems to have been widely available, but used a bit differently than tea and coffee. Chocolate was considered as much food as drink. Surviving records documented all sorts of early Americans having chocolate for breakfast, supper, or refreshment between meals.

[Mid-morning refreshment, Virginia, 1728] We drank our Chocolate at one Jones's.[45]

[North Carolina backcountry, 1754] I treated the Brethren with Chocolate, which I had got to use upon my journey.[46]

[Delaware Valley, 1759] Chocolate is in general use for breakfast and supper. It is drunk with a spoon. Sometimes prepared with a little milk, but mostly only with water.[47]

[Tidewater Virginia, 1774] Sup'd on chocolate, & hoe-Cake.[48]

[Salem, North Carolina, 1781] As we are to have a visit from the Assembly the necessary preparations should be made, for example the potter should make a quantity of chocolate cups, bowls, and plates, and we should provide knives and forks.[49]

Although William Byrd's customary breakfast was milk, he served chocolate to guests. On occasion he enjoyed chocolate himself at breakfast or in mid-morning. Before setting out upon a journey William Byrd started his day with up to three dishes of chocolate. Once he drank four cups of chocolate when breakfasting with the governor from Carolina. When visiting Colonel Will Randolph in December 1709, Byrd shared two particularly curious breakfasts: sausage and chocolate, and on the following day, pickled oysters with chocolate. A century later Maria Rundell noted that chocolate "if not made thick, is a very good breakfast or supper."[50]

From the 1771 *Encyclopaedia Britannica* we learn that chocolate was available as "a kind of paste, or cake" but also as the *cacao-nut*. Both forms were offered for sale in American ports. Hannah Glasse's *Art of Cookery Made Plain and Easy* included an involved method for processing the raw cacao bean or nut. An early Virginian penned straightforward directions:[51]

Chocolate to make up

You must wash the Nuts very clean, the rost then to get the huls off, then roul them on the stone till tis a fine past. yu must mix a few of the best huls with it, to make it froth.

Jane Randolph 1743, Harbury, *Virginia's Cooking Dynasty*, 402.

Another Way to make Chocolate

Take six pounds of the best Spanish nuts, when parched and cleaned from the hulls, take three pounds of sugar, two ounces of the best cinnamon, beaten and sifted very fine, to every two pounds of [chocolate] nuts put in three good vanillas, or more or less as you please; to every pound of nuts half a drachm of cardamum seeds, very finely beaten and searced.

Glasse, *Art of Cookery* (1796), 342.

The 1771 *Encyclopaedia Britannica* offered opinion on proper accent flavorings for chocolate. The Spaniards were thought to mix in "too great a quantity of cloves and cinnamon besides other drugs without number, as musk, ambergris, &c." The French, on the other hand, used few of these ingredients but only a small quantity of sugar, vanilla, or cinnamon. "Among us in England, the chocolate is made of the simple cacao excepting that sometimes vanilla, and sometimes sugar is added." Apparently others in England followed the Spanish seasonings. Hannah Glasse's cookbook included a complicated method suggesting a choice from many exotic ingredients—not only the popular sugar, cinnamon, and vanilla, but also anise, pepper, achiote, musk, ambergris, nutmeg, orange-flower water, rose water, almonds, or pistachios.[52]

Today's processed chocolate from Central and South America may be similar to the eighteenth-century product. Check your local Latino *tienda* or international supermarket for plain block chocolate for beverages as well as sweetened and spiced versions. Although we think of hot chocolate and cocoa prepared in milk, our ancestors ordinarily boiled their chocolate in water. Expect a totally different hot chocolate. Unsweetened chocolate prepared in water with just a little cream or milk, more like coffee than cocoa, is a nice little pick me up in either century. Milk and wine were also employed as bases for chocolate beverages.

To Make Chocolate

Scrape four ounces of chocolate and pour a quart of boiling water upon it, mill it well with a chocolate mill and sweeten it to your taste. Give it a boil and let it stand all night, then mill it again very well. Boil it two minutes, then mill it till it will leave a froth upon the top of your cups.

Raffald, Experienced English Housekeeper, 163.

Others directed to drink right away; however, standing overnight may develop deeper flavor. Chocolate was "milled" with a whisk or by repeatedly pouring from one container to another. We surmise that some eighteenth-century cooks had a specific tool for milling chocolate. According to one 1765 cookery book "The best method . . . of whipping any Syllabubs, is to have ready by you a large Chocolate Mill which should be reserved for that particular Purpose." The charmingly carved wooden chocolate mills or *molenillos* available today in Latino markets may well be little changed from mills in use centuries ago.[53]

And speaking of Syllabub . . . I must digress. Syllabub may be the most delectable period concoction we have ever tried. No, not the basic syllabub prepared by milking the cow directly into a bowl of sweetened and spiced wine, ale, or cider, but the Solid or Everlasting Syllabub. An excellent receipt was discovered in a lowcountry South Carolina manuscript. Syllabub is now required by my family at Thanksgiving and Christmas. It is also outrageously good alongside fresh fruits in the summer.[54]

Solid Syllabub

Take a pint of thick Cream & three quarters of a pound of sugar & half a pint of mountain Wine with the juice of two Lemons & the peel of one grated in mix them together & beat it one way till the whisk will stand upright they will keep a fortnight in a cool place from flies.

South Carolina household book.

Solid Syllabub (Interpretation and advice)

    2 cups heavy cream
    1 ½ cups sugar
    1 cup wine (white or red)
    Juice of 2 lemons; grated peel of one (or both)

Beat with whisk (or chocolate mill) until it begins to thicken. (It may not thicken enough for the whisk to "stand upright" at this stage, but will thicken more as it sets.)

Pour the syllabub into your prettiest small stemmed glasses.

Allow to stand for two or three days in "a cool place" (refrigerator) before serving, so that the syllabub divides into two layers—a lovely lemony mousse on top of a delicious sip of sweet wine. (A "fortnight" seems too long for safe keeping.)

✍ Now, Back to Chocolate

Although chocolate was primarily enjoyed as a beverage, there were a rare handful of other options. Wolley in 1672 directed grating chocolate into claret wine, egg yolks, and sugar and heating until thick for "Chaculato." Other interesting chocolate preparations included early Virginia methods for "Chocolate Almonds" and "Chocolate Puffs" (meringues). Raffald also gave a receipt for "Chocolate Puffs." There was even an unusual "Chocolate Tort" with an almond crust. Chocolate "creams" took the form of whipped cream or thin custard.[55]

Chocolate Cream

Take a pt. of cream with a spoonfull of chrapt [scraped or grated] chocolate boyle them well together mix with it ye yolks of 2 eggs & thicken & mill it on ye fire then pour it into yor. chocolate cups.

> Unidentified cookbook, c.1700, Harbury, *Virginia's Cooking Dynasty*, 278.

Similar receipts called for sweetening and flavorings. The lump or block of processed chocolate available to the c.1700 Virginia cook may have contained sugar and vanilla or cinnamon to flavor her chocolate cream. You are likely to also enjoy the tradition of toasts or "chocolate cakes" with your chocolate.

It seems odd that "Chocolate Cakes" did not contain chocolate until one remembers that coffee cakes do not contain coffee, nor is there tea in tea cakes. These little pastry strips were baked to be served with chocolate. Bread or toast continues to be served along with chocolate today in countries where cacao originates. On an occasion with guests at Westover, William Byrd noted having chocolate and cake for breakfast. What sort of cake might that have been? There may have been seed cake or plum cake or any sort of small cakes on hand. Or did Byrd's guests enjoy special cakes for eating with chocolate? Mary Randolph's chocolate cakes are an enjoyable touch. *The Kentucky Housewife* called for only half as much brown sugar in a similar receipt.[56]

Chocolate Cakes

Put half a pound of nice brown sugar into a quart of flour, sift it and make it into a paste with four ounces of butter melted in as much milk as will wet it; knead it till light, roll it tolerably thin, cut it in strips an inch wide, and just long enough to lay in a plate; bake then on a griddle, put them in the plate in rows to checker each other and serve them to eat with chocolate.

M. Randolph, Virginia Housewife, 173.

About one cup of milk wets this dough. Cook the cakes on a griddle as Randolph directs or in an oven as per Bryan. Either method works. These cakes, dunked into your cup of chocolate, are pleasant indeed.

✒ Seasonings from the Garden

Flower Waters and Brandies

The ubiquitous floral flavorings, rose water and orange flower water, were a signature of early recipes. Puddings and cakes were typically fragrant with these waters in the places we might use vanilla today. Floral waters are absolutely enchanting when used sparingly but rather overpowering when added with too heavy a hand. Experience will guide you in their proper use and educate your taste buds.

Flower waters may now be purchased from specialty or ethnic food sources. Some are mixed from synthetic essences; so look for the natural distilled flower waters. Be aware that these vary significantly in quality and strength. As for the strength, your nose will guide you in using more or less of a given batch of rose or orange flower water. Our ancestors may have purchased these waters or distilled them at home.

Eighteenth-century English cookery books included basic directions for distilling roses as well as other herbs. Since these flavorings are manufactured by distillation, we are unlikely to be equipped to produce flower waters in our kitchens. On the other hand rose brandy is a lovely variation that you can easily create at home.[57]

Rose Brandy

Gather leaves [petals] from fragrant roses without bruising, fill a pitcher with them, and cover them with French brandy; next day, pour off the brandy, take out the leaves, and fill the pitcher with fresh ones, and return the brandy; do this till it is strongly impregnated, then bottle it; keep the pitcher closely covered during the process. It is better than distilled rose water for cakes, &c.

M. Randolph, Virginia Housewife, 214.

Storage Jars. By Teresa Myers Armour, courtesy of
the Schiele Museum.

Of course rose brandy is best made with the most fragrant roses. Avoid roses
that have been sprayed with pesticide. Repeat the extraction three or four
times or until the brandy has acquired a strong rose scent. A jar is preferable
to Mary Randolph's pitcher for keeping the brandy tightly covered during extraction and storage. Similar directions for rose brandy were offered by Lettice
Bryan with her special touches.[58]

Mary Randolph was correct: Rose Brandy is indeed better than distilled
rose water. Being a milder flavoring, it is less likely to overwhelm a dish. Since
many receipts call for brandy or wine along with rose water, rose brandy can
fill both needs.

Besides mixing rose brandy directly into a batter, try soaking currants or
raisins in the brandy before adding to your cake. Lovely! Rose brandy can find
regular use in today's kitchen as well as in re-creating dishes from the past.

Another brandy infusion well known to our ancestors, *ratafia*, drew its flavor from fruit kernels, traditionally from bitter almonds. Other, more widely
available fruits entered into ratafias to be employed as flavoring for cakes
or puddings as well as for a cordial. Peach or apricot kernels or cherry pulp

and seeds were recommended; or, according to *The Kentucky Housewife* even the small black wild cherries might be used for ratafia. Diverse ingredients contributed interesting complementary flavors: orange flower or rose water, lemon, nutmeg, cinnamon, or cloves. The following 1810 receipt provides basic instructions.[59]

Ratafia

Blanch two ounces of peach and apricot kernels, bruise, and put them into a bottle, and fill nearly up with brandy. Dissolve half a pound of white sugar-candy in a cup of cold water, and add to the brandy after it has stood a month on the kernels, and they are strained off; then filter through paper, and bottle for use.

Rundell, *New System of Domestic Cookery*, 256.

Not only brandy, but also vinegars and wines were infused with flowers or herbs. These extracts and infusions are convenient liquid flavorings today as well.

Flavored Vinegars and Wines

These are a cheap and agreeable addition to sauces, hashes, and ragouts, and have the convenience of being always at hand, at seasons when herbs are either very costly or not to be procured.

Dods, *Cook and Housewife's Manual*, 256.

Herbed and spiced vinegars and wines were enjoyed as condiments and in receipts as well. These infusions preserve fresh herb flavors more successfully than dried herbs. The tarragon vinegar receipt below provides basic directions for a variety of flavored infusions.

Taragon Vinegar

To a quart of the best white wine vinegar take a small handful of Taragon, stalks and altogether, twist the stalks well with your hands that the vinegar may get out all the strength of the Taragon the quicker, put the Taragon in an earthen jug or pan and pour the vinegar upon it, let it stand to infuse for 24 hours, then you may try if it's strong enough for your tast, if not, stir it up and let it stand longer, or add more Taragon as you think proper, then strain it from the Taragon thro' a fine linnen cloth and bottle it; it will keep as long as you please.

Raper, *Receipt Book*, 60–61.

Interesting garden stuffs for infusing vinegars include roses, gilliflowers (pinks, dianthus), and peppers. *The Virginia Housewife* suggested celery seeds, thyme leaves, or mint with specific directions for preparing each:[60]

Celery Vinegar [also Thyme or Mint, Vinegar or Brandy]

Pound two gills of celery seed, put it into a bottle, and fill it with strong vinegar; shake it every day for a fortnight, then strain it and keep it for use. It will impart a pleasant flavor of celery to any thing with which it is used.

A very delicious flavor of thyme may be obtained, by gathering it when in full perfection; it must be picked from the stalks; a large handful of it put into a jar, and a quart of vinegar or brandy poured on it, cover it very close, next day take all the thyme out, put in as much more, do this a third time, then strain it . . . Mint may be prepared in the same way.   M. Randolph, *Virginia Housewife*, 114–15.

These methods were applicable to many seed and herb vinegars or brandies. Leaves were to be freshly gathered as were most blossoms, such as roses or violets. On the other hand, elder flowers were first dried.

Elderflower Vinegar

In this Month [May] gather Elder-Flowers when they are dry, and pick them from the Stalks; let them dry in the Shade, and then put an Ounce to each Quart of White-Wine Vinegar, to stand in the Vinegar for two Months, then pour the Vinegar from them for use.   Bradley, *Country Housewife*, I: 96–97.

Elizabeth Raffald gave instruction for serving such condiments: "It [elder-flower vinegar] makes a pretty mixture on a side table with tarragon vinegar, lemon pickle, etc." She suggested alegar (malt vinegar) instead of the white wine vinegar. Both types of vinegar work well and produce delicately flavored condiments. Raffald cautioned: "be careful that you don't let any [elder] stalks in."[61]

Elder buds and shoots were pickled. Additionally, elderflowers were used with raisins or sugar to make wine. The berries of the elder were also employed in winemaking.[62]

Our ancestors were fond of assertive condiments of cayenne, shallot, or horseradish. New World peppers were enthusiastically adopted by newcomers to America and in European kitchens. This spice entered cookery books under cayenne, capsicum, long pepper, or an assortment of other names. Peter Kalm noted: "the fruit itself is as sharp as common pepper." Red peppers were widely included in eighteenth-century American gardens:[63]

Capsicum annuum or Guinea pepper is likewise planted in gardens. When the fruit is ripe it is almost red; it is added to a roasted or boiled piece of meat, a little of it being strewed upon it or mixed with the broth. Besides this, cucumbers are pickled with it, or the pods are pounded while they are yet tender, and being mixed with salt are preserved in a bottle.

Kalm, *Travels*, I: 42.

Pepper vinegar

Infuse a hundred red chilies, fresh gathered, in a quart of the best white-wine vinegar for ten days or more, shaking the bottle occasionally.

Dods, *Cook and Housewife's Manual*, 256.

That Scots cook, Meg Dods added, "This makes an excellent and cheap addition to plain melted butter for fish sauce, &c." I would add, not only excellent and cheap, but an easily made sauce. Other flavored vinegars were used similarly in sauces for vegetables and fowl as well as fish. Try other favorites, chopped shallots or horseradish, to flavor vinegars . . . or wines.

To capture stronger flavor, herbs were infused in wine. Any wine meant for sauces or gravies may be infused with appropriate flavors. Sherry with shallots and horseradish was suggested for seasoning beef.

Eschalot [shallot] wine

To four ounces of eschalots dried, chopped and pounded, or merely bruised, put a bottle of sherry. Infuse for a fortnight and strain it off. If for beef only, horseradish sliced may be added, or rather substituted for part of the eschalots.

Dods, *Cook and Housewife's Manual*, 258.

✍ Ketchup, Catsup

The handiest instant seasonings were the ketchups, but not yet tomato ketchup. Tomatoes did not enter such sauces until the end of the eighteenth century and did not become common for another quarter century. The most common early ketchup was of mushrooms. Others were based on immature English walnuts, anchovies or other fish.[64]

We find mushroom ketchup little changed from Glasse's 1747 English method to the simplified directions in *The Carolina Housewife* of 1847. During the century between those two sources Harriot Pinckney Horry copied her mother's ketchup receipt into her own cookery book. Although most mushroom ketchups are similar in composition, the order of preparation varies. Horry's is nicely straightforward.[65]

Mushroom Catchup and Powder

Gather your Mushrooms early in the Morning, wipe them very clean with a Woolen cloth, then mash them with the hand, strew on them a handful of salt, let them lie all night, then put them on the fire ten minutes, keeping them constantly stiring, then squeeze them through a Canvas, and let them settle. Pour it off from the sediment then put it on the fire and clarify it with the whites of 2 Eggs [optional]. Then put in it whole Pepper, Cloves, Mace, Ginger, Allspice and Salt. It must be high season'd. Boil one part [half] of it away, when cold bottle it putting in the Spices.

[Mushroom Powder] Take 4 lb. Mushrooms that have been squeez'd; and dry them with a little spice in the Sun or Oven, and Powder them for Made Dishes.

Horry, *Colonial Plantation Cookbook*, 84.

Few authors bothered with the clarifying step. If you are fine with cloudy ketchup, as we are, and apparently many early cooks were, you may omit the egg whites. Alternate combinations of spices involved pepper, Jamaica pepper (allspice), cayenne, ginger, mace, nutmeg, and cloves. Some ketchups contained vinegar, wine, or stale beer for tartness. Spicy mushroom powder was a convenient instant seasoning, as was the ketchup.[66]

Dry mixtures of spices or herbs have a long history. "French cooks keep their seasonings mixed, and even pounded together, not from convenience, but to blend the flavours intimately: much may be said for this practice."[67]

These convenient blends were known as *kitchen pepper, cook's pepper,* or *fine herbs.* Harriott Horry suggested a kitchen pepper of ginger, pepper, cinnamon, cloves, and nutmeg. A Scots version was identical but for the addition of Jamaica pepper (allspice). Another, for white sauces, was of white pepper, nutmeg, mace, and grated lemon peel, perhaps with ginger and cayenne. Horry mixed salt into her kitchen pepper, Dods did not. Dods' herb mixture combined dried parsley, lemon thyme, winter savory, sweet marjoram, basil, and lemon peel. You may wish to assemble a personal combination of spices or herbs, reflecting both your particular tastes and an historical touch.[68]

✺ Pickling

Always use Stone jars for all Sorts of Pickles that require hot Pickle, for Vinegar and Salt will penetrate through all earthen Vessels . . . Let your Brass Pan for any Pickles be very bright and clean, and your Pan for white Pickles well tinned: Use the very best Vinegar, and when they are in the Jars, and cold, melt Sewet [suet], and when it is as cold that it will but just pour on them, put it over them, then cover them with wet Bladders.

Cleland, *New and Easy Method*, 165.

Cleland's advice is sound whether working with hot or cold pickle. A tin lined pot is best when heating acid or salt solutions. Earthenware deteriorates with extended exposure to pickling liquid. When it begins to leak both pickle and earthenware jar will be ruined.

A wet bladder does perform rather like modern plastic wrap, but we have found insects and other vermin will attack it. Some authors advised tying a leather cover over the bladder.

The Carolina Housewife left us a general cold pickling method reflecting the previous century. You will find some receipts direct a similar solution poured on hot, especially on those pickles meant for longer keeping.

Universal Pickle

To six quarts of vinegar, one pound of salt, a quarter of a pound of ginger, one ounce of mace, half a pound of shalots; one table-spoonful of cayenne pepper, two ounces of white pepper, two ounces of mustard seed; boil these with the vinegar, and when cold, put it into a jar; you may put in whatever green fruit or vegetables you please, fresh gathered from time to time, only wiping off the dust. If you put in carrots, they should be half boiled. [Cauliflower and green beans were among other vegetables boiled prior to pickling.]

Rutledge, Carolina Housewife, 183–84.

The piquant seed pods of nasturtiums and of radishes were enjoyed raw and pickled. Cookery books commonly included receipts for pickling both pods. According to *The Country Housewife's Family Companion* nasturtium pods "correct" cooling foods, such as cucumbers, making them more wholesome.[69]

Popular English authors gave comparable methods for nasturtium seed pods. Most advised three days in brine before going into the vinegar. Some directed boiling the salt water or the vinegar.[70]

To pickle Nasturtiums

Gather the nasturtium berries soon after the blossoms are gone off, put them in cold salt and water, change the water once a day for three days. Make your pickle of white wine vinegar, mace, nutmeg sliced, peppercorns, salt, shallots and horse-radish. It requires to be made pretty strong as your pickle is not to be boiled. When you have drained them put them into a jar and pour the pickle over them.

Raffald, Experienced English Housekeeper, 182.

Sliced or quartered nutmeg cropped up routinely in all sorts of period receipts. While slicing a cold nutmeg is difficult, when heated (by the fire or in boiling water) the nutmeg slices easily.

The English *Country Housewife* proposed flavoring the vinegar with mace, ginger and bay leaves for pickling nasturtium pods. As usual, *The Frugal Colonial Housewife* simplified recipes for the colonies. She omitted the soaking in salt water, instead directed putting the seed pods straight into white wine vinegar "with what spice you please." The German traveler, von Rumohr, noted "Nasturtium flowers can be pickled in vinegar and used like capers." [71]

A taste for pickled nasturtium seeds remained in vogue. *The Virginia Housewife* included a receipt much akin to Raffald's but flavored with only mace and pepper. *The Kentucky Housewife* in 1839 described both their preparation and use in a sauce. Her pickling method involved simply packing tender nasturtium pods in a jar of plain cold vinegar. The sauce certainly followed earlier tradition. Stewed mutton dishes typically called for capers, so it was not surprising to find a nasturtium seed sauce for mutton. [72]

Nasturtian [*sic*] Sauce

Having drawn your butter in the usual manner, make it as thick as you desire it with pickled nasturtian seeds, add a little of the vinegar in which they were pickled, a small portion of pepper, and serve it warm. It is a fine sauce for boiled mutton.

Bryan, *Kentucky Housewife*, 167.

Pickled nasturtium pods could substitute for capers while pickled radish pods were recommended for garnishing meats. Young radish seed pods should be cut in bunches or gathered singly as soon as fully formed. Both English and American authors proposed the same method for pickling the pods. From Glasse we received good guidance for preparing the brine: "Make a strong pickle, with cold spring-water and bay-salt, strong enough to bear an egg, then put your pods in." [73]

To pickle Radish-Pods

Gather your radish pods when they are quite young and put them in salt and water all night. Then boil the salt and water they were laid in, and pour it upon your pods and cover your jars close to keep in the steam. When it grows cold, make it boiling hot, and pour it on again. Keep doing so till your pods are quite green, then put them on a sieve to drain, and make a pickle for them of white wine vinegar with a little mace, ginger, long pepper, and horseradish. Pour it boiling hot upon your pods. When it is almost cold, make your vinegar twice hot as before and pour it upon them, and tie them down with a bladder.

Raffald, *Experienced English Housekeeper*, 182.

In the first half of the nineteenth century *The Virginia Housewife* and *The Kentucky Housewife* added turmeric to the above pickling mix along with a little sweet oil (olive oil) "which will impart to the pickles rather a resplendent appearance." Such pods would indeed be "very pretty for garnishing meats." [74]

"The best things to give a sauce tartness are mushroom-pickle, white walnut-pickle, elder-vinegar, lemon-juice, or lemon-pickle." A c.1799 Baltimore manuscript included Lemon Pickle straight from published English sources. A lowcountry South Carolina manuscript offered a basic method: [75]

Lemon Pickle Mrs Rose

Take the Lemons quarter but do not separate them stuff them full of Salt put them on a board to dry in the sun or in an oven when the great heat is off they will take long time in drying & must be very dry before the pickle is put to them—Boil the vinegar at least a sufficient quantity to cover the Lemons & let it be cold before you put it to the Lemons [strongly season vinegar with mustard seed, India pepper, garlic, ginger] . . . when you judge the full virtue out of the Lemon strain off the Liquor & bottle it this is excellent to put in to most Sauces.

South Carolina household book.

English cookery books gave more details. Two dozen lemons and half a pound of salt in two quarts of white wine vinegar was spiced with "one ounce of mace, half an ounce of cloves beat fine, one ounce of nutmegs cut in thin slices, four ounces of garlic peeled, half a pint of mustard seed bruised a little and tied in a muslin bag" in identical receipts from Raffald and Glasse. [76]

During the nineteenth century a greatly simplified method was circulated. *The Southern Gardner and Receipt-Book* of 1859 directed simply "Slice six lemons; rub them with salt," dispensing with the drying before packing into a jar. Typical spices with optional garlic or shallots were added and hot vinegar poured over all. After only two days standing the liquid was to be strained and ready for use. Rundell's (1810) method produces a similar but more concentrated sauce. [77]

Lemon Pickle

Wipe six lemons, cut each into eight pieces; put on them a pound of salt, six large cloves of garlick, two ounces of horse-radish, sliced thin, likewise of cloves, mace, nutmeg, and Cayenne, a quarter of an ounce each, and two ounces of flour of mustard; to these put two quarts of vinegar. Boil a quarter of an hour in a will-tinned sauce-pan; or which is better, do it in a strong jar, in a kettle of boiling water: or set the jar on the hot hearth till done. Set the jar by, and stir it daily for six weeks; keep the jar close covered. Put it into small bottles.

Rundell, *New System of Domestic Cookery*, 178.

The uses were extensive. "It may be put in any white sauce and will not hurt the colour. It is very good for fish sauce and made dishes, a teaspoonful is enough for white, and two for brown sauce for a fowl. It is a most useful pickle and gives a pleasant flavor. Be sure you put it in before you thicken the sauce, or put any cream in, lest the sharpness makes it curdle." Some authors used the pickled lemon as well as the liquid. A chicken was larded with preserved lemon in "To boile a Capon larded with Lemons." In other words, slivers of pickled lemon were stuffed into slits in the bird. The broth was seasoned with white wine, herbs, mace, and verjuice (juice of unripe fruits). A little of the liquid from the lemon pickle might fill the place of spice and verjuice. Lemon pickle (the lemon itself or the liquid sauce) was called for in such varied dishes as "Egg Pie" and a sauce "To barbecue a Leg of Pork."[78]

Many savory dishes calling for lemon peel will benefit from preserved lemon. Considering the intermittent availability of fresh lemons in centuries past, historical cooks may have routinely substituted preserved lemon. This interesting condiment may become one of your new favorite touches.

𝒔 Sweetmeats

Conserves

Dry conserves (flavored sugars) were made from blossoms of roses, violets, lavender, borage, rosemary, gilliflowers (pinks), betony, sage, marjoram, and more. Seville orange rind was pounded with double the weight in sugar for "Conserve of Orainges." Proportions varied from equal weight sugar and herb to three times as much sugar as in the receipts below. Conserves were considered medicines as well as sweetmeats.[79]

To Make Consarve of Lavinder flowers mb

Take the flowers being new gathred as many as you Please and beat them very fine take three times their Wheight of white Sugar putt in a little at a time and Beat it till it is all in then put it in your potts Stir it some times else it will Spoyle.

Unidentified cookbook, c.1700, Harbury,
Virginia's Cooking Dynasty, 196.

To make Conserve of Red Roses

Take their Buds and clip off the Whites, then take three times their weight in Sugar double refin'd; beat the Roses well in a Mortar, then put in the Sugar by little and little, and when you find it well incorporated, put it into Gally-pots, and cover it with Sugar, and so it will keep seven years.

Wolley, *Queen-like Closet*, 39.

Wet conserves were closely related to preserves and marmalades. Receipts abounded for spreadable fruits and floral syrups. Cherry and raspberry receipts were especially numerous.

☙ Preserved Fruits

Cherries were cherished fruits, then as now. William Byrd wrote of gorging on cherries in season, as on May twelfth (1711) when he ate cherries midday and again in late afternoon. On one particular morning Byrd noted enjoying cherries with wine. They were also served with afternoon tea. He and his wife were fond of eating cherries straight from the trees when walking in their garden.

One November Byrd and his wife "had some cherries which had been scalded in hot water which did not boil and then [put] in bottles without water in them they were exceedingly good." In a 1743 Virginia cookery manuscript we discovered a related method for attempting to keep cherries until winter. This poses an interesting experiment for the more patient and curious cooks among us.[80]

Mrs. Lanhorns way to Bottle Cherrys

Fill the Bottles, cork, & lash them down [with?] Pack thread, then put them in a Kettle [of] cold Water, & let them stand till they be[gin?] to simmer, then take them off & let them stand till the Water is cold, then Rosin the Corks, & put them in a Cellar.

Jane Randolph 1743, Harbury, *Virginia's Cooking Dynasty*, 414.

The Randolphs and other Virginians must have enjoyed cherries as much as the Byrds, judging by multiple receipts for preserving cherries in sugar syrup. These preserves were packed into ceramic jars with paper tied over the tops.[81]

Morello Cherries

Take out the stones with a quill over a deep dish, to save the juice that runs from them; put to the juice, a pound of sugar for each pound of cherries, weighed after they are stoned; boil and skim the syrup, then put in the fruit and stew till quite clear.

M. Randolph, *Virginia Housewife*, 197.

One patient researcher found stoning cherries with a quill tedious, but possible. The careful Scot, Mistress Dods directed, "take out the stones with a silver toothpick or bodkin as gently as possible; or if this be too troublesome, prick the fruit with a needle." Having no silver toothpick or bodkin at hand, simply leaving the stone in and pricking cherries with a needle worked well. When leaving the stone, the stem was customarily clipped in half.[82]

Mary Randolph's preserved cherries can be seen as a family heirloom from the previous century. Jane Randolph's 1743 manuscript included three similar receipts and the related Unidentified Cookbook c. 1700 gave methods "To Preserve Cherrys with out Stone" and "To Preserve Cherrys with Stones."[83]

Old world receipts frequently combined cherries with currant jelly but were otherwise similar to the Virginia and Carolina methods. In comparative trials, with and without currant jelly, little difference was noted. Lower South climates are not ideal for currants.[84]

There were many, many other methods for preserving or drying cherries. Preserving in brandy rather than sugar syrup is an interesting variation.

Cherries were commonly used to flavor brandy. Hannah Glasse proposed preserving cherries in sweetened brandy, with the cherries themselves as the product. Brandied cherries are festive and pretty for garnishing a cake or pudding. Their flavor is nice; however, beware, these cherries are heady. As a bonus the brandy remaining in the jar is wonderful for mixing into puddings, pastries, or cakes.[85]

To preserve Cherries in Brandy

Cut the stalks half off, put them in a jar. And fill them up with brandy sweetened to your taste with sugar candy, pour in a little currant jelly, dissolved [melted], at the top, and tie them down for use.

Glasse, *Art of Cookery* (1796), 357.

This receipt continued in popularity. In Rundell's similar receipt the cherries were first pricked with a needle. The sugar (three-quarters the weight of cherries) was sprinkled over cherries in the jar before filling with brandy. Raffald gave similar instructions for preserving bunches of grapes "not too ripe" with sugar in brandy, adding that cherries were done the same way. "Tie it close down with a bladder."[86]

Raspberries seem to have been nearly as beloved as cherries. In some locales, blackberries filled the same niche. We found multiple receipts for raspberry

English Wine Bottle Chronology. This collection illustrates the entire range of styles from mid-17th century to late 18th century, dated from left to right c. 1650, c. 1680, 1695, 1718, 1723, 1752, 1772, 1780, 1795. Collection of the Museum of Early Southern Decorative Arts, Old Salem Museums & Gardens.

preserves, jam, or jelly in historical cookbooks and personal manuscripts. The proportion below, three-fourths cup sugar to one pound fruit, was typical although Harriott Horry and an early eighteenth-century Virginian recommended equal weights raspberries and sugar. Reminder: powdered sugar does not refer to confectioners sugar, but to loaf sugar beaten to a powder. Granulated sugar is a reasonable choice from today's standard options.[87]

Rasberry Jam

Take a pound of fruit to three quarters of a pound of best powdered sugar strew the sugar over the fruit and put a very little water just to assist in dissolving the sugar then let it boil slowly over the fire till the fruit and syrup jellies which you must try very frequently when you think they are nearly done.

Stockton receipt book, 56.

The receipt is so simple one wonders why early cooks felt it necessary to record. On the other hand, the technique of cooking sugared fruit just to the jelling point is not so simple without a thermometer. Skill at judging the jelling point is nearly lost to present generations. Look to whatever basic cookbook you rely on today (such as my tattered *Joy of Cooking*) to provide advice on testing jams and jellies.

Jams and preserves and marmalades were made from blackberries, strawberries, cherries, peaches, pears, and other fruits using the same method as for raspberry jam. Prepare these fruit preserves in a copper, brass, or tin lined pot. Iron discolors these sweetmeats.

✍ Frosted Fruits

We have long enjoyed frosting grapes with egg white and sugar to use as garnish. American manuscripts included methods for frosting currants and even currant leaves or boxwood (not edible) "to ornament your dishes." From 1733 England we learned that "all Sorts of small Fruit" were considered appropriate to frost. The frosted fruits were spread out in a warm, dry place for the crust to harden. They should be prepared a day or so ahead to allow time to dry. Dods gave a Scots method for delightful tidbits to add to a party table or as a garnish during fresh cherry season:[88]

Cherries in chemise, a very pretty little dish

Take the largest ripe cherries you can get. Cut off the stalks with scissors, leaving about an inch to each cherry. Beat the white of an egg to a froth, and roll them in it one by one, and then roll them lightly in sifted sugar. . . . The same may be done with currants, strawberries.

Dods, *Cook and Housewife's Manual*, 438–39.

And there, you have it—the final touch, the cherry on top.

Afterword

This curious collection of historical recipes is a rich inheritance, although admittedly opinionated and arbitrary. Miscellanies, musings, and whimsies have been included along with bits of advice. Perhaps your special interests have been neglected. Did you wish for more breads or meat puddings? Maybe you are looking for elegant made dishes or elaborate sweets.

You, dear reader, are invited to join this quest for the historical cook. There are many, many, many more receipts waiting for you to investigate—fascinating or fanciful, useful or outrageous, delectable or questionable. You may choose to begin with works consulted for this study and follow wherever they may lead. Perhaps you are the fortunate curator of a box of old family recipes—barely remembered, pushed into the very back on the top shelf in your cupboard. It is time to pull those down and see where they fit among ancestral foodways. Now is your turn to go to period sources to expand your personal collection.

I hope this volume heightens curiosity and introduces skills and attitudes that will prove useful when attempting to interpret the past. And, of course, *attempting* and *interpreting* is the best we can ever accomplish. We cannot *live* history, but perhaps we may capture vivid glimpses of past lives. Perhaps we may transport ourselves to Mary Randolph's kitchen as we catch the delightful fragrance of roses infusing in brandy. We may recreate a backwoods frolic to feast on a hodgepodge of venison, pork, and turkey amid "the greatest hilarity." Or we may sit down to a plantation dinner and marvel at the choices: roast shoat with green peas pudding, pigeon pie, hashed mutton and sallet, or squirrel and asparagus, imagining William Byrd at the head of the table. There is no doubt that exploring foodways is a most pleasant mode of time travel.

These very arbitrary comments of mine should indeed give free rein to the judgement and imagination of my reader.

Karl Von Rumohr, *Essence of Cookery*, 101

Fireside Advice

There are fire builders and fire doodlers. Have you noticed a fire builder who quickly selects wood, lays a fire, adds the spark or match, and goes on to other tasks while the fire matures and coals gather? You have certainly seen the fire doodler, for this bungling soul is likely to be long at work on a barely smoking heap of sticks. There are three simple bits of advice that, if heeded, will reform a doodler into a builder.

Much has been written and discussed on the best fire woods, techniques for laying the fire, and the science of burning. Certainly, dry seasoned hardwood is a must, and there are many "right" ways to lay a fire. What separates the fire builder from the fire doodler is an understanding of the science, the basic needs of a fire. Beyond that, a fireside cook must develop fire maintenance skills to provide coals or flame as needed.

Fireside cooks have strong opinions about building and tending their fires. Many systems work well. Some arrange fuel as a teepee, others prefer a log cabin stack, the less particular fire builder just lays the wood in a loose, higgledy-piggledy manner. All result in a workable cooking fire, if the three basics of fire are kept in mind:

Fire needs fuel

This may seem too obvious to state; however, starving the fire is a common failing. One must be alert to feeding the fire whenever it is hungry. Add wood regularly, before the fire dies down, a few sticks at a time. The goal is to keep a fairly constant heat under each pot and beside roasting foods while at the same time producing fresh coals as needed for baking.

The experienced cook develops a habit for keeping a supply of coals. Fuel may be added to the back of the fire while pulling coals to the front. Alternately the cook may choose to keep a lively fire going at one side, sliding coals to the other side of the fireplace. At a fire ring one has more access to coals all around the fire and may simply keep the active fire in the center.

Cooking School Hearth. John C. Campbell Folk School, Brasstown,
North Carolina. Author photograph.

Each fire has a character of its own. One simply needs to remain watchful
of its needs for fuel and for oxygen as well.

Fire requires oxygen

The apt fire builder develops a knack for loosely arranging firewood so that
oxygen can reach the fire. On the other hand, the fire doodler stacks fuel
ever more tightly, smothering a developing flame. One must allow the fire to
breathe.

Fire burns up

The fire builder competently lays a fire with the most flammable material (the
tinder) on the bottom and increasingly larger fuel loosely arranged on top
(kindling, then firewood). Skill is demonstrated when one match or a spark
from flint and steel is adequate to start the fire. A thrifty and constant fire is
maintained with moderate quantities of fuel added as needed.

You may see the doodler attempting to start a fire by arranging small fuel
on top of logs. Multiple matches light multiple short lived flames. Once a fire
is finally going the doodler often waits until it nearly dies before piling on fuel.
The resulting hot-cool-hot-cool fire will not work well for the cook.

One must simply remember: Fire burns up. The hottest area is near the tip of the flame.

The accomplished hearth cook is ever attentive to the needs of the fire— fuel, oxygen, and geometry. Once these concerns become intuitive, the cook can concentrate on creating extraordinary meals at the open hearth.

APPENDIX B

Ingredients Defined

❧ Equivalents, Measures, Weights

Weights and Measures

      3 teaspoons = 1 tablespoon
         (1 *spoonful* = approximately 1 tablespoon)*
      (1 *desert spoon* = approximately 1 teaspoon)
      4 tablespoons = ¼ cup
            (1 *glass* = approximately ¼ cup)
               1 gill = ½ cup
            (1 *teacup* = approximately 5 or 6 fluid ounces
                        = 10–12 tablespoons)
               1 cup = 8 fluid ounces (volume)
      16 tablespoons = 1 cup
            2 cups = 1 pint
            2 pints = 1 quart
            4 quarts = 1 gallon
            8 quarts = 1 peck
            1 pound = 16 ounces (weight)

Equivalents

      1 pound flour = 3 to 4 cups**
      1 pound sugar = 2 cups
      1 pound butter = 2 cups
            1 nutmeg = 1 to 2 teaspoons
         blade of mace = varies greatly, perhaps ⅛ or ¼ teaspoon powdered mace
         1 *penny loaf* = ½ to ¾ pound bread (depended on price of flour)
            manchet = fine white bread of varying size

❧ A Spoonful*

A typical eighteenth-century spoon holds about one tablespoon measure. Six level spoonfuls may be interpreted as one third cup, while six heaping spoonfuls is nearer one cup.

🖎 Flour measure**

Just what volume equals one pound of flour? Well, it depends. Flours differed then and differ now. And the weight of a given volume of flour will also vary depending on humidity and how tightly packed. Historic foodways researcher, Karen Hess, determined one pound of flour to be about three cups. That is a good measure to begin with, although we frequently find more flour needed. Often three and a half cups is a good estimate for one pound. To confuse the matter further, we find receipts which are identical except one calls for one pound of flour while another calls for one quart. This implies four cups flour to a pound. [1]

With these variables in mind, one must rely on experience to judge when a batter or dough is of the right stiffness. Don't be timid, for cakes, breads, or pastries generally turn out fine using a range of flour measures. You will find interpretations that have worked well for us accompanying receipts in this volume.

Unbleached flour is a reasonable choice. A little whole wheat flour may be added to simulate less thorough processing.

🖎 Sugar

Measuring sugar is much simpler than measuring flour. Two cups granulated sugar conveniently weighs approximately one pound.

Sugar was not the standard granulated white crystals we know. Raw sugar, turbinado, Demerara, or muscavado may come closer to eighteenth-century grades, although it would have been purchased as loaf or cone rather than crystals. After pounding with mortar and pestle, the sugar would have had a rather different texture from the coarse crystals which we find today. You may wish to experiment by grinding crystallized raw sugar with mortar and pestle or even in a blender in order to produce a finer and less uniform texture that may more closely approach the sugar available to early cooks.

Powdered sugar was not confectioners sugar but finely pounded and sifted loaf sugar. *Brown* sugar in period sources was not the brown sugar of today but a less refined raw sugar. Some maple sugar was produced locally, although maple syrup was more ordinary, even in parts of the south.

🖎 Molasses, Treacle

Treacle was the common eighteenth-century *molasses*. Both names referred to sugar cane syrup, not the sorghum syrup that became the usual molasses by the mid-1800s, the syrup we know as molasses today. West Indian molasses, a byproduct of sugar manufacture, was available in early America. Today cane sugar syrup is available in some grocery stores and in specialty markets.

Molasses was a general term for any liquid sweetening agent. A sort of molasses was produced from corn stalks at least by the 1770s. In experimenting with crushing corn stalks and concentrating the juice by long boiling, we have found the resulting syrup to be similar to sorghum molasses. Maple syrup was another *molasses* available to early southerners, and may be used in some receipts calling for molasses or treacle.[2]

✎ Eggs

Among pudding and cake receipts some call for whole eggs, others omit part or all of the whites. You will find this true even between otherwise identical receipts. The difference will be in texture. The yolks give a tender, delicate consistency, while whites make the foodstuff sturdier or tougher. You may wish to experiment to decide whether you prefer using whole eggs or omitting half the whites. Apart from preferences regarding consistency, some early authors considered the whites to be an unwholesome food.[3]

✎ Yeast

Barm, ale yeast, yeast is the most problematical ingredient in reproducing eighteenth-century breads and cakes. Most of us find it necessary to adapt historic recipes to modern preservative-free dry yeast. We follow the lead of those wiser and more experienced bakers, Elizabeth David and Karen Hess. Both experts agreed that reasonably accurate baked goods can be produced, but that modern recipes call for much more yeast than needed. With less yeast and the resulting longer rising time, taste and texture will be better and more historically accurate, and the bread or cake will keep longer.[4]

Modern American dry yeast packets contain one fourth ounce or three teaspoonfuls. One teaspoonful yeast for three cupfuls flour should be plenty. Dissolve the yeast in a little warm water, adjusting the volume according to yeast measure and liquids called for in the given receipt, and proceed according to historical method.

✎ Fats

Suet, marrow, lard, drippings, and/or butter were considered interchangeable in many receipts. For example, Sippet Pudding is identical to Bread and Butter Pudding save for the choice between marrow, suet, or butter for layering with bread and currants. Compare egg pie receipts (Chapter 1) to see flexible usage of suet, marrow, and butter.[5]

Ellis, in *The Country Housewife's Family Companion,* suggested many such options. A baked rice pudding might be made rich with chopped suet or butter. As sauce for a plain flour batter pudding "some farmers wives melt hogs-lard

Sugar Chest. Kentucky, c. 1800. Although outwardly similar to cellarets (cases for storing a dozen or more bottles),
sugar chests were divided into only two or three sections
for safeguarding loaf sugar and brown sugar, and perhaps
coffee or spices. This unusual furniture form appeared in
remote parts of the Southern backcountry as wealthy cotton and tobacco plantation society spread over the mountains at the end of the eighteenth century. The sugar chest
remained a status symbol for a quarter century. Courtesy of
the Museum of Early Southern Decorative Arts (MESDA)
at Old Salem.

and lade it over the pudding . . . or instead of lard, they melt some sweet pot-fat-dripping. This sort of fat is preferred by some to butter, as being cheaper, heartier, and more ready at hand, when butter cannot be had." And when white gut puddings were made with marrow instead of suet they were said to become "a repast for the rich." On the other hand Kettilby noted "Hog's-Lard . . . eats as well as Marrow" for an orange and almond pudding in skins. When preparing meat for roasting Dods reminded the cook to trim excess fat to save "for dripping or puddings."[6]

Sweet oil (olive oil) was available to those who could afford it. Primarily used in sauces for salads, hot and cold, olive oil sometimes replaced butter or other fat in soups and made dishes. Such foods were said to be prepared in the Spanish or Italian way. Frontier settlers noted, "Bear fat, with salad, is as good as Olive Oil."[7]

✍ Sweetbreads, Sweetmeats

Sweetbreads are not breads and sweetmeats are not meats.

Sweetbreads consist of the pancreas and thymus gland of an animal. These were popular along with other organ meats.

Sweetmeats, on the other hand, include a wide range of sweets: cakes, pastries, confections, and all sorts of preserved fruits and sugared nuts. Dried currants and raisins, candied lemon, orange, or citron peels, and almonds are sweetmeats commonly called for in period receipts.

Their Usual and Best Food for Breakfast and Supper

In this quest for the historical cook we have examined common, and a few uncommon, dishes. Most were for the main meal of the day, dinner, generally served in mid afternoon. Breakfast, supper, and between meal refreshments complete the picture.

🕊 Breakfast

[Dutch in interior New York, 1750s] drank tea in the customary way by putting brown sugar into the cup of tea. With the tea they ate bread and butter and radishes; they would take a bite of the bread and butter and would cut off a piece of the radish as they ate.... They sometimes had small round cheeses (not especially fine tasting) on the table, which they cut into thin slices and spread upon the buttered bread.[1]

[Moravians traveling in North Carolina, 1755] We had chocolate for breakfast.[2]

[Mr. Carter, plantation owner, 1773] breakfasted late, and on Oysters.[3]

[When breakfasting at a "Dutch house" in western Virginia, 1770s] Nothing to drink but Whiskey.[4]

[Near Halifax, North Carolina, 1782] It would have made you laugh, to have seen us at our repast, three gentlemen on a journey, sitting on an old log, breaking our fast, on bacon and bread, and bread and bacon.[5]

[A French lady noted the Tidewater Virginians] Generally breakfast on a glass of hot water colored with tea or coffee, but just colored, and quite tasteless, and on hot bread, half-baked and soaked in melted butter which they all seem to like and to swallow without chewing. To this they add cheese, pickled pork and fish, all served together, most of the time on the same plate.[6]

[A Frenchman describing typical American meals, 1790s] They breakfast at nine o'clock on ham or salt fish, herring, for example, which is accompanied by coffee or tea, and slices of toasted or untoasted bread spread with butter.[7]

[George Washington] breakfasts about seven o'clock on three small Indian hoe cakes and as many dishes of tea[8]

[At the new University of North Carolina, 1797] Coffee and tea, or chocolate and tea, one warm roll, one loaf of wheat or corn flower, at the option of the student, with a sufficiency of butter.[9]

[Tennessee, 1797] Coffee and some fried rashers of bacon served up with Indian bread: a common breakfast in this part of the country, where nothing better is to be had.[10]

[At the Salem girls boarding school, 1804] for breakfast, milk, butter and bread, coffee, tea, and sugar.[11]

[Served to visitors in the Moravian settlement of Salem, North Carolina, 1827] a breakfast which would not have disgraced the reign of Queen Elizabeth, such a variety of meats, hashes, pickles, salads &c &c.[12]

[West of Morganton, North Carolina, 1827] the meal was well adapted for hardy mountaineers and would not have disgraced the highlands in the 16 century—but would certainly have given the vapours to a modern fine lady to think of a boiled ham, cabbages, potatoes, corn, pickles &c. &c, for breakfast.[13]

When at home on his Virginia plantation William Byrd customarily consumed only milk (as a young man) or tea or coffee (in later years) for breakfast. However, when setting out on a journey, he breakfasted on chocolate to fortify himself.

Supper

[Dutch, above Albany, New York, mid-1700s] In the evening they made a porridge of corn, poured it as customary into a dish, made a large hole in the center into which they poured fresh milk, but more often buttermilk. ... This was their supper nearly every evening. After that they would eat some meat left over from the noonday meal, or bread and butter with cheese.[14]

[New Sweden, 1759] Suppers are not much in use. Where one is so invited, chocolate is the most reliable. Whole pots of it are sometimes made, but little or no milk in it, chiefly of water.[15]

[In Tidewater Virginia we find a plantation tutor ending his day with widely varied suppers, 1773–74] A Bowl of hot Green Tea, & several Tarts. … Supp'd on Oysters …. sup'd on Crabs & an elegant dish of Strawberries & cream…. supt on Artichoks, & Huckleberries & Milk…. We have omitted Supper, & in its place substituted Coffee which we commonly take about seven in the evening[16]

[Between Salisbury and Charlotte, North Carolina, 1782] The families here, in one respect, resemble the low Dutch in their way of eating—that is the whole family sup their Mush and Milk out of one large dish for that purpose. No tea or coffee was to be had here.[17]

[At the University of North Carolina, 1797] Coffee, tea, or milk at the option of the Steward, with the necessary quantity of bread or biscuit.[18]

[At the Salem, North Carolina, girls boarding school, 1804] In the evening, milk, warmed-overs, pie, pancakes, mush, chocolate, etc.[19]

Tidewater Virginia plantation suppers varied with the season and the company. William Byrd noted choosing his supper from a wide range of elegant dishes (perhaps leftover from dinner), including broiled or roasted lamb, mutton, veal, fowl, pork, or beef; pies of chicken, turkey, mince, or apple; hashed or fricasseed lamb; or oysters. On other occasions he simply had pone and milk, bread with butter or cheese, toast and mead, cake and wine, eggs, broth, custard, or fruit. Later in life Byrd vowed to eat only fresh fruit for supper during the summer months, often with milk.

While many receipts in this volume graced dinner tables, leftovers were likely to have shown up at supper, breakfast, or for hungry travelers. Each meal depended on seasonal availability, locale, cultural influences, and social or economic conditions.

NOTES

Chapter 1: Interpreting Historical Reciepts

1. Other quaking pudding receipts suggested varying seasoning combinations: sugar, nutmeg, and salt in *Martha Washington's Booke*, 108–109; nutmeg, salt, and rose water (no sugar) in Glasse, *Art of Cookery* (1744), 112; nutmeg, cinnamon, mace, sack (or sherry or madeira), sugar, salt, almond flour in Smith, *Compleat Housewife,* 30–31.

2. Pre-1744 Virginia cookbook, 62; see also Moss and Hoffman, *Backcountry Housewife*, 106.

3. Glasse, *Art of Cookery* (1747), 71, 113; Smith, *Compleat Housewife*, 149–50; *Martha Washington's* Booke, 91; C. Carter, *Complete Practical Cook*, 138; Moxon, *English Housewifry*, 37–38; Horry, *Colonial Plantation Cookbook*, 73; Wolley, *Queenlike Closet*, 127; S. Carter, *Frugal Colonial Housewife*, 97; Ellis, *Country Housewife's Family Companion*, 454; &c.

4. Unidentified cookbook, c. 1700, Harbury, *Virginia's Cooking Dynasty*, 154, 162, 232; Pre-1744 Virginia cookbook, 55.

5. Kettilby, *Above Three Hundred Receipts*, 28; Rundell, *New System of Domestic Cookery*, 158; Glasse, *Art of Cookery* (1747), 116; Ellis, *Country Housewife's Family Companion*, 454; May, *Accomplisht Cook*, 182.

6. Pinckney household book; Smith, *Compleat Housewife*, 149–50.

7. Unidentified cookbook, c. 1700, Harbury, *Virginia's Cooking Dynasty*, 154, 232.

8. Kettilby, *Above Three Hundred Receipts*, 19; Glasse, *Art of Cookery* (1747), 142, (1796), 251; Cleland, *New and Easy Method*, 134; Raffald, *Experienced English Housekeeper*, 84; Schober commonplace book; Leslie, *Directions for Cookery*, 15–17; Rutledge, *Carolina Housewife*, 126; Hill, *Southern Practical Cookery*, 273–75; *Charleston Receipts*, 228; Brown, *Southern Cookbook*, 297; Rombauer and Becker, *The Joy of Cooking* (1953), 572; *Ladies Home Journal Dessert Cookbook*, ed. Carol Truax (New York: Doubleday, 1964), 104; *Charlotte Cookbook*, 250; Patricia Veasey, Clover, South Carolina.

9. For examples see Glasse, *Art of Cookery* (1747), 142; Horry, *Colonial Plantation Cookbook*, 72.

Chapter 2: Developing an Eighteenth-Century Mindset

1. The size of a penny loaf varied with the price of flour. Approximately one half to three quarters pound may be considered as a rough weight of a penny loaf. In 1775 Salem, North Carolina, a four penny loaf weighed three pounds four ounces. Prices were higher in 1795 "if wheat costs 5 shillings a bushel.... A four-penny loaf should weigh two pounds and thirteen ounces." *Records of the Moravians,* II:899, VI:2540.

2. Brown, *Southern Cookbook,* 184–85. This source is not meant to be a historical cookbook but is one of the best for noting evolution of Southern foods into the twentieth century.

Chapter 3: From a Pot of Boiling Water

1. Smith, *Compleat Housewife,* 130; M. Randolph, *Virginia Housewife,* 164.

2. Glasse, *Art of Cookery* (1747), 112; Moss and Hoffman, *Backcountry Housewife,* 68; *Martha Washington's Booke,* 108–109; Raffald, *Experienced English Housekeeper,* 87.

3. Glasse, *Art of Cookery* (1747), 248.

4. William Salmon, *Botanologia* (London: 1710), as quoted in Hess, *The Carolina Rice Kitchen,* 17; Moss and Hoffman, *Backcountry Housewife,* 131–134.

5. Cleland, *New and Easy Method,* 117; S. Carter, *Frugal Colonial Housewife,* 112; Glasse, *Art of Cookery* (1747), 111, 124; Chadwick, *Home Cookery,* 50.

6. Glasse, *Art of Cookery* (1796), 341; Rundell, *New System of Domestic Cookery,* 185.

7. Ellis, *Country Housewife's Family Companion,* 293.

8. "To make a dry Oatmeal Pudding," Wolley, *Queen-like Closet,* 91; "An Herb Pie for Lent," Raffald, *Experienced English Housekeeper,* 76; "To make an Oatmeal Pudding boil'd," May, *Accomplisht Cook,* 154.

9. Wolley, *Queen-like Closet,* 91.

10. Glasse, *Art of Cookery* (1747), 247; Moss and Hoffman, *Backcountry Housewife,* 67.

11. May, *Accomplisht Cook,* 149 and Pre-1744 Virginia cookbook, 52; "White Puddings in Skins," Raffald, *Experienced English Housekeeper,* 87.

12. Von Rumohr, *Essence of Cookery,* 133.

13. Unidentified cookbook, c. 1700, Harbury, *Virginia's Cooking Dynasty,* 242; Jane Randolph 1743, Harbury, *Virginia's Cooking Dynasty,* 394; M. Randolph, *Virginia Housewife,* 148–49.

14. Von Rumohr, *Essence of Cookery,* 133; Maussion, *They Knew the Washingtons,* 126; Kalm, *Travels,* II: 603.

15. Glasse, *Art of Cookery* (1747), 108; Leslie, *Directions for Cookery,* 28; Child, *American Frugal Housewife,* 61, 64.

16. Von Rumohr, *Essence of Cookery,* 133.

17. Bryan, *Kentucky Housewife*, 252–53.

18. Cresswell, *Journal*, 107.

19. Baily, *Journal*, 70.

20. Glasse, *Art of Cookery* (1805), "An Indian Pudding boiled" 137.

21. M. Randolph, *Virginia Housewife*, 153–54.

22. Glasse, *Art of Cookery* (1747), 109.

23. See pigeon and apple dumplings: Moss and Hoffman, *Backcountry Housewife*, 37, 65; Bradley, *Country Housewife*, I: 12, II: 163–64; Glasse, *Art of Cookery* (1747), 113; and others.

24. Dods, *Cook and Housewife's Manual*, 410.

25. Ellis, *Country Housewife's Family Companion*, 311.

26. Dods, *Cook and Housewife's Manual*, 399.

27. Glasse, *Art of Cookery* (1747), 125, 126; from Aristophanes in "The Clouds," as quoted in McNeill, *Scots Kitchen*.

28. Smith, *Compleat Housewife*, 134–135.

29. Moss and Hoffman, *Backcountry Housewife*, 48; Glasse, *Art of Cookery* (1747), 73.

30. Raffald, *Experienced English Housekeeper*, 67; Glasse, *Art of Cookery* (1747), 46.

31. S. Carter, *Frugal Colonial Housewife*, 63.

32. Dods, *Cook and Housewife's Manual*, 88; Ude, *French Cook*, 86; Bryan, *Kentucky Housewife*, 212.

33. Bradley, *Country Housewife*, II: 142–43; Wolley, *Queen-like Closet*, 107; The pre-1744 Virginia cookbook mentions boiling "Colleyflowers" in a cloth preparatory to pickling, 85.

34. Von Rumohr, *Essence of Cookery*, 86; Glasse, *Art of Cookery* (1747), 33, 34; Johnson, *Every Young Woman's Companion*, 80; Dods, *Cook and Housewife's Manual*, 78; Cameron, "Friend to the Memory," 13; Moss and Hoffman, *Backcountry Housewife*, 109.

35. Similar to "How to Boil a Turkey," Moxon, *English Housewifry*, 22–23.

36. Dods, *Cook and Housewife's Manual*, 78–79.

37. Johnson, *Every Young Woman's Companion*, 80; Dods, *Cook and Housewife's Manual*, 78.

38. Fisher, *What Mrs. Fisher Knows*, 54–55.

39. Glasse, *Art of Cookery* (1747), 21; Cleland, *New and Easy Method*, 89, 99; Wolley, *Queen-like Closet*, 123, 126, 161; La Varrene, *French Cook*, 52–53 and more.

40. Today's recipes for spoon bread generally call for more eggs, as in Brown, *Southern Cookbook*, 211; *Charlotte Cookbook*, 157; *Charleston Receipts*, 314; and others.

41. Simmons, *American Cookery*, 64; M. Randolph, *Virginia Housewife*, 153–54; Bryan, *Kentucky Housewife*, 249.

42. See variation of "Pigeons in a Hole," Glasse, *Art of Cookery* (1747), 46.

43. Moss and Hoffman, *Backcountry Housewife*, 37, 65; Raffald, *Experienced English Housekeeper*, 66.

44. Variations of "Virginia Chicken Pudding" can be found in Bryan, *Kentucky Housewife*, 124; Hill, *Southern Practical Cookery*, 147; Thornton, *Southern Gardener*, 216.

45. Byrd, *Another Secret Diary*, 87.

46. Glasse, *Art of Cookery* (1747), 27; Jane Randolph 1743, Harbury, *Virginia's Cooking Dynasty*, 394; M. Randolph, *Virginia Housewife*, 153.

Chapter 4: With a Good Bed of Coals

1. *The Memoirs of Lieut. Henry Timberlake* (Who accompanied the Three Cherokee Indians to England in the Year 1762) (London: 1765), 57.

2. Dods, *Cook and Housewife's Manual*, 445.

3. Rutledge, *Carolina Housewife*, 195.

4. South Carolina household book; Glasse, *Art of Cookery* (1747), 140; Moss and Hoffman, *Backcountry Housewife*, 73.

5. Byrd, *Secret Diary*, 423.

6. Fries, *Records of the Moravians*, II: 834; Glasse, *Art of Cookery* (1747), 139, (1796) 310, (1805) 163.

7. Rutledge, *Carolina Housewife*, 187, 199.

8. Glasse, *Art of Cookery* (1747), 140; Horry, *Colonial Plantation Cookbook*, 72, 79; Rutledge, *Carolina Housewife*, 197–199; Cleland, *New and Easy Method*, 164; Dods, *Cook and Housewife's Manual*, 447–48; Ashfield, *Pleasures of Colonial Cooking*, 132.

9. May, *Accomplisht Cook*, 205; Wolley, *Queen-like Closet*, 80; Markham, *English Housewife*, 120.

10. Hill, *Southern Practical Cookery*, 296–298.

11. As "Cinnamon Cakes" and other German *cakes* in Schmidt household book; Von Rumohr, *Essence of Cookery*, 130–31.

12. Similar to Glasse, *Art of Cookery* (1747), 141; Unidentified cookbook, c. 1700, Harbury, *Virginia's Cooking Dynasty*, 170.

13. Jane Randolph 1743, Harbury, *Virginia's Cooking Dynasty*, 366; M. Randolph, *Virginia Housewife*, 146; Pre-1744 Virginia cookbook, 30; *Martha Washington's Booke*, 341; Cleland, *New and Easy Method*, 163; Rutledge, *Carolina Housewife*, 203.

14. "Naples Biskets," Unidentified cookbook, c. 1700, Harbury, *Virginia's Cooking Dynasty*, 210–11 and Horry, *Colonial Plantation Cookbook*, 104; "Savoy Biskets," C. Carter, *Complete Practical Cook*, 171; Unidentified cookbook, c. 1700 Virginia, Harbury, *Virginia's Cooking Dynasty*, 204, and Kettilby, *Above Three Hundred Receipts*, 90; "Drop-Biscuits," Glasse, *Art of Cookery* (1747), 140 and Johnson, *Every Young Woman's Companion*, 142; "Sponge Biscuits," *Art of Cookery* (1747), 139

and Rutledge, *Carolina Housewife*, 205–206; "Common Biscuit," Glasse, *Art of Cookery* (1747), 140, Johnson, *Every Young Woman's Companion*, 142, S. Carter, *Frugal Colonial Housewife*, 106, and Van Rensselaer, *Score of Hospitality*, 28; "Biscuit," La Varenne, *French Cook*, 240; "Lady's Fingers," Hill, *Southern Practical Cookery*, 296.

15. Hesse, note in *Martha Washington's Booke*, 336; Schober commonplace book; Cameron, "Friend to the Memory," 24.

16. La Varenne, *French Cook*, 240; Unidentified cookbook, c. 1700, Harbury, *Virginia's Cooking Dynasty*, 210–11; Bryan, *Kentucky Housewife*, 290–91.

17. M. Randolph, *Virginia Housewife*, 163; Evelyn, *Acetaria;* Byrd, *Histories of the Dividing Line*, 83.

18. Wolley, *Queen-like Closet*, 72; W. M., *A Queens Delight*, 66.

19. "To make Almond Puddings with French Rolls or Naples Biskets," Wolley, *Queen-like Closet*, 99; Kettilby, *Above Three Hundred Receipts*, 86.

20. Cleland, *New and Easy Method*, 137; Glasse, *Art of Cookery* (1796), 328.

21. Moss and Hoffman, *Backcountry Housewife*, 37; Rundell, *New System of Domestic Cookery*, 247.

22. "Wine biscuit," Dods, *Cook and Housewife's Manual*, 448; "Dutch Biscuits," Cleland, *New and Easy Method*, 162; "Tavern Biskett," Pre-1744 Virginia cookbook, 90; "Biscuit Bread," Goelet household book, 5; "Miss Butler's biscuit," Cameron, "Friend to the Memory," 28; "Nice Biscuit," M. Randolph, *Virginia Housewife*, 169; Rutledge, *Carolina Housewife*, 33; Jane Randolph recorded a decidedly different "Tavern Biskets," Harbury, *Virginia's Cooking Dynasty*, 372.

23. Dods, *Cook and Housewife's Manual*, 448.

24. William Stephens, "Journal of the Proceedings in Georgia," in *Setting Out to Begin a New World*, 62.

25. Simmons, *American Cookery*, 78; Bryan, *Kentucky Housewife*, 312; Rutledge, *Carolina Housewife*, 19–28; Moss and Hoffman, *Backcountry Housewife*, 9–13.

26. Francois Andre Michaux, "Travels 1801–1802," in *Early Western Travels 1748–1846. Vol. 3*, trans. and ed. Reuben Gold Thwaites (Cleveland: 1906; New York: AMS Press, 1966), 147.

27. Davidson, *Private Journal*, 92.

28. Jane Randolph 1743, Harbury, *Virginia's Cooking Dynasty*, 298; Glasse, *Art of Cookery* (1747), 151.

29. Rutledge, *Carolina Housewife*, 16, 24, 25, 29, 30.

30. Rutledge, *Carolina Housewife*, 29.

31. Avery poetry and receipt book; M. Randolph, *Virginia Housewife*, 169.

32. Leslie, *Directions for Cookery*, 71; Dods, *Cook and Housewife's Manual*, 453; Glasse, *Art of Cookery* (1747), 151; M. Randolph, *Virginia Housewife*, 169.

33. Glasse, *Art of Cookery* (1747), 151; Leslie, *Directions for Cookery*, 71; Bryan, *Kentucky Housewife*, 308–9.

34. See Ellis, *Country Housewife's Family Companion*, 85–87 for complete poem.

35. Von Rumohr, *Essence of Cookery*, 128; Glasse, *Art of Cookery* (1747), 75; Johnson, *Every Young Woman's Companion*, 102; C. Carter, *Complete Practical Cook*, 127.

36. Ashfield, *Pleasures of Colonial Cooking*, 133; Pre-1744 Virginia cookbook, 23.

37. Von Rumohr, *Essence of Cookery*, 129.

38. Moss and Hoffman, *Backcountry Housewife*, 70; Glasse, *Art of Cookery* (1747), 75; Cleland, *New and Easy Method*, 130–31.

39. C. Carter, *Complete Practical Cook*, 127; *Martha Washington's Booke*, 156; Ellis, *Country Housewife's Family Companion*, 91; Cameron, "Friend to the Memory," 14.

40. Ellis, *Country Housewife's Family Companion*, 91; Bradley, *Country Housewife*, II: 127; S. Carter, *Frugal Colonial Housewife*, 92.

41. *Martha Washington's Booke*, 159.

42. For example Rundell, *New System of Domestic Cookery*, 134; S. Carter, *Frugal Colonial Housewife*, 99; Montefiore, *The Jewish Manual*, 104; Dods, *Cook and Housewife's Manual*, 390–91.

43. Kettilby, *Above Three Hundred Receipts*, 30.

44. Glasse, *Art of Cookery* (1796, also later editions), 243, 245.

45. Within a bread and butter pudding receipt, Rundell, *New System of Domestic Cookery*, 138.

46. Dods, *Cook and Housewife's Manual*, 399.

47. Bryan, *Kentucky Housewife*, 232, 235, 236, 239, 245, and more.

48. From "Of Apple-Pyes: A poem, by Mr. Welsted" in Ellis, *Country Housewife's Family Companion*, 86.

49. *Oxford English Dictionary;* Unidentified cookbook, c. 1700, Harbury, *Virginia's Cooking Dynasty*, 240 and others.

50. See Kay Moss, *Decorative Motifs*, 2001.

51. Wolley, *Queen-like Closet*, 103, 164–65, 171; Markham, *English Housewife*, 107–9; Dods, *Cook and Housewife's Manual*, 390–91, Glasse, *Art of Cookery* (1747), 76; Raffald, *Experienced English Housekeeper*, 72–76; Leslie, *Directions for Cookery*, 25–27; Bryan, *Kentucky Housewife*, 273–74.

52. May, *Accomplisht Cook*, 181.

53. Doddridge, *Notes on the Settlement*, 88.

54. Von Rumohr, *Essence of Cookery*, 113.

55. For more early chicken pie receipts with sweetmeats see Wolley, *Queen-like Closet*, 102–3; Markham, *English Housewife*, 115. Mutton, sweetbreads, calf udder, oysters, and veal enter a 1671 chicken pie, along with preserved fruits and spices. W.M., *Compleat Cook*, 35–36.

56. Ude, *French Cook*, 150, 178, etc.

57. Byrd, *Secret Diary*, chicken pie for breakfast 467, for dinner 58, 352, 451 etc., for supper 88, 351, 436 etc.

58. Dods, *Cook and Housewife's Manual*, 387.

59. Byrd, *Secret Diary*, 267, 292, etc.; Unidentified cookbook, c. 1700, Harbury, *Virginia's Cooking Dynasty*, 152; Pre-1744 Virginia cookbook, 56.

60. Glasse, *Art of Cookery* (1747), 72; Rundell, *New System of Domestic Cookery*, 133; Cleland, *New and Easy Method*, 82–83; Dods, *Cook and Housewife's Manual*, 387.

61. Markham, *English Housewife*, 100–103; On the other hand Wolley's 17th-c. oyster pie was savory rather than sweet.

62. Doddridge, *Notes on the Settlement*, 88.

63. Glasse, *Art of Cookery* (1747), 113–14.

64. Cleland, *New and Easy Method*, 85; Ellis, *Country Housewife's Family Companion*, 315.

65. Kalm, *Travels*, I: 97; Byrd, *The Secret Diary*.

66. Markham, *English Housewife*, 104–5, 108.

67. Ellis, *Country Housewife's Family Companion*, 86–87.

68. Moss and Hoffman, *Backcountry Housewife*, 119; S. Carter, *Frugal Colonial Housewife*, 69.

69. Ellis, *Country Housewife's Family Companion*, 92–93.

70. Child, *American Frugal Housewife*, 68.

71. Simmons, *American Cookery*, 61, 71.

72. Brown, "Journal of Travel," 284–313. A Pennsylvanian, agent for land speculators, Brown spent over 6 months traveling the region of Salisbury, Statesville, Wilkesboro, Morganton, and Ashville; Simmons, *American Cookery*, 61; Rutledge, *Carolina Housewife*, 160–161; Horry, *Colonial Plantation Cookbook*, 112.

73. This double-boiler method is described for "Egg Cream," Bryan, *Kentucky Housewife*, 326.

74. Van Rensselaer, *Score of Hospitality*, 35; Rutledge, *Carolina Housewife*, 135; Hammond, *Modern Domestic Cookery*, 150; Rundell, *New System of Domestic Cookery*, 138; Smith, *Compleat Housewife*, 127. Glasse, *Art of Cookery* (1747), 111.

75. Hammond, *Modern Domestic Cookery*, 150.

76. Bryan, *Kentucky Housewife*, 247–48.

77. Raffald, *Experienced English Housekeeper*, 83.

78. Dods, *Cook and Housewife's Manual*, 408.

79. Horry, *Colonial Plantation Cookbook*, 136; Rundell, *New System of Domestic Cookery*, 151; M. Randolph, *Virginia Housewife*, 155; "Apple Brown Betty" is a more recent member of this family of dishes.

80. Ashfield, *Pleasures of Colonial Cooking*, 98.

81. Dods, *Cook and Housewife's Manual*, 408.

Chapter 5: At the Fireside: Broiling and Roasting

1. Dods, *Cook and Housewife's Manual*, 95.

2. Dods, *Cook and Housewife's Manual*, 116–18.

3. Dods, *Cook and Housewife's Manual*, 120.

4. Bryan, *Kentucky Housewife*, 141; or "a little chalk, or flour" 146; Dods, *Cook and Housewife's Manual*, 118.

5. See La Varenne, *French Cook*, 144–156; Glasse, *Art of Cookery* (1747), 155–57, 159; Ude, *French Cook*, 255, 272, 276; M. Randolph, *Virginia Housewife*, 71; Bryan, *Kentucky Housewife*, 141–47.

6. Byrd, *Secret Diary*, 388, 458, 585.

7. Dods, *Cook and Housewife's Manual*, 122.

8. Bryan, *Kentucky Housewife*, 29, 74; Ude, *French Cook*, 86; Dods, *Cook and Housewife's Manual*, 93.

9. Cleland, *New and Easy Method*, 65; M. Randolph, *Virginia Housewife*, 64.

10. Cleland, *New and Easy Method*, 101, Raffald; *Experienced English Housekeeper*, 33; Glasse, *Art of Cookery* (1747), 5; Smith, *Compleat Housewife*, 21; La Varenne, *French Cook*, 70; Lawson, *New Voyage*, 58, 144.

Chapter 6: Soups, Stews, and Made Dishes

1. Fries, *Records of the Moravians*, I: 104, 110–111, 123

2. Fries, *Records of the Moravians*, I: 194.

3. As laid out in the first "Plan of Studies." Kemp P. Battle, *History of the University of North Carolina* (Spartanburg, South Carolina: The Reprint Co., 1974), 51, 52.

4. Bailey, *Journal*, 90.

5. Bailey, *Journal*, 90–91.

6. Smyth, *Tour*, 171–172.

7. Maussion, *They Knew the Washingtons*, 126, 156.

8. Maussion, *They Knew the Washingtons*, 145.

9. Cresswell, *Journal*, 20.

10. Conner, *Diary*, 11.

11. Maussion, *They Knew the Washingtons*, 153.

12. Stearns, *American Oracle*, 481.

13. Byrd, *Secret Diary*, beaver 488, etc.

14. Byrd, *Secret Diary*; also *London Diary*.

15. Pinckney, *Letterbook*, 39.

16. Bailey, *Journal*, 55.

17. Henry Melchior Muhlenberg, *The Notebook of a Colonial Clergyman*. (1750) Trans. and ed. Theodore C. Tappert and John W. Doberstain. Philadelphia: Muhlenberg Press, 1959, 34–35; Kalm, *Travels*, I: 52, 53; Fries, *Records of the Moravians*, II: 578; Smyth, *Tour*, 149.

18. Byrd, *Secret Diary*, squirrel and onions 286, 392; hare and onions 469; one April he dined on asparagus with squirrel 21.

19. As Raffald, *Experienced English Housekeeper*, 68–69.

20. Glasse, *Art of Cookery* (1747), 77, (1796) 207; Cleland, *New and Easy Method*, 9; Bradley, *Country Housewife*, I: 180; Ashfield, *Pleasures of Colonial Cooking*, 80.

21. English cookery receipt book, c.1730–1760; Bradley, *Country Housewife*, I: 180.

22. Glasse, *Art of Cookery* (1796), 211; Raffald, *Experienced English Housekeeper,* 8; C. Carter, *Complete Practical Cook,* 19.

23. *Martha Washington's Booke,* 68.

24. Dods, *Cook and Housewife's Manual,* 77.

25. Glasse, *Art of Cookery* (1747), 18, 19, 36; Dods, *Cook and Housewife's Manual,* 155–56; Simmons, *American Cookery,* 52, 53; Stockton receipt book, 20; Moss and Hoffman, *Backcountry Housewife,* 107.

26. Rutledge, *Carolina Housewife,* 61–62; Cleland, *New and Easy Method,* 49–50; Glasse, *Art of Cookery* (1747), 20.

27. La Varenne, *French Cook,* 47–48; M. Randolph, *Virginia Housewife,* 97; Hill, *Southern Practical Cookery,* 65–66.

28. "Breast of Mutton into an aricot," La Varenne, *French Cook,* 48; "A Harrico of Mutton," Glasse, *Art of Cookery* (1747), 24; "A haricot of mutton," Dods, *Cook and Housewife's Manual,* 296–97; "To Harrico Mutton," M. Randolph, *Virginia Housewife,* 59–60; Note: *Stew* was formerly seldom used as a noun, but often as a verb.

29. Byrd, *Histories of the Dividing Line,* 178.

30. Byrd, *Histories of the Dividing Line,* 194.

31. Wolley, *Queen-like Closet,* 104; May, *Accomplisht Cook,* 28–29.

32. C. Carter, *The Complete Practical Cook,* 3–4; Glasse, *Art of Cookery* (1747), 17, 65, (1796) 51, 73, 127, 184; "A Pepper-pot," several "Hotch-potches," and "An olio," Dods, *Cook and Housewife's Manual,* 155, 277–78, 365–66, 374–75; "Hotche-pot Soup," Ude, *French Cook,* 62; "Hotch-potch" and "Pepper-pot," Rundell, *New System of Domestic Cookery,* 75, 100, 207. Pepperpot appeared in early 19th-century sources, along with variations of the earlier olio and hodge-podge.

33. "A Spanish Olio," W.M., *Compleat Cook,* 92–93; C. Carter, *Complete Practical Cook,* 3–4; May, *Accomplisht Cook,* 28–29; Wolley, *Queen-like Closet,* 104.

34. Cleland, *New and Easy Method,* 13; Markham, *English Housewife,* 77.

35. Glasse, *Art of Cookery* (1747), 17.

36. Hill, *Southern Practical Cookery,* 69–70; Edgeworth, *Southern Gardener,* 131.

37. Dods, *Cook and Housewife's Manual,* 79–89; Baily, Journal, 55.

38. Dods, *Cook and Housewife's Manual,* 271.

39. Byrd, *Secret Diary,* 6.

40. As in W.M., *Compleat Cook,* 85- 86; Wolley, *Queen-like Closet,* 127.

41. Richard Bradley recounted an anecdote of a cook's accidentally partially roasting and then cutting up mutton for stewing to hurry the meal. The result was said to have been extraordinarily tasty; thus this was said to have become the favored method. *Country Housewife,* II: 141–142; "To make hashed Meat," Wolley, *Queen-like Closet,* 127; Rutledge, *Carolina Housewife,* 37; for example see Glasse, *Art of Cookery* (1747), 20, 22, 24.

42. La Varenne, *French Cook,* many examples, 41–77 etc.

43. Glasse, *Art of Cookery* (1747), 40, (1796) 105; Raffald, *Experienced English Housekeeper*, 63.

44. Maussion, *They Knew the Washingtons*, 126.

45. Glasse, *Art of Cookery* (1796), 136; Moss and Hoffman, *Backcountry Housewife*, 52.

46. Glasse, *Art of Cookery* (1747), 13.

47. Smith, *Compleat Housewife*, 31; Glasse, *Art of Cookery* (1747), 104; Cleland, *New and Easy Method*, 59.

48. Cleland, *New and Easy Method*, 59.

49. Smith, *Compleat Housewife*, 31; Glasse, *Art of Cookery* (1747), 57, 104; Moss and Hoffman, *Backcountry Housewife*, 32.

50. Rombauer and Becker, *The Joy of Cooking* (1953), 171; Conversations with Margaret Gell, John C. Campbell Folk School, November 2009, April 2010.

51. Pre-1744 Virginia cookbook, 61.

52. Smith, *Compleat Housewife*, 62, 134.

53. Glasse, *Art of Cookery* (1747), 104.

54. Glasse, *Art of Cookery* (1747), 84.

Chapter 7: Vegetables: Salads, Potherbs, Sauces, *Meagre* Dishes

1. Glasse, *Art of Cookery* (1747), 98.

2. Moreau de St. Méry, *American Journey*, 265; Bryan, *Kentucky Housewife*, 192–93; Hill, *Southern Practical Cookery*, 182–83.

3. Markham, *English Housewife*, 64

4. Rundell, *New System of Domestic Cookery*, 171.

5. M. Randolph, *Virginia Housewife*, 123; Von Rumohr, *Essence of Cookery*, 147.

6. Dods, *Cook and Housewife's Manual*, 212; Raffald, *Experienced English Housekeeper*, 183.

7. Harbury, *Virginia's Cooking Dynasty*, 272, 388; La Varenne, *French Cook*, 204; Glasse, *Art of Cookery* (1747), 133; Hill, *Southern Practical Cookery*, 180; Fisher, *What Mrs. Fisher Knows*, 33–34.

8. Markham, *English Housewife*, 64–67; Wolley, *Queen-like Closet*, 154; Evelyn, *Acetaria*, appendix, 35.

9. Evelyn, *Acetaria*, 64 and appendix 35; May, *Accomplisht Cook*, 134–37.

10. Rundell, *New System of Domestic Cookery*, 203–4; Evelyn, *Acetaria*, 12.

11. Rundell, *New System of Domestic Cookery*, 174; Wolley, *Queen-like Closet*, 159.

12. "Salomongundy," Pre-1744 Virginia cookbook, 74; "Salmagundy," Glasse, *Art of Cookery* (1747), 59–60, 84; "Solomon-Gundy," Raffald, *Experienced English Housekeeper*, 142; "Sallad-Magundy," Kettilby, *Above Three Hundred Receipts*, 81; "Solomon-Gundie to eat in Lent," Moxon, *English Housewifry*, 74; "Salmy-Gundy," Bradley, *Country Housewife*, II: 71; and nearly a century later "Salmagundy," Rundell, *New System of Domestic Cookery*, 203–4; "Salmagundi," M. Randolph, *Virginia Housewife*, 189; Unidentified cookbook, c. 1700, Harbury, *Virginia's*

Cooking Dynasty, 282, includes "Salmongandy" and "Solomon gundy" along with "A Grand sallad," "A grand Sallad of Pickles," and "A salad & butter" in the order for serving dinner.

13. Raffald, *Experienced English Housekeeper,* 142; Glasse, *Art of Cookery* (1747), 59–60, 84; Dods, *Cook and Housewife's Manual,* 197.

14. Rundell, *New System of Domestic Cookery,* 203–4.

15. Kettilby, *Above Three Hundred Receipts,* II: 81; Raffald, *Experienced English Housekeeper,* 142; Moxon, *English Housewifry,* 74; Dods, *Cook and Housewife's Manual,* 197.

16. Von Rumohr, *Essence of Cookery,* 106–107; Montagne, *Larousse Gastronomique* (1961), 826; Hill, *Southern Practical Cookery,* 145–146.

17. Bryan, *Kentucky Housewife,* 120; Dods, *Cook and Housewife's Manual,* 224.

18. Von Rumohr, *Essence of Cookery,* 164.

19. Von Rumohr, *Essence of Cookery,* 160; Ude, *French Cook,* 17–18 gave two French sorrel purees; Byrd, *Secret Diary,* 388.

20. Von Rumohr, *Essence of Cookery,* 160.

21. Glasse, *Art of Cookery* (1747), 5; Dods, *Cook and Housewife's Manual,* 229; Rutledge, *Carolina Housewife,* 91.

22. M. Randolph, *Virginia Housewife,* 112–13; Ude, *French Cook,* 33.

23. Dods, *Cook and Housewife's Manual,* 240–41; Rutledge, *Carolina Housewife,* 89; "To make Sauce for Partridges," Wolley, *Queen-like Closet,* 160; "Sauce for Wild Fowl," M. Randolph, *Virginia Housewife,* 108; "To make celery sauce for turkey or fowles," Stockton receipt book, 25; Cleland, *New and Easy Method,* 65 (for roast pork), 93 (for roasted turkey); Bryan, *Kentucky Housewife,* 168 (for pig, for poultry and game).

24. Raffald, *Experienced English Housekeeper,* 29; Rutledge, *Carolina Housewife,* 157–58; Dods, *Cook and Housewife's Manual,* 359; Glasse, *Art of Cookery* (1796), 34.

25. Glasse, *Art of Cookery* (1747), 34, 35; Dods, *Cook and Housewife's Manual,* 237; M. Randolph, *Virginia Housewife,* 112; Bryan, *Kentucky Housewife,* 169; Wolley, *Queen-like Closet,* 77–78.

26. Glasse, *Art of Cookery* (1747), 98, 101; Pre-1744 Virginia cookbook, 66; Unidentified cookbook, c. 1700, Harbury, *Virginia's Cooking Dynasty,* 152.

27. Dods, *Cook and Housewife's Manual,* 213.

28. Raffald, *Experienced English Housekeeper,* 29; Glasse, *Art of Cookery* (1747), 34; S. Carter, *Frugal Colonial Housewife,* 55; M. Randolph, *Virginia Housewife,* 110; Dods, *Cook and Housewife's Manual,* 235–36; Rundell, *New System of Domestic Cookery,* 115; and others.

29. Harbury, *Virginia's Cooking Dynasty,* 228.

30. Maussion, *They Knew the Washingtons,* 126.

31. Evelyn, *Acetaria,* 5; Pre-1744 Virginia cookbook, 92, 93.

32. Anburey, *Travels,* 2: 218.

33. Bryan, *Kentucky Housewife*, 202–3, 204; and lifetime experience.

34. Byrd, *The Secret Diary;* basic asparagus method detailed by Glasse, M. Randolph, Raffald, Bryan, & others.

35. Von Rumohr, *Essence of Cookery*, 150.

36. C. Carter, *Complete Practical Cook*, 30.

37. Bradley, *Country Housewife*, I: 69; Raffald, *Experienced English Housekeeper*, 39; Apicius, *Cooking and Dining in Imperial Rome*, 83; Glasse, *Art of Cookery* (1747), 98.

38. Von Rumohr, *Essence of Cookery*, 152.

39. Von Rumohr, *Essence of Cookery*, 151.

40. Baily, *Journal*, 242; Byrd, *Secret Diary*, 42, 45, 50, and many more entries.

41. Glasse, *Art of Cookery* (1747), 11; Dods, *Cook and Housewife's Manual*, 208–9; Raffald, *Experienced English Housekeeper*, 40; Smith, *Compleat Housewife*, 16; S. Carter, *Frugal Colonial Housewife*, 34; M. Randolph, *Virginia Housewife*, 126; (with pork) Bryan, *Kentucky Housewife*, 208–209.

42. Fries, *Records of the Moravians*, II: 522.

43. Fithian, *Journal and Letters*, 169; Brown, "Journal of Travel," 312.

44. Fries, *Records of the Moravians*, VI: 2854; Doddridge, *Notes on the Settlement*, 82.

45. Bradley, *Country Housewife*, I: 138; Smith, *Compleat Housewife*, 14–15; Ude, *French Cook*, 337; Von Rumohr, *Essence of Cookery*, 141.

46. Dods, *Cook and Housewife's Manual*, 217–19.

47. Kalm, *Travels*, I: 96; Castiglioni, *Viaggio*, 171.

48. M. Randolph, *Virginia Housewife*, 145; Rutledge, *Carolina Housewife*, 131; Simmons, *American Cookery*, 65.

49. Castiglioni, *Viaggio*, 171; Pickney, *Letterbook*, 97.

50. Moreau de St. Méry, *American Journey*, 56; Kalm, *Travels*, I: 96; Fries, *Records of the Moravians*, II: 575.

51. Von Rumohr, *Essence of Cookery*, 146, 152; Dods, *Cook and Housewife's Manual*, 211.

52. Pre-1744 Virginia cookbook, 48.

53. Pre-1744 Virginia cookbook, 48; Horry, *Colonial Plantation Cookbook*, 75; Jane Randolph 1743, Harbury, *Virginia's Cooking Dynasty*, 388; Unidentified cookbook, c. 1700, Harbury, *Virginia's Cooking Dynasty*, 170, 242.

54. Maussion, *They Knew the Washingtons*, 160.

55. Von Rumohr, *Essence of Cookery*, 141.

56. Byrd, *Secret Diary*, 358.

57. Rutledge, *Carolina Housewife*, 97–98, 102; Bryan, *Kentucky Housewife*, 212–13; Dods, *Cook and Housewife's Manual*, 207–208, 358.

58. Kalm, *Travels*, II: 607; Fries, *Records of the Moravians*, I: 123, 194.

59. La Varenne, *French Cook*, 128, 213–14; Von Rumohr, *Essence of Cookery*, 139, 143–44.

60. Von Rumohr, *Essence of Cookery*, 143; M. Randolph, *Virginia Housewife*, 132; Bryan, *Kentucky Housewife*, 214.

61. Kalm, *Travels*, II: 607.

62. Leslie, *Directions for Cookery*, 21; Glasse, *Art of Cookery* (1805), 138; Simmons, *American Cookery*, 66.

63. Kalm, *Travels*, I: 183.

64. Castiglioni, *Viaggio*, 172.

65. Von Rumohr, *Essence of Cookery*, 140; Moss, *Southern Folk Medicine*.

Chapter 8: For Special Occasions

1. Fithian, *Journal and Letters*, 147, 150, 156, 162, 168, 172, 183 etc.

2. Glasse, *Art of Cookery* (1747), 90; Dods, *Cook and Housewife's Manual*, 191; Bradley, *Country Housewife*, I: 108; Ude, *French Cook*, 267; Raffald, *Experienced English Housekeeper*, 19; also "Waterzooteje" (Flemish cookery), Montagne, *Larousse Gastronomique* (1961), 1004.

3. Von Rumohr, *Essence of Cookery*, 87.

4. La Varenne, *French Cook*, 142–62.

5. Glasse, *Art of Cookery* (1796), 278; Bryan, *Kentucky Housewife*, 149.

6. The Virginia "Sallmon Pye" was closely related to Hannah Glasse's carp pie in which a similar forcemeat filled the belly of the fish. Glasse, *Art of Cookery* (1747), 115.

7. S. Carter, *Frugal Colonial Housewife*, 97–98; C. Carter, *Complete Practical Cook*, 152–57; Smith, *Compleat Housewife*, 162; La Varenne, *French Cook*, 160–62; Glasse, *Art of Cookery* (1747), 114–15.

8. Lawson, *New Voyage*, 161; Moreau de St. Méry, *American Journey*, 68; Glasse, *Art of Cookery* (1747), 115; Raffald, *Experienced English Housekeeper*, 77; S. Carter, *Frugal Colonial Housewife*, 98; English cookery receipt book, c. 1730–1760, 29.

9. Glasse, *Art of Cookery* (1747), 94–95.

10. Wolley, *Queen-like Closet*, 106; Cleland, *New and Easy Method*, 37; Bradley, *Country Housewife*, II: 26–27.

11. "To dress a Crab," Glasse, *Art of Cookery* (1747), 95; "To Stew Crabs," Rutledge, *Carolina Housewife*, 56–57.

12. Von Rumohr, *Essence of Cookery*, 130; Dods, *Cook and Housewife's Manual*, 196 notes that dressed crab was also known as "Scotch Partan-pie."

13. Fisher, *What Mrs. Fisher Knows*, 16–19.

14. Moreau de St. Méry, *American Journey*, 266.

15. "Pottage of Oysters" and "Oyster-Loaves," or "Oyster-Bread," C. Carter, *Complete Practical Cook*, 28, 79; "To stew a Turky brown the nice Way," Glasse, *Art of Cookery* (1747), 36.

16. Raffald, *Experienced English Housekeeper*, 20–21; Jane Randolph 1743, Harbury, *Virginia's Cooking Dynasty*, 408; Moxon, *English Housewifry*, 59; Smith, *Compleat Housewife*, 39; Pre-1744 Virginia cookbook, 35, 73.

17. Cleland, *New and Easy Method*, 24; Ashfield, *Pleasures of Colonial Cooking*, 97–98.

18. Hammond, *Modern Domestic Cookery*, 140; Kettilby, *Above Three Hundred Receipts*, 80–81; Cleland, *New and Easy Method*, 80.

19. Rutledge, *Carolina Housewife*, 55; Ashfield, *Pleasures of Colonial Cooking*, 97–98, 100.

20. Hannah Glasse termed the turtle "the King of Fish." *Art of Cookery* (1796), 145.

21. Woodmason, *Carolina Backcountry*, 237, 244.

22. Burnaby, *Travels*, 80–81.

23. Pinckney, *Letterbook*, 113, 119; Schaw, *Journal of a Lady of Quality*, 96.

24. Raffald, *Experienced English Housekeeper*, 10–11; Glasse, *Art of Cookery* (1796), 145–47.

25. Schaw, *Journal of a Lady of Quality*, 95–96; Simmons, *American Cookery*, 53–56; Hill, *Southern Practical Cookery*, 45.

26. Schaw, *Journal of a Lady of Quality*, 186.

27. Cresswell, *Journal*, 74; Byrd, *Histories of the Dividing Line*, 278.

28. *What Mrs. Fisher Knows About Old Southern Cooking*, 1881, is thought to be the first cookbook from an African-American. Originally from South Carolina, Abby Fisher became an acclaimed cook in San Francisco.

29. Fries, *Records of the Moravians*, II: 578.

30. Stephens, "Journal of the Proceedings in Georgia," in *Setting out to Begin a New World*, 62; Moreau de St. Méry, *American Journey*, 58; Asbury, *Journal and Letters* 2: 248; Burnaby, *Travels*, 26; Fithian, *Journal and Letters*, 183.

31. Mary Clay to Nancy, November 9, 1782 (Camden, South Carolina ?), Clay Papers, Southern Historical Collection, University of North Carolina, Chapel Hill; Letter, Lawrence Butler, Westmoreland County, Virginia, to Madam [---], England, 15 October, 1784, *Virginia Magazine of History and Biography*, Vol. 40:266–67.

32. M. Randolph, *Virginia Housewife*, 62–63.

33. Doddridge, *Notes on the Settlement*, 104.

34. Kalm, *Travels*, II: 677.

35. Schober commonplace book; Raffald, *Experienced English Housekeeper*, 134–35; Rutledge, *Carolina Housewife*, 196.

36. Bryan, *Kentucky Housewife*, 279–80; Montagne, *Larousse Gastronomique* (1961), 205; *Charleston Receipts*, 237; Farmer, *Boston Cooking School*, 646–47.

37. Eaton, *Complete and Universal Dictionary*, 479; Bryan, *Kentucky Housewife*, 276–77.

38. Bryan, *Kentucky Housewife*, 301; Unidentified cookbook, c. 1700, Harbury, *Virginia's Cooking Dynasty*, 208; Beeton, *Everyday Cookery*, 160; Horry, *Colonial Plantation Cookbook*, 63; Ashfield, *Pleasures of Colonial Cooking*, 131.

39. Bryan, *Kentucky Housewife*, 280, 202–301; Beeton, *Everyday Cookery*, 160.

40. Beeton, *Everyday Cookery*, 160.

41. Moreau de St. Méry, *American Journey*, 54.

42. Maussion, *They Knew the Washingtons*, 144–45.

43. Pre-1744 Virginia cookbook, 88; Jane Randolph 1743 (and *Several Hands, A Collection of Above Three Hundred Receipts in Cookery Physick and Surgery* (London: 1714)), Harbury, *Virginia's Cooking Dynasty*, 382–385.

44. Ellis, *Country Housewife's Family Companion*, 127; Tusser, *Good Husbandry*, 273.

45. Tusser's *furmenty, frumity*, or *furmity* were early variations of *flummery*. A simple rustic flummery was prepared from finely ground oats, wheat, rice, or other grain soaked and boiled to a smooth jelly or pudding-like consistency. This smooth porridge was sweetened, perhaps flavored, and served with milk or cream, wine, or ale. The American "porridge of corn" or mush was also commonly eaten with milk, or buttermilk, and syrup or sugar. Ashfield, *Pleasures of Colonial Cooking*, 141; W.M., *Compleat Cook*, 59–60; Ellis, *Country Housewife's Family Companion*, 279–80; Kalm, *Travels*, II: 602–3.

46. Dods, *Cook and Housewife's Manual*, 445; Glasse, *Art of Cookery* (1747), 139; Cleland, *New and Easy Method*, 158–161; Bradley, *Country Housewife*, II: 91–92; Raffald, *Experienced English Housekeeper*, 135, 138; Moxon, *English Housewifry*, 77, 79; Johnson, *Every Young Woman's Companion*, 138–39, 141; Ashfield, *Pleasures of Colonial Cooking*, 135; Goelet household book, 3; Pre-1744 Virginia cookbook, 28, 33; Jane Randolph 1743, Harbury, *Virginia's Cooking Dynasty*, 402–4; Unidentified cookbook, c. 1700, Harbury, *Virginia's Cooking Dynasty*, 212, 246.

47. Glasse, *Art of Cookery* (1747), 141; Raffald, *Experienced English Housekeeper*, 139; Cleland, *New and Easy Method*, 155–56; Horry, *Colonial Plantation Cookbook*, 104–5; Goelet household book, 4; Unidentified cookbook, c. 1700, Harbury, *Virginia's Cooking Dynasty*, 210, 248; Rutledge, *Carolina Housewife*, 209–10; and others.

48. Dods, *Cook and Housewife's Manual*, 450–51.

49. Doddridge, *Notes on the Settlement*, 88; Moss and Hoffman, *Backcountry Housewife*, 37–38.

50. Blackford, "Recipes in the Culinary Arts," 12.

51. M. Randolph, *Virginia Housewife*, 95.

52. Moreau de St. Méry, *American Journey*, 99.

53. Glasse, *Art of Cookery* (1747), 85, 146; Lee, *Cook's Own Book*, 124.

54. Cleland, *New and Easy Method*, 148; Moxon, *English Housewifry*, 125.

55. "Allmond Puding" and "Calves feet Puding," Pre-1744 Virginia cookbook, 51; "To make a green Pudding to Butter" and "To make an Almond Tart," Wolley, *Queen-like Closet*, 165; "Plum Pudding," Leslie, *Directions for Cookery*, 14–15; and others: "To Make a Light Pudding," *Martha Washington's Booke*, 109; "To make an Almond pudding" and "To make a quaking Pudding," W.M., *Compleat Cook*, 48, 25–26.

56. Dods, *Cook and Housewife's Manual,* 451.

57. Margaret Steele, December 24, 1804, Special Collections Library, Duke University.

58. "Lemon Puffs," Cleland, *New and Easy Method,* 151; "Lemon Puffs," Rundell, *New System of Domestic Cookery,* 162; "Cream Cakes," Raffald, *Experienced English Housekeeper,* 138; "Lemon Biskett," Pre-1744 Virginia cookbook, 27; "Lemon Biskits," Van Rensselaer, *Score of Hospitality,* 28; "Kisses," Leslie, *Directions for Cookery,* 58; "Kiss Cakes," Rutledge, *Carolina Housewife,* 188; "Kisses," Blackford, "Recipes in the Culinary Arts," 3.

59. Raffald, *Experienced English Housekeeper,* 138.

60. Bryan, *Kentucky Housewife,* 299.

61. Fries, *Records of the Moravians,* I: 233, 409, 745, 783; II: 834.

62. Fries, *Records of the Moravians,* I: 233.

63. Glasse, *Art of Cookery* (1747), 73; Raffald, *Experienced English Housekeeper,* 73; Dods, *Cook and Housewife's Manual,* 388; Rutledge, *Carolina Housewife,* 85; Rundell, *New System of Domestic Cookery,* 133.

64. Rundell, *New System of Domestic Cookery,* 133; Cleland, *New and Easy Method,* 80.

65. Bradley, *Country Housewife,* II: 146–47; Smith, *Compleat Housewife,* 146–47; Pre-1744 Virginia cookbook, 56–57; Blackford, "Recipes in the Culinary Arts," 32; Horry, *Colonial Plantation Cookbook,* 76, 100.

66. Glasse, *Art of Cookery* (1747), 74.

67. Dods, *Cook and Housewife's Manual,* 399.

68. Dods, *Cook and Housewife's Manual,* 374; Smith, *Compleat Housewife,* 29–30.

69. Pre-1744 Virginia cookbook, 60.

70. Cresswell, *Journal,* 52–53.

71. Montagne, *Larousse Gastronomique* (1961), 204–5; *Glasgow Cookery Book,* 234; Brown, *Southern Cookbook,* 247–48.

72. Byrd, *Secret Diary,* 549; Receipt from John Lewis Beard to Elizabeth Steel 1773 for purchase of funeral foods. John Steel Papers, 689, Southern Historical Collection, University of North Carolina, Chapel Hill.

73. Fries, *Records of the Moravians,* I: 361.

Chapter 9: Miscellanies and Musings

1. Woodmason, *Carolina Backcountry,* 13.

2. Waightstill Avery travel diary, 1769, typescript. Lyman Draper Papers, Wisconsin Historical Society, Madison.

3. William Tennent. Journal, 1775, Caroliniana Collection, University of South Carolina, Columbia.

4. Anburey, *Travels,* 2: 198.

5. Marquis de Chastellux, *Travels . . . ,* Vol. 2.

6. Baily, *Journal,* 22.

7. Baily, *Journal,* 42.

8. Maclean, "William Maclean's Travel Journal," 378–388.

9. Maclean, "William Maclean's Travel Journal," 383.

10. Georgia Trustees agreement with John Thomas, shipmaster, 1732, in *Setting Out to Begin a New World,* 14.

11. Francis Moore, *Voyage to Georgia,* in *Setting Out to Begin a New World,* 42. Moore was storekeeper for a group of colonists headed for Georgia, 1735.

12. Thomas Christie, journal of 1732 voyage, in *Setting Out to Begin a New World,* 16–20. Christie was one of Oglethorpe's first Georgia colonists.

13. Woodmason, *Carolina Backcountry,* 39.

14. Franklin, *Autobiography,* 110.

15. Dods, *Cook and Housewife's Manual,* 128; Glasse, *Art of Cookery* (1747), 98, 99; See "Asparagus Forced in French Role" in chapter 7.

16. Pre-1744 Virginia cookbook, 74; Cleland, *New and Easy Method,* 128–29; Raffald, *Experienced English Housekeeper,* 148; M. Randolph, *Virginia Housewife,* 106–7, 236; Rutledge, *Carolina Housewife,* 107; Bryan, *Kentucky Housewife,* 228–29; Wolley, *Queen-like Closet,* 102.

17. Raffald, *Experienced English Housekeeper,* 148.

18. Kalm, *Travels,* I: 320, II: 646–47; Byrd, *The Secret Diary;* Maussion, *They Knew the Washingtons,* 145.

19. Dods, *Cook and Housewife's Manual,* 322.

20. Raffald, *Experienced English Housekeeper,* 144; Von Rumohr, *Essence of Cookery,* 132.

21. M. Randolph, *Virginia Housewife,* 100; Rutledge, *Carolina Housewife,* 110–12.

22. Glasse, *Art of Cookery* (1747), 97; Cleland, *New and Easy Method,* 155; La Varenne, *French Cook,* 91; Dods, *Cook and Housewife's Manual,* 320–23.

23. Woodmason, *Carolina Backcountry,* 39; Franklin, *Autobiography* 110; Martin, *Journey,* 10.

24. Kalm, *Travels,* I: 189.

25. Acrelius, *History of New Sweden,* 163, 158.

26. Acrelius, *History of New Sweden,* 163.

27. Acrelius, *History of New Sweden,* 163.

28. Acrelius, *History of New Sweden,* 160.

29. Fithian, *Journal and Letters,* 54.

30. Fries, *Records of the Moravians,* VI: 2512.

31. Reeves, "Extracts from the Letterbooks," 65.

32. Byrd, *Secret Diary,* 442–43.

33. Fries, *Records of the Moravians,* II: 522.

34. Acrelius, *History of New Sweden,* 162.

35. Stearns, *American Oracle,* 481.

36. Kalm, *Travels,* I: 370.

37. Acrelius, *History of New Sweden,* 164.

38. Castiglioni, *Viaggio*, 179.

39. Byrd, *Histories of the Dividing Line*, 42.

40. Johann David Schoepf, *Travels*, 114.

41. Moreau de St. Méry, *American Journey*, 266.

42. Doddridge, *Notes on the Settlement*, 89–90.

43. Acrelius, *History of New Sweden*, 164.

44. Fithian, *Journal and Letters*, 158.

45. Byrd, *Histories of the Dividing Line*, 123.

46. Fries, *Records of the Moravians*, II: 531.

47. Acrelius, *History of New Sweden*, 164.

48. Fithian, *Journal and Letters*, 55.

49. Fries, *Records of the Moravians*, IV: 1726.

50. Byrd, *Secret Diary*, 121, 418, etc.; Rundell, *New System of Domestic Cookery*, 284.

51. Kalm, *Travels*, II: 661, 670 noted *cocoa* for sale by the pound in Boston and *chocolate* by the dozen in New York. For extensive cultural and natural history of chocolate see Maricel E. Presilla, *The New Taste of Chocolate*. Berkeley: Ten Speed Press, 2001.

52. *Encyclopaedia Britannica* (1771) 193; Glasse, *Art of Cookery* (1796), 341–42.

53. Johnson, *Every Young Woman's Companion*, 152.

54. Moss and Hoffman, *Backcountry Housewife*, 123.

55. Wolley, *Queen-like Closet*, 60; Ashfield, *Pleasures of Colonial Cooking*, 137; Unidentified cookbook, c. 1700, Harbury, *Virginia's Cooking Dynasty*, 278, 188; Smith, *Compleat Housewife*, 181; Raffald, *Experienced English Housekeeper*, 125, 141; C. Carter, *Complete Practical Cook*, 125; Pre-1744 Virginia cookbook, 17.

56. Byrd, *Secret Diary*, 467; M. Randolph, *Virginia Housewife*, 173, Bryan, *Kentucky Housewife*, 307. Bryan also gave a receipt for "Coffee Cakes" which were cracker-like.

57. Glasse, *Art of Cookery* (1796), 376–377; Raffald, *Experienced English Housekeeper*, 191.

58. "To make the liquid more odoriferous, you may add some fragrant pink leaves [dianthus petals], sweet Williams, &c.," Bryan, *The Kentucky Housewife*, 388.

59. Cleland, *New and Easy Method*, 201–202; Dods, *Cook and Housewife's Manual*, 458; Horry, *Colonial Plantation Cookbook*, 82, 95; Rutledge, *Carolina Housewife*, 172; Bryan, *Kentucky Housewife*, 403–404; Rundell, *New System of Domestic Cookery*, 256.

60. Wolley, *Queen-like Closet*, 98; May, *Accomplisht Cook*, 133; M. Randolph, *Virginia Housewife*, 114–15.

61. Raffald, *Experienced English Housekeeper*, 176; *Martha Washington's Booke*, 168; W.M., *Compleat Cook*, 21.

62. Kettilby, *Above Three Hundred Receipts*, 34; Moxon, *English Housewifry*, 130; Raffald, *Experienced English Housekeeper*, 165, 169, 182; Harbury, *Virginia's Cooking*

Dynasty, 160; Von Rumohr reported, but did not condone, another use: "Some people add elderflowers... to sweet dishes. They impart a rather flat, sweet flavor which is inclined to become unpleasant." *Essence of Cookery*, 163.

63. Kalm, *Travels*, I: 42; Fries, *Records of the Moravians*, II: 575.

64. Sara Few Davidson made few food notes in her diary but noted on July 6, 1837 she was occupied "making ketshup for myself & sister Mary." By this date she may have been making tomato ketchup. The time of year also supports this likelihood. Davidson, *Private Journal*, 110.

65. Glasse, *Art of Cookery* (1747), 121–22, 156; Rutledge, *Carolina Housewife*, 185.

66. Cleland, *New and Easy Method*, 195; Raffald, *Experienced English Housekeeper*, 175; Dods, *Cook and Housewife's Manual*, 259–60; M. Randolph, *Virginia Housewife*, 202–3; Bryan, *Kentucky Housewife*, 172–174; Rundell, *New System of Domestic Cookery*, 183–84; Horry, *Colonial Plantation Cookbook*, 84 (from Pinckney); another mushroom powder, Glasse, *Art of Cookery* (1747), 122.

67. Dods, *Cook and Housewife's Manual*, 254.

68. Horry, *Colonial Plantation Cookbook*, 140; Dods, *Cook and Housewife's Manual*, 254.

69. Ellis, *Country Housewife's Family Companion*, 450.

70. Von Rumohr, *Essence of Cookery*, 164; Glasse, *Art of Cookery* (1747), 135; Smith, *Compleat Housewife*, 106; Moxon, *English Housewifry*, 141; Raffald, *Experienced English Housekeeper*, 182.

71. Bradley, *Country Housewife*, I: 122; S. Carter, *Frugal Colonial Housewife*, 128; Von Rumohr, *Essence of Cookery*, 164.

72. M. Randolph, *Virginia Housewife*, 207; Bryan, *Kentucky Housewife*, 167, 183.

73. Glasse, *Art of Cookery* (1747), 132–33; Raffald, *Experienced English Housekeeper*, 182; M. Randolph, *Virginia Housewife*, 207–8; Bryan, *Kentucky Housewife*, 182–83.

74. M. Randolph, *Virginia Housewife*, 207; Bryan, *Kentucky Housewife*, 182–83; S. Rutledge, *Carolina Housewife*, 182.

75. Glasse, *Art of Cookery* (1796), 37; Smith, *Compleat Housewife*, 119; Kettilby, *Above Three Hundred Receipts*, 63–64; Purviance household book; Raffald, *Experienced English Housekeeper*, 42; South Carolina household book.

76. Raffald, *Experienced English Housekeeper*, 42; Glasse, *Art of Cookery* (1796), 37–38.

77. Edgeworth, *Southern Gardener*, 146; Rundell, *New System of Domestic Cookery*, 178, 181.

78. Raffald, *Experienced English Housekeeper*, 42; W.M., *Compleat Cook*, 4; Unidentified cookbook, c. 1700, Harbury, *Virginia's Cooking Dynasty*, 232; Glasse, *Art of Cookery* (1747), 133; (1796), 37–38, 87.

79. Equal weight of sugar and flowers, Markham, *English Housewife*, 117; double weight sugar to orange rind, Pre-1744 Virginia cookbook, 11; 2 ½ times as much sugar as flowers, Glasse, *Art of Cookery* (1747), 153; different sugar to herb

proportions—from equal weights to three times sugar, W.M., *A Queen's Delight*, 18, 39–43.

80. Byrd, *Secret Diary*, 103.

81. Unidentified cookbook, c. 1700, Harbury, *Virginia's Cooking Dynasty*, 176, 178; Pre-1744 Virginia cookbook, 3; Jane Randolph 1743, Harbury, *Virginia's Cooking Dynasty*, 332–34, 340; M. Randolph, *Virginia Housewife*, 196–97.

82. Dods, *Cook and Housewife's Manual*, 438–39; Rutledge, *Carolina Housewife*, 164–65.

83. Jane Randolph 1743, Harbury, *Virginia's Cooking Dynasty*, 332–34, 340, 404; Unidentified cookbook, c. 1700, Harbury, *Virginia's Cooking Dynasty*, 176, 178.

84. Dods, *Cook and Housewife's Manual*, 438.

85. Bradley, *Country Housewife*, I: 124–25; Raffald, *Experienced English Housekeeper*, 173.

86. Rundell, *New System of Domestic Cookery*, 216; Raffald, *Experienced English Housekeeper*, 107.

87. Ashfield, *Pleasures of Colonial Cooking*, 145; Horry, *Colonial Plantation Cookbook*, 101; Bryan, *Kentucky Housewife*, 362; Unidentified cookbook, c. 1700, Harbury, *Virginia's Cooking Dynasty*, 196, 198.

88. Moss and Hoffman, *Backcountry Housewife*, 124; Stockton receipt book, 6; South Carolina household book; Eale, *Receipts*, 99.

Appendix B

1. Karen Hess, notes in *Martha Washington's Booke*, 157, 312, 319. For an example of similar receipts, one with quart measure of flour and other with weight, see gingerbread receipts from Unidentified cookbook, c. 1700, Harbury, *Virginia's Cooking Dynasty*, and Cameron, "Friend to the Memory."

2. Fries, *Records of the Moravians*, I: 90, IV: 1864; Maryland Journal and Baltimore Adviser (Baltimore, 2 December, 1777).

3. Karen Hess, note in *Martha Washington's Booke*, 104; Eaton, *Complete and Universal Dictionary*, 281.

4. David, *English Bread and Yeast Cookery*, (Hess, introductory notes, x–xi), 114–18; Hess, notes in *Martha Washington's Booke*, 113–115, 118, 312.

5. M. Randolph, *Virginia Housewife*, 165; Raffald, *Experienced English Housekeeper*, 83.

6. Ellis, *Country Housewife's Family Companion*, 81, 84, 271; Kettilby, *Above Three Hundred Receipts*, 86; Dods, *Cook and Housewife's Manual*, 91.

7. For example Glasse, *Art of Cookery* (1796), "To fricassee Pigeons the Italian Way," 119, (1747 & 1796) "Cullis the Italian Way," 54, (1796) "A Spanish Peas-Soup" and "To make Onion-Soup the Spanish Way," 211; Fries, *Records of the Moravians*, II: 577.

Appendix C

1. Kalm, *Travels*, II: 602.

2. Fries, *Records of the Moravians*, I: 142–146.

3. Fithian, *Journal and Letters*, 40.

4. Cresswell, *Journal*, 61.

5. Reeves, "Extracts from the Letterbooks," 64.

6. Maussion, *They Knew the Washingtons*, 126.

7. Moreau de St. Méry, *American Journey*, 265.

8. Stearns, *American Oracle*, 481.

9. Kemp P. Battle, *History of the University of North Carolina* (Spartanburg, South Carolina: The Reprint Co., 1974), 51.

10. Baily, *Journal*, 252.

11. Fries, *Records of the Moravians*, VI: 2779.

12. Conner, *Diary*, 26.

13. Conner, *Diary*, 37.

14. Kalm, *Travels*, II: 602.

15. Acrelius, *History of New Sweden*, 158.

16. Fithian, *Journal and Letters*, 33, 39, 110, 114, 128.

17. Reeves, "Extracts from the Letterbooks," 86.

18. Kemp P. Battle, *History of the University of North Carolina* (Spartanburg, South Carolina: The Reprint Co., 1974), 51.

19. Fries, *Records of the Moravians*, VI: 2779.

Selected Bibliography

General Cookery Books

Apicius. *Cookery and Dining in Imperial Rome.* Edited by and Translated by Joseph Dommers Vehling. New York: Dover Publications, 1977.

Beeton, Isabella Mary. *Mrs. Beeton's Every Day Cookery and Housekeeping Book.* 1865. New York: Gallery Books, 1984.

Boston Housekeeper (Mrs. N. K. M. Lee). *The Cooks Own Book.* 1832. Merrifield, Virginia: Rare Book Republishers.

Bradley, Richard. *The Country Housewife and Lady's Director.* 1736. Vol. I & II. London: Prospect Books, 1980.

Brown, Marion. *The Southern Cookbook.* Chapel Hill: The University of North Carolina Press, 1951.

Bryan, Lettice. *The Kentucky Housewife.* 1839. Columbia: University of South Carolina Press, 1991.

Carter, Charles. *The Complete Practical Cook: Or, A New System of the Whole Art and Mystery of Cookery.* 1730. London: Prospect Books, 1984.

Carter, Susannah. *The Frugal Colonial Housewife.* 1772. Garden City, N.Y.: Doubleday, 1976.

Chadwick, Mrs. J. *Home Cookery: a Collection of Tried Receipts.* 1853. Birmingham, Ala.: Oxmoor House, Antique American Cookbooks, 1984.

Charleston Receipts. Charleston, S.C.: Junior League of Charleston, 1950.

The Charlotte Cookbook. Charlotte, N.C.: Charlotte Junior League, 1969.

Child, Mrs. (Lydia Maria). *The American Frugal Housewife.* 1832. Boston: Carter, Hendee, 1980.

Cleland, Elizabeth. *A New and Easy Method of Cookery.* Edinburgh: C. Wright and Co., 1759. Gale ECCO Print Editions, 2010.

Dods, Mistress Margaret. *The Cook and Housewife's Manual.* Fourth edition, 1829. London: Rosters Ltd., 1988.

Eale, Mary. *Mrs. Mary Eale's Receipts.* 1733. London: Prospect Books, 1985.

Eaton, Mary. *The Cook and Housekeeper's Complete and Universal Dictionary.* Bungay: J. and R. Childs, 1823.

Edgeworth, Mrs. Mary L. *The Southern Gardener and Receipt-Book.* Philadelphia: J. B. Lippincott, 1859.

Ellis, William. *The Country Housewife's Family Companion.* 1750. Devon, U.K.: Prospect Books, 2000.

Evelyn, John. *Acetaria: A Discourse of Sallets.* London: B. Tooke, 1699.

Farmer, Fannie Merritt. *The Boston Cooking-School Cook Book.* Boston: Little, Brown, 1924.

Fisher, Abby. *What Mrs. Fisher Knows about Old Southern Cooking.* 1881. Edited by Karen Hess. Bedford, Mass.: Applewood Books, 1995.

The Glasgow Cookery Book. Glasgow and West of Scotland College of Domestic Science. Glasgow: John Smith & Son, 1951.

Glasse, Hannah. *The Art of Cookery Made Plain and Easy.* 1747. London: Prospect Books, 1983.

———. *The Art of Cookery Made Plain and Easy.* 1796. Hamden, Conn.: Archon, 1971.

———. *The Art of Cookery Made Plain and Easy.* First American edition 1804. Bedford, Mass.: Applewood Books, 1997.

Hammond, Elizabeth. *Modern Domestic Cookery and Useful Receipt Book.* London, c. 1830.

Hill, Annabella P. *Southern Practical Cookery and Receipt Book.* 1872. Columbia: University of South Carolina Press, 1995.

Johnson, Madam. *Madam Johnson's Present; or, Every Young Woman's Companion in Useful and Universal Knowledge.* London: J. Fuller & W. Nicoll, 1765.

Kettilby, Mary. *A Collection of Above Three Hundred Receipts in Cookery, Physick, and Surgery; For the Use of All Good Wives, Tender Mothers, and Careful Nurses.* 1734. LaVergne, Tenn.: General Books, 2010.

La Varenne, Francois Pierre. *The French Cook.* "Englished by I.D.G. 1653." Lewes, East Sussex: Southover Press, 2001.

Lee, Mrs. N. K. M. "A Boston Housekeeper." *The Cook's Own Book.* 1832. Merrifield, Va.: Rare Book Publishers, 1997.

Leslie, Miss [Eliza]. *Directions for Cookery in Its Various Branches.* First edition. 1828 Philadelphia: Cary & Holt, 1837.

Macleod, Iseabail. *Mrs. McLintock's Receipts for Cookery and Pastry-Work.* 1736. Aberdeen: The University Press, 1986.

Markham, Gervase. *The English Housewife.* 1631. Kingston and Montreal: McGill-Queen's University Press, 1986.

May, Robert. *The Accomplisht Cook; or, The Art & Mystery of Cookery.* London 1685. Lexington, Ky.: Filiquarian Publishing, 2010.

[Montefiore, Judith Cohen] ("Edited by a Lady"). *The Jewish Manual.* 1846. New York: Nightingale Books, 1983.

Moxon, Elisabeth. *English Housewifry.* Leeds: James Lister, 1742.

Raffald, Elizabeth. *The Experienced English Housekeeper.* 1769. Lewes, East Sussex, U.K.: Southover Press, 1997.

———. *The Experienced English Housekeeper.* 1782. Newport Pagnell, U.K.: Paul Minet Reprints, 1970.

Randolph, Mary. *The Virginia Housewife*. 1824. Edited by Karen Hess. Columbia: University of South Carolina Press, 1984.

Rombauer, Irma S., and Marion Rombauer Becker. *The Joy of Cooking*. Indianapolis: Bobbs-Merrill, 1953.

[Rundell, Maria Eliza] ("By a Lady"). *A New System of Domestic Cookery; formed upon Principles of Economy; and Adapted to the Use of Private Families*. Boston, 1807; London, 1810.

Rutledge, Sarah. *The Carolina Housewife*. 1847. Columbia: University of South Carolina Press, 1980.

Simmons, Amelia. *American Cookery, 1796*. Green Farms, Connecticut: Silverleaf Press, 1984.

Smith, E[liza]. *The Compleat Housewife: or Accomplish'd Gentlewoman's Companion*. London: 1742.

———. The *Compleat Housewife*. London: 1758.

Thornton, P. *The Southern Gardener and Receipt Book*. Newark, N.J., 1845.

Tusser, Thomas. *Five Hundred Points of Good Husbandry with a Book of Huswifery*. 1580. London, 1812.

Ude, Louis Eustache. *The French Cook*. 1828. New York: Arco Publishing, 1978.

Von Rumohr, Karl Friedrick. *The Essence of Cookery*. 1822. Translated by Barbara Yeomans. London: Prospect Books, 1993.

W. M., *The Compleat Cook and A Queens Delight*. (Two titles of the trilogy *The Queens Closet Opened*) 1671. London: Prospect Books, 1984.

Wolley, Hannah. *The Queen-like Closet*. 1672. Charleston, S.C.: Bibliobazaar, 2006.

Personal Cookery Books

Alston household book, 1818. South Carolina. Ms. Alston Family Papers, Caroliniana Collection, University of South Carolina, Columbia.

Ashfield family (c.1720–1775). *Pleasures of Colonial Cooking*. Newark, N.J.: Miller Cory House Museum and the New Jersey Historical Society, 1982.

Avery, Harriet Erwin. Poetry and receipt book, c.1815–1858. Ms. Avery Family of North Carolina Papers. Southern Historical Collection, University of North Carolina, Chapel Hill.

Blackford, Lancelot Minor. "Recipes in the Culinary Art, Together with Hints on Housewifery &c." 1852. Ms. Blackford Family Papers, Southern Historical Collection, University of North Carolina, Chapel Hill.

Burling, Polly. "A Book of Receipts April 1770." Edited by Sue Huesken and Mercy Ingraham. *Colonial Burlington Cookery*. Riverside, N.J.: RanMer Publishing, 2008.

Cameron. "A Friend to the Memory, Recipes, Mrs. R. Cameron, Fairntosh, Orange Co. No. Carolina." October the 15th 1816. Also recipes attributed to Annie Cameron c. 1834. Ms. Cameron Family Papers, Southern Historical Collection, University of North Carolina, Chapel Hill.

Devereux, Margaret Mordecai. Receipt book, c.1842. Raleigh, N.C. Ms. Devereux Family Papers, Special Collections Library, Duke University, Durham, North Carolina.

English cookery receipt book, c.1730–1760. (TP.1950.074.006) Tryon Palace, New Bern, North Carolina.

Goelet [Elizabeth?] household book, 1756. North Carolina. Ms. Goelet-Buncombe Papers, Southern Historical Collection, University of North Carolina, Chapel Hill.

Horry, Harriot Pinckney. *A Colonial Plantation Cookbook: The Receipt Book of Harriott Pinckney Horry, 1770.* Edited by Richard Hooker. Lowcountry South Carolina. Columbia: University of South Carolina Press, 1984.

Martha Washington's Booke of Cookery. Edited by Karen Hess. New York: Columbia University, 1981.

Pinckney, Eliza Lucas. Household book, 1756–?. South Carolina Lowcountry. Ms. South Carolina Historical Society, Charleston.

Pre-1744 Virginia cookbook. Ms & Ts. Old Salem Museums & Gardens, Winston-Salem, N.C.

Price, Rebecca. *The Compleat Cook: or the Secrets of a Seventeenth-Century Housewife* c.1681–1740. London: Routledge & Kegan Paul, 1974.

Purviance, Elizabeth Isabella. Household book, c.1799. Baltimore, Maryland. Ms. Purviance-Courtaney Papers, Special Collections Library, Duke University, Durham, N.C.

Randolph, Jane (Bolling). "Jane Randolph her Cookery Book" 1743. Virginia Historical Society, Richmond. Edited by Katharine E. Harbury. *Colonial Virginia's Cooking Dynasty* (pp. 285–421). Columbia: University of South Carolina Press, 2004.

Raper, Elizabeth. *The Receipt Book of Elizabeth Raper.* Edited by Bartle Grant. Soho: Nonesuch Press, 1924.

Schmidt, Dorothea Christina. Household book, c.1772. Germany & Liberty County, Georgia. Ms. Alexander & Hillhouse Papers, Southern Historical Collection, University of North Carolina, Chapel Hill.

Schober, Anna Paulina. Commonplace book, 1805–1821. Ms. Old Salem Museums & Gardens, Winston-Salem, N.C.

South Carolina household book, c.1778–85. Ms. Preston-Davie Papers, vol.1, Southern Historical Collection, University of North Carolina, Chapel Hill.

Stockton receipt book, c. 1762. New Jersey. Ms. Bryan Family Papers, Special Collections Library, Duke University, Durham, N.C.

Unidentified cookbook, c.1700. Virginia Historical Society, Richmond. Edited by Katharine E. Harbury, *Colonial Virginia's Cooking Dynasty* (pp. 145–283). Columbia: University of South Carolina Press, 2004.

Van Rensselaer family. *Score of Hospitality.* 1785–1835. Albany, N.Y.: Historic Cherry Hill, 1986.

Winkler family recipe collection, late 1700s & 1800s. Ts. Archives of the Moravian Church in America, Southern Province, Winston-Salem, N.C. Translated by Old Salem, Inc., Winston-Salem, N.C.

Related Primary Sources

Acrelius, Israel. *A History of New Sweden*. 1759. Translated by William M. Reynolds, 1874. Ann Arbor: University Microfilms, 1966.

Anburey, Thomas. *Travels through the Interior Parts of America*. 1789. Boston: Houghton Mifflin, 1923.

Asbury, Francis. *The Journal and Letters of Francis Asbury: Volume I, The Journal 1771 to 1793*. London: Epworth Press and Nashville: Abingdon Press, 1958.

Baily, Francis. *Journal of a Tour in Unsettled Parts of North America in 1796 & 1797*. Carbondale: Southern Illinois University Press, 1969.

Brown, John. "John Brown's Journal of Travel in Western North Carolina in 1795." Edited by A.R. Newsome. *North Carolina Historical Review*, XI: 4 (October 1934): 284–313.

Burnaby, Rev. Andrew. *Travels through the Middle Settlements in North-America in the Years 1759–1760*. London, 1775. Ithaca, N.Y.: Cornell University Press, 1960.

Byrd, William. *Histories of the Dividing Line Betwixt Virginia and North Carolina*. 1728. Gloucester, Mass.: Peter Smith, 1984.

———. *The London Diary (1717–1721) and Other Writings*. Edited by Louis B. Wright and Marion Tinling. New York: Oxford University Press, 1958.

———. *The Secret Diary of William Byrd of Westover 1709–1712*. Edited by Louis B Wright and Marion Tinling. Richmond, Va.: The Dietz Press, 1941.

———. *Another Secret Diary of William Byrd of Westover 1739–1741: With Letters & Literary Exercises 1696–1726*. Edited by Maude H. Woodfin, decoded by Marion Tinling. Richmond, Va.: The Dietz Press, 1942.

Castiglioni, Luigi. *Viaggio: Travels in the United States of North America 1785–1787*. Translated by Antonio Pace. Syracuse: Syracuse University Press, 1983.

Chastellux, Marquis de. *Travels in North America in the Years 1780, 1781, and 1782*. Chapel Hill: University of North Carolina Press, 1963.

Conner, Juliana Margaret. Diary from June 10–October 17, 1827 in North Carolina and Tennessee. Ts. Conner Papers, Southern Historical Collection, University of North Carolina, Chapel Hill.

Cresswell, Nicholas. *The Journal of Nicholas Cresswell 1774–1777*. New York: The Dial Press, 1926.

Davidson, Sarah Few. *A Life in Antebellum Charlotte: The Private Journal of Sarah F. Davidson, 1837*. Edited by Karen M. McConnell, Janet S. Dyer, and Ann Williams. Charleston, S.C.: History Press, 2005.

Doddridge, Joseph. *Notes on the Settlement and Indian Wars of the Western Parts of Virginia and Pennsylvania from 1763 to 1783. . . .* 1824. Pittsburgh: John S. Titenour and William T. Lindsey, 1912.

Fithian, Philip Vickers. *Journal & Letters of Philip Vickers Fithian 1773–1774: A Plantation Tutor of the Old Dominion.* Edited by Hunter Dickinson Farish. Charlottesville: The University Press of Virginia, 1968.

Franklin, Benjamin. *The Autobiography of Benjamin Franklin.* Edited by Philip Smith. Mineola, New York: Dover, 1996.

Humelbergius, Dick Secundus. *Apician Morsels; or, Tales of the Table, Kitchen, and Larder.* New York: J. & J. Harper, 1829.

Kalm, Peter. *Peter Kalm's Travels in North America.* Vols. I–II. 1770. Edited by Adolph B. Benson. New York: Dover, 1937.

Lawson, John. *A New Voyage to Carolina.* 1701. Chapel Hill: University of North Carolina Press, 1984.

Maclean, William. "William Maclean's Travel Journal from Lincolnton, North Carolina, to Nashville, Tennessee, May–June, 1811." Edited by Alice Barnwell Keith. *North Carolina Historical Review,* XV: 4 (October 1938), 378–388.

Martin, William D. *A Journey from South Carolina to Connecticut in the Year 1809: The Journal of William D. Martin.* Charlotte, N.C.: Heritage House, 1959.

Maussion, Gaston and Helene de. *They Knew the Washingtons: Letters from a French Soldier with Lafayette and from His Family in Virginia.* 1777–1799. Translated and edited by Princess Radziwill. Indianapolis: The Bobbs-Merrill Company, 1926.

Moreau de St. Méry's American Journey 1793–1798. Translated and edited by Kenneth Roberts and Anna M. Roberts. Garden City, N.Y.: Doubleday & Company, 1947.

Pinckney, Eliza Lucas. *The Letterbook of Eliza Lucas Pinckney, 1739–1762.* Edited by Elise Pinckney. Chapel Hill: University of North Carolina Press, 1972.

Records of *the Moravians in North Carolina.* Vol. 1–6. Edited by Adelaide L. Fries. Raleigh: North Carolina State Department of Archives and History, 1968–1970.

Reeves, Enos. "Extracts from the Letter-books of Lieutenant Enos Reeves, of the Pennsylvania Line," *Pennsylvania Magazine of History and Biography,* 20:3 (1896), 61–92.

Schaw, Janet. *Journal of a Lady of Quality: from Scotland to the West Indies, North Carolina, and Portugal 1774–1776.* Edited by Evangeline Walker Andrews. New Haven: Yale University Press, 1923.

Schoepf, Johann David. *Travels in the Confederation (1783–1784).* Philadelphia: William J. Campbell, 1911.

Setting Out to Begin a New World: Colonial Georgia. A Documentary History. Edited by Edward J. Cashin. Savannah: The Beehive Press, Library of Georgia, 1995.

Smyth, John Ferdinand Dalziel. *A Tour in the United States of America.* Vol. 1. (London: 1784) New York: New York Times and Arno Press, 1968.

Stearns, Samuel. *The American Oracle.* New York: 1791.

Tusser, Thomas. *Five Hundred Points of Good Husbandry & A Book of Huswifery.* 1580. Edited by William Mavor. London: 1812.

Woodmason, Charles. *The Carolina Backcountry on the Eve of the Revolution: The Journal and Other Writings of Charles Woodmason, Anglican Itinerant. 1766–1768.* Edited by Richard J. Hooker. Chapel Hill: The University of North Carolina Press, 1953.

Secondary Sources

Crump, Nancy Carter. *Hearthside Cooking.* Chapel Hill: University of North Carolina Press, 2008.

David, Elizabeth. *English Bread and Yeast Cookery.* New York: The Viking Press, 1977.

Harbury, Katharine E. *Colonial Virginia's Cooking Dynasty.* Columbia: University of South Carolina Press, 2004.

Hess, Karen. *The Carolina Rice Kitchen: The African Connection.* Columbia: University of South Carolina Press, 1992.

Hess, Karen. Editorial notes. *Martha Washington's Booke of Cookery.* New York: Columbia University, 1981.

Luard, Elisabeth. *The Old World Kitchen: The Rich Tradition of European Peasant Cooking.* New York: Bantam Books, 1987.

McNeill, F. Marian. *The Scots Kitchen: Its Traditions and Lore with Old-Time Recipes.* Bungay, Suffolk: Blackie & Son: 1929.

Montagne, Prosper. *Larousse Gastronomique.* Edited by Charlotte Turgeon and Nina Froud. New York: Crown Publishers, 1961.

Moss, Kay. *Decorative Motifs from the Southern Backcountry, 1750–1825.* Gastonia, N.C.: Schiele Museum, 2001.

———. *Southern Folk Medicine, 1750–1820.* Columbia: University of South Carolina Press, 1999.

Moss, Kay, and Kathryn Hoffman. *The Backcountry Housewife: A Study of Eighteenth-Century Foods.* Gastonia, N.C.: Schiele Museum, 1985, 1994, 2001.

Presilla, Maricel E. *The New Taste of Chocolate: A Cultural and Natural History of Cacao with Recipes.* Berkeley: Ten Speed Press, 2001.

Smith, Andrew F. *Pure Ketchup: A History of America's National Condiment.* Washington: Smithsonian Institution Press, 2001.

Weaver, William Woys. *Sauerkraut Yankees.* Philadelphia: University of Pennsylvania Press, 1983.

INDEX

Index listings in bold are followed by receipts for those categories.